INSTRUMENTS OF
MONETARY POLICY
IN THE UNITED STATES

Instruments of Monetary Policy in the United States

The Role of the Federal Reserve System

by Ralph A. Young

International Monetary Fund
Washington, D. C., 1973

International Monetary Fund
Washington, D. C. 20431, U.S.A.

$1.25 (or the equivalent
in most other currencies)

Young, Ralph Aubrey
    Instruments of monetary policy in the United States: the
role of the Federal Reserve System. Washington, D. C., International Monetary Fund, 1973.
    xiv, 196 p.

    1. Monetary policy—U.S. 2. Federal Reserve System. 3. Federal
Reserve banks. I. Title. II. International Monetary Fund.

Second Printing, July 1974

CONTENTS

Preface   xi

1 Organization of U.S. Central Banking   1

The Board of Governors   3
   Role of the Chairman   4
   Duties of the Board   6
    Supervisory and regulatory duties   6
    Responsibility for monetary instruments   8
    Reporting to Congress and the public   10
The Federal Open Market Committee   10
   Emergence as a top-level policy forum   11
   Adaptations required   12
The Federal Reserve Banks   13
   The Reserve Bank directorates   16
    Selection of directors   16
    Principal duties   17
The Federal Advisory Council   18
Structure and Monetary Operations   19
   Rationale of operational focus   22
   Influence on monetary operations   24
Relations with the U.S. Treasury   25
Independence of the Federal Reserve   26

2 The Banking System and the Credit Market   28

The Commercial Banking System   28
   General characteristics   29
    Concentration of banking resources   32
    Correspondent banking   33
   The many nonmember banks   34
    Lower reserve requirements   35
    Other factors favoring nonmember status   36
    Concern over nonmember banking   37
The U.S. Credit Market   39
   Market features   39
   The banking system as an influence   42

The Money Market   45
   Principal features   45
      The role of the banks   47
      Special role of large city banks   48
      Reserve Bank practice in member bank discounting   49
   Service to the Treasury and Federal Reserve   49
The Money Market and Monetary Policy   50
   Effect on bank policies   51
   The market's performance   52

3 Open Market Operations   **54**

Procedures in Open Market Operations   55
   Scope of authorized transactions   55
   Steps in policy making   58
   Market strategy for the Manager   59
The Account Manager's Transactions   61
   Committee transactions in securities   61
   Two-way transactions   64
   Transactions for Treasury and foreign central banks   67
   Manager's role in market surveillance   68
Orderly Market Interventions   68
   Market factors in operations   69
   Conduct of orderly market operations   70
   Interaction of market and policy operations   72
   Justificaton of orderly market transactions   72
Committee Guidance of Policy Operations   74
   "Money market conditions" guideline   74
   One monetary aggregate for guidance   75
   New pattern for instructing the Manager   76
Difficulties with the Open Market Instrument   79
   The agent's instruction and money creation   80
   Risks in orderly market operations   81
   Limits to active open market operations   82
   Risks in facilitating government financing   83
   Difficulties from central banking structure   83
   Coordination with other instruments   84
Public Disclosure of Market Operations   85

4 Open Market Operations in Foreign Currencies   **86**

Administrative Arrangements   87
Interest of the U.S. Treasury   88
Exchange Market Interventions   89
The Swap Network   90
Effect of Suspension of Dollar Convertibility   92

5 Discount Operations   97

General Features   98
Fixing the Discount Rate   100
  Meaning of "review and determine"   100
  Coordination of Reserve Bank rates   101
Administrative Rules in Discounting   102
  Discounting procedures   103
  Surveillance of member bank borrowing   104
  Follow-up on outstanding advances   104
  Uniformity and stability of surveillance   105
  Uncertainty about Reserve Bank lending   107
Changing the Discount Rate   108
  Discount and other money market rates   108
  Review of discount rate changes   111
  Government interest in rate changes   113
Emergency Discounting   114
Reform of the Discount Mechanism   117

6 The Variable Reserve Instrument   123

Authority of the Board of Governors   123
  Rationale of the demand deposit differential   125
  Graduated pattern of requirements   126
  Joint reform of check clearance   130
Special Problems of the Variable Reserve   134
  Distinctive features   134
  Administrative dfficulties   136
  Use of reserve requirement change   138
Adaptations in the Requirement Base   140
  Techniques of large city banks   140
  Practices adopted by large city banks   142
  Regulatory reaction by the Federal Reserve   143
Proposed Legislative Reform   145

7 Instruments for Selective Regulation   147

Regulation of Stock Market Credit   147
  How the regulation works   150
  Administration of margin requirements   152
  Criteria for margin changes   153
Interest Rate Ceilings on Time Deposits   155
  Administration of ceilings   155
  Regulation Q ceilings and city banks   158

Restraint on Foreign Lending and Investing   159
The Federal Reserve program   160
Record of the Federal Reserve program   162

8 Coordinated Use of Policy Instruments   **165**

Financial Aims in Instrument Coordination   166
Strategy in Instrument Coordination   167
Coordination of Bank Reserve Instruments   168
Recast of the instruments after World War II   169
Coordination in the short run   171
Problems in coordinating reserve ratio changes   172
  Coordination with other reserve instruments   174
  *Impact of joint reserve ratio and open market action
    on bank reserve positions*   176
  *Ratio change and response of the monetary
    aggregates*   176
Coordination for longer-run objectives   177
  Under balanced economic conditions   177
  *Under conditions of destabilizing boom with
    inflationary trends*   177
  To cope with recession and potential deflation   179
  Adaptations in coordination   179
Coordination with Treasury debt management   181
Coordination of Selective and Major Instruments   183
Influences of International Monetary Developments   185
Outlook for Instrument Coordination   187

Index   **191**

Charts

1 Boundaries of Federal Reserve Districts and Their Branch
  Territories   15
2 Organizational Arrangement of Authority Within the
  Federal Reserve System   20
3 Structure of Federal Reserve Authority for Credit and
  Monetary Regulation   21
4 Changes in the U.S. Commercial Banking Structure,
  1950, 1960, and Mid-1972   31
5 Total Outright Transactions of the Federal Open Market
  Committee in the Market for U.S. Government
  Securities, 1961-72   63
6 Selected Money Market Interest Rates, 1963 to
  August 1973   109
7 Member Bank Borrowing from Reserve Banks, 1961-72   120
8 Effective Ratios of Reserve Requirements Before and After
  Restructuring, November 9, 1972   129

Tables

1 The Federal Reserve Banks Ranked by Size, End of Year, 1971   2
2 Banks and Competing Thrift Deposit Institutions in the United States, Mid-1972   30
3 Major Types of Debt Claims Utilized in the U.S. Credit Market, End of Year, 1968-71   40
4 Participation in the U.S. Credit Market by Investor Category and Type of Deposit, End of Year, 1968 and 1971   41
5 Sources of Supply and Demand Funds in the U.S. Credit Market, 1968-71   43
6 Major U.S. Money Market Claims Outstanding, End of Year, 1968-71   46
7 Open Market Transactions of the Federal Reserve System in U.S. Government Securities, 1961-71   62
8 Factors Affecting Member Bank Reserves, 1970   71
9 Federal Reserve Network of Reciprocal Currency Arrangements: Total Swap Drawings, March 1, 1962 to August 15, 1971, and Amount of Arrangements on August 15, 1971 and July 11, 1973   93
10 Annual Average Borrowing by Member Banks from Federal Reserve Banks, 1961-72   119
11 Basic Reserve Requirements of Federal Reserve Member Banks Before and After the Restructuring Effective November 9, 1972   128
12 Effective Ratios of Reserve Requirements Against Demand Deposits of Selected Federal Reserve Member Banks Before and After the Restructuring Effective November 9, 1972   129
13 Changes in Member Bank Reserve Ratios, 1962-70   173
14 Estimated Short-Run Effects of Concurrent Reserve Requirement and Open Market Action on Marginal Reserve Measures and on Associated Expansion of Total Bank Credit and the Active Money Stock, 1962-70   175

CENTRAL BANKING in the United States, as conducted by the Federal Reserve System in implementing national monetary policy, has several features that distinguish it from central banking to implement monetary policy in other countries. For one thing, the central banking institution has been fitted onto a complex governmental structure in which the federal authority unites the 50 state governments. Consequently, the organization of the Federal Reserve System has the quite distinctive form of twelve regional units operating under centralized supervision and policy administration.

The structure of banking in the United States, comprising many thousands of commercial banks distributed over a very wide area, is also unique. Less than half of these banks are members of the Federal Reserve System, the more numerous nonmember banks being chartered and regulated by supervisory authorities under the jurisdiction of the state governments. All commercial banks offer customers both check payment and time deposit services. In their savings and time deposit business, however, they are in competition with thousands of specialized thrift institutions, including mutual savings banks, savings and loan associations, and credit unions. Each type of institution, as well as the commercial banks, may have its deposit or share liabilities partially insured with a special federal agency.

A third exceptional feature of the financial system in the United States is the very large size of the credit market. This market, which is centered in New York City and encompasses a wide range of specialized financing activities and types of credit obligation, provides a capacious, fluid, and efficient facility for handling both domestic and international business. The importance of the credit market to U.S. central banking lies in the role it performs—through the interest rates and conditions of credit availability established there—in guiding the lending and investing activities of both the banks and the nonbank financial institutions. Within the credit market is a money market dealing in standardized financial claims of very short maturity. All financial institutions, most large nonfinancial corporations, and many state and local government funds operate in the money market to acquire or sell the standardized liquid claims that can serve as payments reserves in meeting their operating adjustments or contingencies.

Over the years the U.S. money market has attained an exceptional volume of trading activity at a low cost of transactions and for that reason has come to play a key role in the implementation of the monetary policy of the Federal Reserve System. Its existence, in fact, enables the Federal Reserve to rely on open market operations as the principal instrument for carrying out its policy. The funds supplied to the credit market by these open market operations affect the aggregate cash reserve position of all commercial banks—member banks directly and nonmembers indirectly.

The open market operations of the Federal Reserve System encompass transactions in marketable convertible currencies as well as in authorized money market claims. Such transactions, however, mainly have the purpose of maintaining orderly market conditions for the currencies. Thus, any bank reserve funds released or absorbed by them are ordinarily compensated by offsetting transactions in the liquid claims of the money market.

The central bank discount or lending facility in the United States, which serves Federal Reserve member banks as a safety valve through which short-term adjustment and contingency credit is available to them, is closely coordinated with the System's open market operations. Since resort to the discount facility by individual member banks is governed by standard rules of access and administrative surveillance of each bank's borrowing, the Federal Reserve discount rate is not used as a deterrent to such borrowing. Hence, the U.S. discount rate is typically positioned within the band of money market rates, and changes in the discount rate reflect the apparent liquidity needs and expectations that affect this special sector of the credit market.

Another major instrument for implementing monetary policy is the Federal Reserve System's authority to vary the required reserve ratios of the member banks. The Federal Reserve authorities, however, have found that frequent use of this instrument is ill-suited to U.S. commercial banking, and it is regarded purely as a supplement to open market and discount operations. Ordinarily, the variable reserve instrument is held on a stand-by basis, to be used when needed as a reinforcement of the other two policy instruments that are applied more flexibly and actively.

In addition, the Federal Reserve System has three selective credit regulations that can be used to support its general policy—covering the financing of stock market trading, rates of interest on member bank time deposits, and lending abroad by financial institutions. Only one of these, designed to prevent undue dependence on stock market trading financed by credit, is applied continuously. Authority to regulate interest rates paid on time deposits by member banks may, however, be used on occasions when credit conditions are being influenced restrictively in order to limit or contract the issue by large city banks of negotiable money market claims. Voluntary limitation on lending abroad by banks and other financial institutions (under temporary authority) has been employed in recent years to moderate capital outflow but is officially scheduled to be terminated by the end of 1974.

In the course of time each policy instrument has been adapted not only to adjust to functional, structural, or technological changes in the U.S. financial system but also to serve more responsively the aims of national monetary policy. As the Federal Reserve System is continuously evolving, it is to be assumed that policy instruments will continue to be adapted to changing circumstances in the years ahead.

Over the past decade U.S. monetary policy has been subject in public to active critical examination and vigorous controversy. To the central banker, the practical issue was the extent to which conditions in the money market, especially interest rates, should guide open market operations or whether primary guidance should derive from the interrelated trends of the major monetary aggregates—particularly the trends shown by bank credit and the money stock. Through much of the 1960s, the Federal Reserve authorities had focused on the maintenance of orderly money market conditions as the proximate objective of their market operations. In response to public debate, the authorities reconsidered intensively all the issues raised from the standpoint of their customary practices in market intervention.

As a result of this review, the Federal Reserve System has adopted a combination strategy for guiding its open market policy that emphasizes the performance of the monetary aggregates as tactical targets for a longer period, while placing a short-run stress both on the current trend in bank reserves and on an orderly process of interest rate formation in the money and credit markets. Accordingly, its present view explicitly recognizes that central bank monetary operations necessarily influence economic activity through both channels and that an effective domestic payments system under modern conditions requires a balanced consideration of both.

The author is indebted to many staff colleagues and also to the staff of the Board of Governors of the Federal Reserve System for numerous criticisms and suggestions during the preparation of this study. The staff of the Board of Governors also provided special tabulations of data and some other materials not otherwise available. While gratefully acknowledging the assistance and counsel received, the author wishes to stress that he alone is responsible for any imperfections in the final text and for the views expressed.

August 1973   RALPH A. YOUNG
                                     Consultant
                                     International Monetary Fund

1 Organization of U.S. Central Banking

THE FEDERAL RESERVE SYSTEM, as the central bank of the United States, is primarily responsible for the formulation and implementation of U.S. monetary policy. By statute, the Board of Governors is the System's administrative and regulative head. By organizational adaptation, however, the Federal Open Market Committee, a statutory body, has become the organ that determines the broad objectives of monetary policy. The headquarters of the Federal Reserve System is in Washington, which is the seat of the governing and policy-making bodies. Twelve regional Federal Reserve Banks conduct U.S. central banking operations; their activities are supervised, regulated, and coordinated by the Board of Governors.

The Federal Reserve Banks differ widely in size (Table 1). Those located in the major financial centers—New York, Chicago, and San Francisco—rank first, second, and third, respectively, and account for over half of the combined assets of all twelve. The Reserve Banks carry common public responsibilities: individually they perform a contributory role in shaping national monetary policy and jointly they serve as the agencies through which that policy is implemented. To discharge these public functions, each Reserve Bank is organized in accordance with a pattern prescribed by statute and is subject to identical regulation and supervision by the Board of Governors; more-

1

over, each provides the same range of banking and monetary services to its member banks and to the U.S. Government. Among the twelve, nevertheless, the Reserve Bank of New York gains extra prominence because: (1) it is located in the economy's central financial market; (2) it acts as agent for the other eleven in all market transactions of the Federal Reserve System; (3) it provides similar agency services to the U.S. Treasury; and (4) it serves as official correspondent of foreign central banks and the international institutions of which the United States is a member.

The Federal Reserve System has a virtual monopoly on the issuance of the nation's currency (with the exception of some authorized issues of coins and notes by the Treasury). Federal Reserve notes are legal tender, constituting the major segment (approximately 88 per cent) and the elastic component of the U.S. public's hand-to-hand means of payment.

Commercial banks' currency holdings and their deposit accounts with the Federal Reserve Banks serve as the reserve cash against the checking and other deposit accounts which the community at large holds with these banks. This reserve cash gives to those deposits the

Table 1. The Federal Reserve Banks Ranked by Size, End of Year, 1971

Bank	Total Resources (billion U.S. dollars)[1]	Number of Branch Offices	Official District Number[2]	Number of Employees
New York	23.9	1	2	4,815
Chicago	16.0	1	7	3,100
San Francisco	13.1	4	12	1,955
Cleveland	7.7	2	4	1,378
Richmond	7.4	2	5	1,941
Atlanta	6.0	4	6	2,006
Philadelphia	5.3	0	3	1,063
Boston	5.0	0	1	1,380
Dallas	4.5	3	11	1,132
Kansas City	4.5	3	10	1,456
St. Louis	4.0	3	8	1,423
Minneapolis	2.1	1	9	831
All Reserve Banks	99.5	24		22,480

Sources: *Federal Reserve Bulletin*, January 1972, p. A 13 and Board of Governors, Federal Reserve System, *Annual Report, 1971*, p. 256.

[1] Since total resources amount to $99.5 billion, the figures in this column also represent the approximate percentage share of each Reserve Bank.

[2] Districts are first numbered north to south in the eastern region of the country and then from east to west (see Chart 1, p. 15).

quality of convertibility, either into currency or into deposits with other banks. But only commercial banks that are members of the Federal Reserve System are eligible to hold reserve accounts with the Reserve Banks. Nonmember banks, which accounted for about 30 per cent of the growth in U.S. bank deposits over the past five years, hold part of their cash reserves in vault but hold the major part in the form of demand deposits with correspondents selected from among the larger banks. In an overall banking sense, therefore, the reserve cash held by the member banks plus their deposits with the Federal Reserve serve as the primary base on which the entire U.S. monetary system operates.

The member banks of the Federal Reserve System comprise all commercial banks operating under federal charter (national banks) and, in addition, those chartered by a state government that have voluntarily elected to assume membership responsibilities, have qualified, and have been formally admitted to membership by the Board of Governors. Principal advantages of membership are the exclusive availability to members, in non-crisis periods, of their discount or lending facility in the Reserve Bank and full use of the facilities of the Federal Reserve System for custody of marketable assets, transfer of funds, check clearance, and collection of cash items. Member banks are required to become stockholders in the Reserve Bank of their region, and they are its sole stockholders.[1] Ownership of Reserve Bank stock, unlike that of private corporations, carries only limited rights: to participate in the election of six of nine directors of a member's Reserve Bank and to receive a dividend of 6 per cent on its stock holdings in that Bank.

THE BOARD OF GOVERNORS

The Board of Governors is the apex of the Federal Reserve System for administration and for ultimate policy making. Its seven members are appointed by the President of the United States, and their appointment is confirmed by the Senate. Board members have terms of office of 14 years so arranged that the term of one member expires every two years, and their salaries are fixed by law. After serving a

---

[1] A member is liable to a stock subscription equivalent to 6 per cent of its capital stock issue and accumulated surplus, although only 50 per cent of such amount has been called. Its holdings of Reserve Bank stock are not transferable by sale.

full term of office, a member is ineligible for reappointment, but if he is initially appointed as a member to fill an unexpired term, he may be reappointed to a full term. During his term no member may be removed from office by the President "except for cause."

The President may select not more than one member of the Board of Governors from any Federal Reserve district. Further, he is obliged by statute to give "due regard to a fair representation of the financial, agricultural, industrial, and commercial interests and geographical divisions of the country." No Board member may retain an officership or directorship of any bank, banking institution, or trust company nor hold any stock in a banking institution, and his "entire time" must be devoted to "the business of the Board."

The funds to defray the Board's expenses are not voted upon by Congress but are levied against and paid by the twelve Reserve Banks in accordance with their respective earnings; hence, they may not be construed as appropriated funds of the Federal Government. To ensure Congress that expenditures are properly accounted for and controlled in relation to the Board's functions and responsibilities, the Board authorizes an annual audit of its accounts by a prominent firm of certified public accountants and, after each audit, submits the reports made to the Banking and Currency Committee of the House and the Banking, Housing, and Urban Affairs Committee of the Senate.

Role of the Chairman

Each member of the Board of Governors has equal voting power on all policy matters, but one member serves as its presiding officer and chief executive. Accordingly, the Federal Reserve Act provides that the President shall designate one member of the Board to serve as Chairman and another as Vice-Chairman, both to serve a term of four years, with presidential redesignation possible upon expiration of their terms as long as they remain members of the Board. For instance, a recent Chairman held office for four successive presidential terms and parts of two other terms, and a recent Vice-Chairman through two successive presidential terms and part of another. As the law is not fully explicit on the scope of the Chairman's executive responsibilities,[2] these must be defined by the Board as a whole, be limited by the

---

[2] Mentioning only a responsibility for assigning the performance of any function that the Board has decided to delegate to another member, a Board employee, or a Reserve Bank.

budget which the Board has adopted as well as by its regulatory determinations, and remain subject to the Board's general supervision.

The Chairman of the Board of Governors personifies to the public the Federal Reserve System's responsibility for maintaining the integrity of its money and, therefore, he is accorded a special status among Board members. This status is much enhanced by two other attributes of his office: (1) the Chairman of the Board is traditionally selected to be Chairman of the Federal Open Market Committee, which has come to play a central role in the formulation and implementation of Federal Reserve monetary policy; and (2) he acts as liaison on behalf of the Board, in accordance with established governmental protocol, within the structure of the Federal Government. In this latter role, he serves both as the Board's primary contact with the Executive Branch of Government and as the official medium of communication with the interested committees of Congress.

Thus, the Chairman keeps in especially close touch with the three officials of the Executive Office of the President who have primary responsibility for shaping and implementing the Federal Government's overall financial policy: namely, the Secretary of the U.S. Treasury (who as of January 11, 1973 is also designated Special Assistant to the President and acts as his coordinator for national economic policies), the Chairman of the President's Council of Economic Advisers, and the Director of the President's Office of Management and Budget. From time to time the Chairman and these three officials attend informal discussions with the President to consider and evaluate the major elements in the Government's overall financial policy. All of these intragovernmental contacts and discussions have the purpose of exchanging viewpoints rather than arriving at policy decisions (for example, concerning any altered emphasis that might be given to either fiscal or monetary policy), since the Chairman has no legal authority to commit the Board of Governors with regard to their future policy. Nevertheless, they afford an opportunity for representation of the Federal Reserve System in top-level discussion of economic policy within the Government and, as communicated back to the Board, help to facilitate coordination between fiscal, monetary, and other economic policies.

Equally important to the Chairman's official contacts within the Executive Branch of the Government are his liaison relationships with the chairmen and members of committees of Congress dealing with, or interested in, banking and monetary affairs or in the relative reliance to be placed by the Federal Government on fiscal and monetary action in fostering economic stability. In carrying out this duty, he serves as main spokesman for the Board of Governors and the Federal Reserve System on banking and monetary matters coming before the relevant congressional committees and, as appropriate, he conveys to them the Board's views and judgments with respect to legislation under consideration bearing on the organization, responsibilities, functions, or instruments of monetary regulation of the Federal Reserve System.

Duties of the Board

The Board of Governors has three areas of responsibility: (1) supervision and regulation of the operating units of the domestic payments and credit mechanism—the Reserve Banks directly, the member banks at a stage once removed, and such other institutions (or persons) as are placed under the regulatory jurisdiction of the Board; (2) formulation of national policy as delegated to the Board by Congress under that body's constitutional authority; and (3) formal reporting to Congress and the public on its trusteeship of the monetary authority assigned to the Federal Reserve System by Congress.

Supervisory and regulatory duties. With regard to the operational units of the Federal Reserve System—the Federal Reserve Banks—the first duty of the Board of Governors is to assure that the top management of each is of the highest possible caliber. In executing this responsibility, the Board selects and appoints three of each Reserve Bank's directors, one of whom is designated to be chairman and another deputy chairman. Furthermore, the Board approves the appointments and salaries of each Reserve Bank president (the chief executive officer) and first vice-president, as proposed by the respective directorates, and approves the overall salary schedules of the second line of officers.

As a second duty, the Board of Governors is obligated to maintain close supervision and regulation of all phases of each Reserve Bank's activities, including review and approval of its annual budget, examination and audit once a year, and review at that time of internal operating procedures and controls.[3] In addition, the Board keeps

---

[3] On occasion, the Board's examiners are accompanied by outside auditors of established repute to assure that each Reserve Bank's auditing procedures and controls adhere to the highest standards of the auditing profession.

under review the adequacy and uniformity of the services rendered by the Reserve Banks to their members and explores with their presidents the possibilities for improvement.

Thirdly, to maintain a commercial banking structure that comprises individually strong and sound banks, the Board of Governors directs the practices of each Reserve Bank in examining state-chartered member banks in the field or in reviewing the examination of national member banks chartered by the Office of the Comptroller of the Currency of the Department of the Treasury.[4] Achievement of a continuing adequate inspection of the widely dispersed banks in the United States calls for uniformly high examination standards among the federal and state supervisory authorities. The Board actively cooperates in all efforts within the Government toward this end.

Finally, the Board of Governors fosters and coordinates the economic intelligence function of all the Reserve Banks. Its emphasis here is on the helpfulness of their combined intelligence program in enlarging and refining the factual base for banking and monetary policy and in assessing the current alternatives for policy action facing the Federal Reserve System. At the same time the Board allows each Reserve Bank appropriate independent latitude to initiate other research, including research related to the regional economy, deemed useful to its officers, directors, and members.

Concerning the general functioning of the Federal Reserve member institutions, the Board of Governors is directed by law to issue a wide range of detailed regulations to govern or limit specific phases of member bank activities or business. In addition, it has special responsibilities in connection with changes in the status of state member banks and foreign affiliates of all members.[5]

---

[4] The Federal Reserve Act assigns to the Comptroller of the Currency primary responsibility for examining the national member banks that he charters. On the other hand, the Board derives from the Act a primary responsibility for the examination of state-chartered member banks and examines each one annually.

[5] For example, the Board of Governors must approve each application for, or withdrawal from, membership of a state-chartered bank; any merger of a state member bank with a nonmember bank; and any merger between member banks where the resulting bank will be a state-chartered member bank. In merger decisions affecting state members, the Board is obliged to take into account possible effects on banking competition and potential local monopoly and on the convenience and needs of the public to be served. In addition, any member bank seeking to establish either a foreign banking company as an affiliate or a direct foreign branch must seek the approval of the Board and be subject to such supervision and regulation as it may require.

At various points, moreover, the supervisory and regulatory responsibilities of the Board of Governors extend beyond the area of member banks. For instance, all bank holding companies, including companies holding only one bank, are subject to its supervision and regulation. The Board must determine and approve the nonbanking activities in which these companies or their subsidiaries may engage as incidental or closely related to their banking business, taking into account public convenience, effects on competition of any new activities or financial services permitted, and the gains in efficiency of the economy's financial mechanism from such additional activities. Then, for all banks and other consumer credit lenders, the Board regulates disclosure of the elements making up the financing charge and other credit terms for the purpose of making clear to the borrower the true annual rate of interest to be paid and the terms of repayment. The regulation of stock market credit is a further area extending beyond member bank activity; here, the Board's regulatory authority reaches all lenders and all borrowers of this kind of credit.

Responsibility for monetary instruments. The main responsibilities of the Board of Governors are to formulate domestic monetary policy and to administer the instruments with which the Federal Reserve System implements its policy. These instruments are six in number, three of which may be regarded as major and three of minor importance. The three major instruments are open market operations, discount operations, and changes in member bank reserve requirements.[6] These major tools have come to be called the bank reserve instruments for two reasons: (1) from a national monetary viewpoint, the most important operational impact of their use is on the combined cash reserve position of the member banks; and (2) the coordinated use of these instruments causes any given level of bank reserve cash to have a smaller or larger effect on aggregate bank lending and investing.

The role of the Board of Governors in the use of these instruments is complicated, because authority over two of the major instruments is shared with other bodies in the Federal Reserve System. Open market operations are the responsibility of a separate statutory body, the

---

[6] In the usage of the U.S. financial community, the term "discount operations" refers both to the purchase by a Reserve Bank from a member bank of eligible short-term paper bearing the bank's endorsement and to any direct advance, against appropriate collateral, by a Reserve Bank to a member bank.

Federal Open Market Committee, discussed below; however, the seven members of the Federal Reserve Board of Governors, who are statutory members of that body, constitute a majority of the Committee's membership of twelve. For the instrument of discount or lending operations, the Board determines the standards or principles on which Reserve Banks may extend their credit. It also has ultimate authority for determining the discount rates that Reserve Bank directorates recommend to the Board that their individual Reserve Banks should charge members when discounting paper with or obtaining advances from them. Only the authority to establish member bank ratios of reserve cash to deposit liabilities, within a range fixed by statute, is exclusively vested in the Board of Governors.[7]

The administration of the three minor or limited-objective instruments of monetary action, designed to deal by regulation with selected areas of credit, is also vested entirely in the Board of Governors. One of these, referred to earlier, pertains to the use of credit to finance stock market securities. It thus involves the Board in the detailed regulation of credit against stock collateral by securities brokers and dealers, banks, and other lenders and in setting rules that govern what persons may obtain this credit. A second instrument is the fixing of interest rates that member banks may pay customers on savings and time deposits. Use of this instrument involves consultation with other federal supervisory agencies which have a comparable responsibility for setting the maximum interest rates that institutions regulated by them may pay patrons. The third instrument is that of regulating (under temporary authority) foreign credits made by U.S. financial institutions.

The potential range of these minor instruments is open to much enlargement, however. It fact, legislation enacted in 1969 gives the

---

[7] In executing this responsibility, as discussed in Chapter 6, the Board must deal with matters vital to individual member banks, such as: (a) defining the deposit liabilities subject to differing reserve ratios (demand versus time deposits), a process requiring determination of allowances that may reasonably be deducted from one or both of the categories; (b) determining whether, by their location in selected cities or by their size, individual banks are to be classed as "reserve city banks" or "country banks" and be subject to higher or lower reserve ratios by reason of that classification; (c) determining for each of these bank classes a graduation in reserve ratios up to a maximum falling within the statutory limits; (d) defining and designating the reserve period to which reserve ratios specified in the law are applicable; and (e) setting the penalty applicable to member banks showing a reserve deficiency in any reporting period covering their reserve requirements.

President of the United States authority to direct the Board of Governors to undertake the direct regulation of "any or all" types of credit if he believes it necessary to "prevent or control inflation." Congress itself, with the President's approval, may also add at any time to the selective powers that the Board may exercise at its discretion.

Reporting to Congress and the public. A final duty of the Board of Governors is to keep Congress and the public informed of its activities and performance. This is accomplished by numerous publications, including press releases, an official monthly bulletin, special reports, and an annual report setting forth the policy actions of the Board of Governors and the Federal Open Market Committee as required by law. In addition, the Board frequently submits, at the request of congressional committees, formal statements or pertinent information bearing on the national monetary problem and the policies and actions of the Federal Reserve System in this regard. The Board's views on legislative proposals affecting the banking and monetary mechanism directly or indirectly, as noted above, are also expressed in testimony or letter to these committees, and these views are usually made public.

THE FEDERAL OPEN MARKET COMMITTEE

The Federal Open Market Committee is the body designated by statute to have full charge of Federal Reserve open market operations; indeed, no Reserve Bank may engage in open market operations "except in accordance with the direction of and regulations" adopted by this Committee. The Committee comprises the seven members of the Board of Governors, the president of the Federal Reserve Bank of New York, and four of the other eleven Reserve Bank presidents, among whom the four memberships are rotated annually.

The Reserve Bank members are the presidents by tradition rather than by legal requirement. The statute merely allocates one membership for election by the directors of the Reserve Bank of New York; the other four memberships are allocated on the basis of one each to three groups of three Reserve Bank directorates and one to the remaining two directorates. Since elections are conducted annually, a simple accommodation to this seemingly complex election procedure is for each of the latter directorate groups to elect presidents of their Reserve Banks by rotation, and this practice has long been followed. Thus, the president of the Reserve Bank of New York is a continuing member, three other presidents serve as members every third year, and one serves every second year. Although the Reserve Bank presidents on the Committee are elected by their respective directorates, these members do not attend meetings under instruction from directors and they do not report back to them on the discussions held or on the decisions taken, nor otherwise divulge to their directorates any confidential matter taken up as a part of the Committee's agenda.

The Committee decides upon its own organization, traditionally electing the Chairman of the Board of Governors as its Chairman and the president of the Reserve Bank of New York as its Vice-Chairman. The Committee is not explicitly empowered to have its own budget and accommodates itself to this statutory omission by drawing its secretarial, technical, and advisory staff by assignment from the existing staffs of the Board and the Reserve Banks.

Emergence as a top-level policy forum

Federal Reserve law, as amended in 1935, provides that (1) the Federal Open Market Committee shall determine the "time, character, and purchase or sale" of all securities eligible for holding by the twelve Reserve Banks and (2) these operations "shall be governed with a view to accommodating commerce and business and with regard to their bearing upon the credit situation of the country." The evident intent of this amendment was not only to unify Reserve Bank purchases and sales of U.S. Government securities in the open market under a single administration, but also to ensure that all such transactions serve a national purpose.

At the end of World War II, Congress enacted the Employment Act of 1946, which declared "maximum employment, production, and purchasing power" to be the objectives of national economic policy and directed all agencies of the Federal Government to apply their efforts toward these goals. Upon post-World War II resumption of flexible monetary administration in 1951, this national policy directive was recognized as somewhat awkward for the Federal Reserve System to conform to in practice, because (as noted above) authority over the use of its major instruments for implementing a national monetary policy was vested in three different statutory bodies, though with some interlocking either of participation or of representation among them. With the passage of time, consequently, Federal Reserve officials became increasingly aware that this mechanism for implementing policy was working neither as smoothly nor as promptly as desirable in the light of the objectives stated in the Employment Act. Accordingly, they considered ways of making more effective the coordination of Federal Reserve tools of action for meeting national objectives.

In the early 1950s, the Federal Reserve authorities were also deeply involved in the larger problem of how to use in the period ahead the instruments available to them. In the light of circumstance and experience, they reasoned that the open market operation was the most flexible and adaptable instrument for both short-run and longer-term operations and should be accepted as the main or most actively used means of implementing Federal Reserve policy. It followed that the Federal Open Market Committee might well serve as the Federal Reserve's central body for forming overall monetary policy and coordinating tactically the use of its several monetary instruments; action in this direction was taken in mid-1955.

Adaptations required

It required only a few organizational adaptations for this Committee that was already in charge of Reserve Bank operations in the open market to be converted into a central policy-making body for the Federal Reserve System. The most important changes were (1) that the Committee should hold more frequent meetings (its practice had been to meet quarterly and leave interim decisions to an executive committee); (2) that nonmember Reserve Bank presidents should be invited to attend and participate in policy discussion, though not to vote on the Committee's operating decisions; and (3) that the focus of the Committee's deliberations should be enlarged from the specific conduct of open market operations to embrace national monetary problems against the background of both longer-term and shorter-term prospects, domestic and foreign.

The third of these accommodations was the most important, although not fully accomplished until the early 1960s; it called for the committee members and the presidents participating as nonmembers first to reach a consensus on overall monetary policy objectives, bearing in mind that the Federal Reserve's principal means of attaining them was through the combined use of the three bank reserve instruments.[8] The

---

[8] Supplemented on occasion by the related use of selective measures of action that the Federal Reserve had authority to employ.

statutory members present at a committee meeting could then agree by consensus on an instruction (to apply until the Committee's next meeting) regarding market operations of the Federal Reserve System that would be consistent with overall policy aims. By following this order of agenda, all participants having a responsibility for the use of other instruments or representing bodies having such responsibility would obtain guidance from the policy action taken by the Committee and from the discussion that followed of open market strategy to help attain those objectives.

Whether this altered decision-making procedure has served the Federal Reserve System constructively since that time is a question to be answered in terms of its contribution to the coordination of Federal Reserve policy with national stabilization policy. From this restricted standpoint, Federal Reserve authorities emphasize two advantages in particular: (1) shortening the time required to reach a consensus on policy throughout the Federal Reserve System; and (2) furthering unity within the Federal Reserve in coordinating its monetary objectives with the broader economic objectives of national policy. Considering the unwieldy structure for policy making that had been established by statute, these are not unimportant benefits.

THE FEDERAL RESERVE BANKS

The original decision by Congress to establish a system of eight to twelve Reserve Banks rather than one central bank was the result of compromise, a dominant consideration being the sheer size of the United States and the uneven distribution of its resources and population. Provided with this latitude, an organization committee accepted the larger number, granting to each the authority to set up branches, subject to the approval of the Board of Governors. The committee then divided the country into twelve Reserve Bank districts, fixing the boundaries to accord with "the convenience and customary course of business and . . . not necessarily to be coterminous with the boundaries of groups of states." The Reserve Bank of each district was to be located in a leading financial center.

Since the original determination by Congress of Reserve Bank district boundaries in 1914, few changes have been made (Chart 1), except for the addition of the two newest states, Alaska and Hawaii, assigned to the San Francisco Federal Reserve District.[9] Reflecting growth of the economy since that time, all but two of the Reserve Banks (those in Boston and Philadelphia) have found it desirable to establish one or more branches; at present there are 24 Reserve Bank branches located in additional financial centers throughout the country and one check-clearing facility in Miami, Florida, destined to become a branch.

Under present-day organization of the Federal Reserve System, the twelve Reserve Banks function primarily as the operational units of U.S. central banking.[10] Each acts as both a regional and a local

---

[9] The question is often raised as to why Puerto Rico is not included in this chart. Puerto Rico is a self-governing commonwealth voluntarily associated with the United States, but subject to the U.S. Constitution in exercising its sovereign powers. While not all laws enacted by the U.S. Congress extend in application to Puerto Rico, some of them do apply expressly. In view of ambiguity in U.S. banking statutes in this regard and the omission of explicit mention of Puerto Rico in the Federal Reserve Act, Puerto Rico is excluded from the area embraced by Federal Reserve authority.

The Puerto Rican economy, however, is closely integrated into that of the United States and employs U.S. currency as its legal means of payment and debt settlement. While Puerto Rican local banks and branches of foreign banks operating there are subject to insular supervision, those that carry U.S. deposit insurance (14 local banks, including one new bank chartered under U.S. national banking law and admitted to Federal Reserve membership, and two branches of U.S. banks) are also subject to regulatory supervision by U.S. authorities. All banks in Puerto Rico maintain their supplies of usable currency through the facilities of the Reserve Bank of Atlanta, and the Reserve Bank of New York makes its bank clearing services available to them in collecting checks drawn on U.S. banks. Two of the local Puerto Rican banks have been permitted by the State of New York to have branches in New York City.

[10] In accordance with original legislative conception, each Federal Reserve Bank was to pursue discount rate, lending, and open market actions suited to the banking conditions in its district. The combined actions of the twelve Reserve Banks to implement individual district banking policies, however, would necessarily achieve some national coordination by their mutual response to interregional trade and money flows. Further coordination would presumably derive from overall regulation exercised by the Federal Reserve Board.

Various difficulties with this premise were uncovered during the first two decades of operating experience (1913-33) and, because of numerous bank failures over the second decade and a sharp contraction in the national monetary aggregates toward the end of that decade, the Federal Reserve's process of coordinating its policy actions came under progressive public criticism. Following the disruptive banking and financial crisis of the early 1930s, Congress in 1935 amended the Federal Reserve Act of 1913 to achieve a greater measure of centralized administration, to reinforce and supplement the policy instruments available to the Federal Reserve System, and to ensure that its policy-making process would function in a centripetal—and effectively coordinated—manner toward national stabilization goals.

Chart 1. Boundaries of Federal Reserve Districts and Their Branch Territories

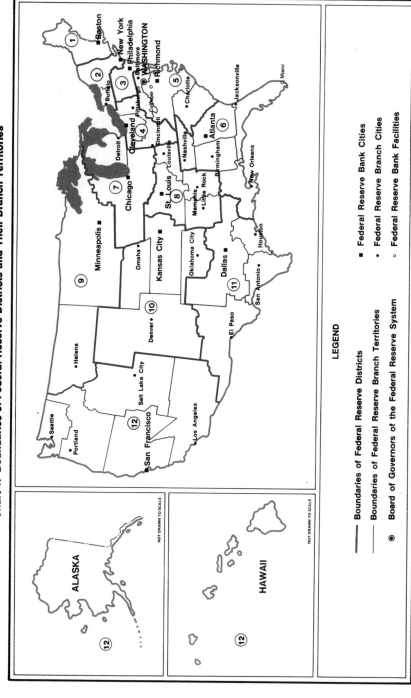

LEGEND

— Boundaries of Federal Reserve Districts

— Boundaries of Federal Reserve Branch Territories

◉ Board of Governors of the Federal Reserve System

■ Federal Reserve Bank Cities

• Federal Reserve Branch Cities

○ Federal Reserve Bank Facilities

Reserve Bank as well as an operating unit of the U.S. central banking system and participates in the formation of national banking and monetary policy. Accordingly, the officers of each Bank are responsible for representing the interests of their district so that the national interest may be shaped in the light of the regional as well as the overall requirements of the country, including those of its international balance of payments.

The Reserve Bank directorates

Each Reserve Bank functions under the direction of a board of nine directors, which is responsible for the conduct of its business and daily operations under the supervision and regulation of the Board of Governors. Each director serves on a part-time basis rather than being a full-time board member as are members of the Board of Governors. Since directorate remuneration consists entirely of nominal fees and expenses for attending meetings of directors, which are typically held once a month—or every two weeks in the case of the executive committee—a director's reward is largely in the knowledge that he renders a public service.

Selection of directors. The directors of a Reserve Bank fall into three classes, with three directors in each class. Class A directors are elected by the member banks of a district; they may be and usually are bankers. Class B directors are likewise elected by the member banks of a district, but they must be individuals actively engaged in commerce, industry, or agriculture rather than officers, directors, or employees of banks. Class C directors are appointed by the Board of Governors, and while serving as Reserve Bank directors, may hold neither other office or employment nor stock in any bank. Two of the three Class C directors are designated by the Board of Governors to serve as chairman and deputy chairman, respectively, of a Bank's board of directors.[11]

Each Reserve Bank director has a three-year term of office, but he may be re-elected or reappointed for successive terms. In the interest of healthy rotation of directorate service, a maximum of one re-election or reappointment is a rule preferred by the Board of Governors.

---

[11] By law, the chairman serves as agent of the Board of Governors (Federal Reserve Agent) and, in this capacity, is its official representative for the continuing performance of the Reserve Bank's functions. In current practice, however, some of the chairman's routine duties have been delegated to assistant Federal Reserve agents, thus alleviating demands upon the part-time chairman.

For election of Class A and Class B directors, the member banks of each district are classed by size as small, medium, and large, with each class being entitled to elect one Class A and one Class B director by a process of preferential voting. Whenever a vacancy occurs, each member bank of the size group in which the vacancy falls is entitled to nominate a candidate; the banks in that group then elect their director by the same process of preferential voting.

Each branch of a Reserve Bank has its own board of directors, comprising either five or seven members. The majority of the directors in a branch is appointed by the head office directorate and the remainder by the Board of Governors, but the term of each branch director, however appointed, is at the pleasure of the Board. By tradition, branch directors appointed by the head office are usually bankers, while those appointed by the Board conform to the pattern of Class C appointments to the head office directorates.

Principal duties. A main duty of the directors is to maintain Reserve Bank management of the highest competence and of demonstrated capacity for leadership in the banking and financial community. Directors appoint their president and first vice-president and also recommend their salaries subject to final approval by the Board of Governors. In addition, they determine and appoint any other officers that their Bank may need to function efficiently and, with the Board's concurrence, decide upon an appropriate salary scale. Furthermore, each Reserve Bank directorate has the duty of selecting (and then electing) individuals of regional prominence to serve as majority directors of its branch or branches and also of selecting from their district one representative of recognized regional distinction to serve as a member of the Federal Advisory Council, discussed below.

In implementing the monetary policy of the Federal Reserve System, a principal duty of Reserve Bank directors is to administer their Bank's discount (or lending) operations. Directors, therefore, are empowered to initiate discount rate changes, and each directorate or its executive committee is obliged, at least every 14 days, to recommend to the Board of Governors for "review and determination" the discount rate it plans to charge as to both discounts for and advances to its member banks. In fulfilling the statutory responsibilities for their Bank's credit extensions to member banks, each Reserve Bank's directorate must see to it that such extensions are administered in conformity with the discount regulations of the Federal Reserve Board of Governors and are made "fairly and impartially without discrimination in favor of or against any member bank or banks." Moreover, the directors must assure themselves that their Bank's credit accommodation of any member is safely and reasonably extended, with due regard to the claims of other member banks, the maintenance of sound credit conditions, and the accommodation of commerce, industry, and agriculture.

Experience shows that the statutory method of electing or appointing directors results in Reserve Bank directorates that possess varied administrative and advisory talents, reflecting the differences among individual members in background, training, and experience. At the operating level, their knowledge of organization, management, and technology in other fields enables them to counsel their Bank on innovations that will keep it abreast of advanced managerial practices and operating techniques whether in banking or business. At the policy level, their differing viewpoints and knowledgeable appraisals of the economic situation are regularly communicated to the Federal Open Market Committee and provide uniquely intimate intelligence about the expectations of regional business leadership for that Committee's use in policy deliberation.[12]

The Reserve Bank and branch directors are also helpful to the Federal Reserve System in interpreting its monetary policy to the banking, business, farm, and labor groups in their respective districts. Their efforts in this area not only help to further public understanding of Federal Reserve policy and operations in the national interest but also to foster a broader public understanding of the interrelation between monetary and other governmental policies for stabilization of the economy.

THE FEDERAL ADVISORY COUNCIL

The Federal Reserve Act of 1913 provided for one further organizational body, the Federal Advisory Council, to serve as a formal channel of communication between the banking and financial community and

---

[12] Under former practice, the Reserve Bank presidents individually reported to the Committee on the expectations of their directorates when this was deemed relevant to policy discussions. In recent years, to ensure that the views both of the Reserve Bank directorates and of the business and financial communities that they represent are systematically made available to the Committee as background information in advance of each meeting, the staff of one Reserve Bank is designated, on a rotating basis, to assemble and collate these viewpoints for that purpose.

the Federal Reserve Board of Governors. The Council has twelve members, one from each Federal Reserve district selected by the directorate of each Reserve Bank. While the statute does not specify qualification (occupational, educational, or other) for council membership, those selected by the Bank directorates are typically active bankers of local and regional prominence. The Council is directed by statute to hold its meetings at least four times a year in Washington, D.C., and to confer there with the Board of Governors.

The statutory role contemplated for the Council entails giving advice on a wide range of topics—from the general state of business to any matter within the jurisdiction of the Board of Governors. Thus, the Council's advice to the Board might extend from broad recommendations regarding the overall banking and monetary objectives of the Federal Reserve System to specific suggestions concerning the administration and use of any one of its policy instruments and any aspects of its regulation of member bank operations.

Although this range of advisory discretion is indeed broad, the emphasis in the functioning of the Federal Reserve System has over the years tended to move from strictly banking affairs toward the wider problems of monetary stabilization. Influenced by this change in emphasis, the Council has gradually come to focus its advisory efforts on business and financial tendencies in relation to the monetary policy of the Federal Reserve System. In particular, it concerns itself with the adverse or acceptable effects of the Federal Reserve's implementing actions on commercial banking activities and on the performance of the money market as prime areas of the economy's initial response.

STRUCTURE AND MONETARY OPERATIONS

The organizational structure of the Federal Reserve System plainly is complex, reflecting the varied political and geographical elements that entered into its founding and also the subsequent adaptations in its structure and authority to make it more responsive to national authority and objectives. Its present form is summarized in Charts 2 and 3; Chart 2 depicts the formal relationship between the several entities of the System and identifies the main functions assigned to each, and Chart 3 sets forth the structure for regulating money and credit. One special technical point should be kept in mind in examining them: while the examination and inspection of member banks are identified in the charts, these functions should not be considered as

Chart 2. Organizational Arrangement of Authority Within the Federal Reserve System

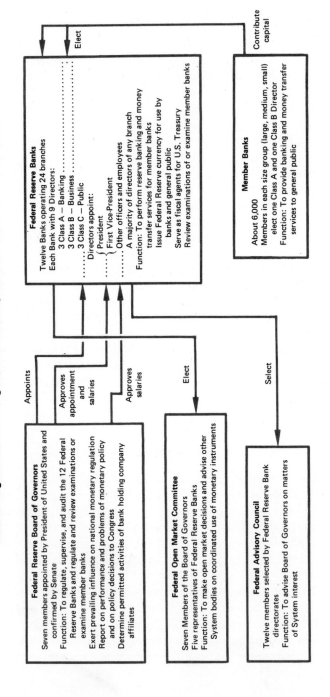

Federal Reserve Board of Governors

Seven members appointed by President of United States and confirmed by Senate

Function: To regulate, supervise, and audit the 12 Federal Reserve Banks and regulate and review examinations or examine member banks

Exert prevailing influence on national monetary regulation

Report on performance and problems of monetary policy and on policy decisions to Congress

Determine permitted activities of bank holding company affiliates

Federal Open Market Committee

Seven Members of the Board of Governors

Five representatives of Federal Reserve Banks

Function: To make open market decisions and advise other System bodies on coordinated use of monetary instruments

Federal Advisory Council

Twelve members selected by Federal Reserve Bank directorates

Function: To advise Board of Governors on matters of System interest

Federal Reserve Banks

Twelve Banks operating 24 branches

Each Bank with 9 Directors:
- 3 Class A — Banking
- 3 Class B — Business
- 3 Class C — Public

Directors appoint:
{ President
{ First Vice-President
Other officers and employees

A majority of directors of any branch

Function: To perform reserve banking and money transfer services for member banks

Issue Federal Reserve currency for use by banks and general public

Serve as fiscal agents for U.S. Treasury

Review examinations of or examine member banks

Member Banks

About 6,000

Members in each size group (large, medium, small) elect one Class A and one Class B Director

Function: To provide banking and money transfer services to general public

Appoints

Approves appointment and salaries

Approves salaries

Elect

Select

Elect

Contribute capital

Chart 3. Structure of Federal Reserve Authority for Credit and Monetary Regulation

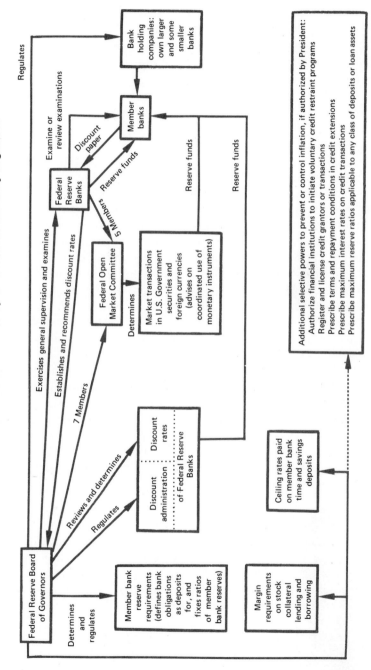

instruments that can be used in any active or flexible way in carrying out monetary policy. Rather, their primary concern is to ensure the consistent adherence of each member institution to the relevant banking statute or regulation and its continuing operating soundness as a going concern.

Together, Charts 2 and 3 give point to a characterization of the structure as a "blend of national authority and regional responsibility." In noting this characterization, it should be re-emphasized that all participants in the decision-making process act in the capacity of public officials,[13] for this is both the explicit and implicit intent of the statutory direction to the Federal Reserve System. Moreover, in the past two decades the Federal Reserve has adopted internal reforms in its procedures for determining policy and taking action that have been aimed at giving practical expression to such intent.

While the organization of the Federal Reserve gives an outward impression of cumbersomeness and complexity, one purpose served by its structure is the inclusion of *checks and balances* in discretionary decision making. These help to keep due deliberation a prominent feature of the Federal Reserve decision-making process and thus protect the public against official actions in the banking and monetary area that could reflect hasty response to transient economic or even political influences.

At the same time, the impression of complexity conveyed by its organization admittedly leaves open two questions that some observers would consider highly relevant: (1) whether this apparent complexity has not, in too many instances, impaired the effectiveness of monetary policy of the Federal Reserve System; and (2) whether the conduct of policy has been coordinated consistently and sufficiently with national economic policy, so that such coordination has been gradually improving.

Rationale of operational focus

The structure of the Federal Reserve System also needs to be viewed in relation to the focus that it accepts for its monetary operations. Simply stated, the Federal Reserve considers that its responsibility in the public interest is to regulate national credit and monetary affairs, as affected especially by the functioning of the commercial banking

---

[13] Even though the Reserve Bank directors in fact serve as quasi-public officials.

system, so as to contribute to the attainment of the nation's economic objectives. Functionally, the Federal Reserve defines this responsibility as a compound of two primary elements: (1) regulating the quantity of cash reserves either held by or potentially accessible to commercial banks and, in turn, the ability of the banks to expand the economy's bank credit and money supply; [14] and (2) influencing simultaneously the overall supply and cost of funds available for borrowing in the general credit market. In this way, monetary policy and the action taken to implement policy have at times facilitated and at other times inhibited investment or other spending financed with credit, thereby influencing vital components of aggregate demand.

The reasons for this focus are pragmatic. The commercial banks are the main participants in the money market and active participants in other sectors of its credit market, and, overall, large suppliers of credit to the entire economy. By bringing about marginal changes in the reserve position of the commercial banking system, the monetary actions of the Federal Reserve System necessarily affect the supply and cost of credit in the whole financial market and the pace of the change in the total stock of money and bank credit in the economy, that is, the two major monetary aggregates. As the member banks, and not the Federal Reserve Banks, act as depositories of the main part of the reserves of nonmember banks, member bank holdings of cash reserves constitute, in practice, the principal operating reserves (other than currency in bank vaults) of the entire commercial banking system. The reserve position of the member banks, therefore, is the *de facto* operational focus of monetary policy of the Federal Reserve System.

It has been argued that this focus is too narrow because it excludes from considerations of policy the currency component of the money stock. Currency constitutes the larger part of credit made available by the Reserve Banks, although it is a smaller component of the broader money stock than bank deposits. Moreover, currency moves into public circulation only through the medium of the banks, and the quantity held by the public is as much credit of the combined central and commercial banking system as are the demand and time deposits generated by the banks.

---

[14] Both in the narrow sense of currency in circulation with the public plus private demand deposits and in the broader sense of including in addition the public's savings and other time deposits.

Influence on monetary operations

While this argument is valid in the technical sense that currency is an important form of money, it should be noted that the distribution of the public's holdings of money balances in the form of deposit accounts and personal holdings of currency is a matter of discretionary choice on the part of the public. The Federal Reserve has long accommodated itself to this basic fact by assuming the initiative in supplying circulating currency to the economy, in the first instance through the medium of the member banks, in accordance with the public's demand and convenience. Public demand for currency may vary sharply owing to seasonal or special random influences affecting public attitudes toward their money holdings, but over longer periods it is heavily influenced by the growth in the value and scope of the retail and service trades.

Accordingly, as the public's money balances with the banks are converted into the form of currency, the Federal Reserve typically employs its bank reserve instruments to cushion the impact of the withdrawal on the bank reserve position and specifically on the reserve position of the member banks. Similarly, when the public returns currency from circulation, the Federal Reserve applies its instruments so as to offset the effect on the bank reserve position, particularly that of the member banks.

For practical reasons, therefore, the monetary operations of the Federal Reserve System are immediately directed to affecting the aggregate commercial bank reserve position and the quantity of deposit money, which is much the larger and faster-growing component of the money stock, however defined.[15] In so doing, the Federal Reserve must take into account the growth in the needs of the economy for circulating currency and must adjust bank reserves accordingly. The purpose of its operations is to bring about an expansion in monetary aggregates that is consistently related, as far as possible, to desired changes in economic activity, as reflected in output, employment, and prices. But the influence of the Federal Reserve System on these latter variables is exerted with varying lags, its influence on the monetary aggregates being usually more certain and subject to a shorter lag than on economic activity.

---

[15] As explained in Chapter 3, the operational concept of aggregate commercial bank reserves has undergone special refinement in recent years to abstract from irregular instabilities in the aggregate caused by fluctuations in required reserves against both U.S. Government deposits and total interbank deposits.

RELATIONS WITH THE U.S. TREASURY

The U.S. Government department with which the Federal Reserve System has its closest working relations is the Treasury. Under U.S. monetary law, the Treasury is the ultimate custodian of the international monetary reserves of the United States in gold and foreign exchange and is charged with responsibility for maintaining the international exchange value of the dollar.[16] Moreover, the Treasury is the source of a small part of the circulating note issue and also is responsible for the minting of all coin. Domestic monetization of international reserves, as well as the introduction of all issues of new coins and Treasury notes, proceeds under Treasury authority through the facilities of the Reserve Banks and their member banks.

In addition to a relationship associated with the supervision of international monetary reserves and with the issuance of Treasury currency, other relationships arise from the Treasury's responsibilities that have either a direct or indirect bearing on the functioning of the credit market and monetary mechanism. These include administering: (1) the overall position of the Federal Government's cash balance to keep it as neutral as practicable in relation to the banking system's reserve position; (2) all U.S. Government borrowing operations, including the refinancings of maturing federal debt; (3) the market investment of the Government's various trust funds; (4) the public borrowing of federal credit agencies; (5) direct Treasury lending to such agencies; and (6) interventions in the foreign exchange market for purposes of stabilizing the exchange value of the dollar. Whenever these responsibilities give rise to large transactions in the financial market, the Treasury seeks the advice of officials of the Federal Reserve System before making the final decision to undertake them.

Finally, there is the area of fiscal mechanics handled for the Treasury on an agency basis by the Federal Reserve Banks. These

---

[16] In support of this responsibility, the Secretary of the Treasury is authorized to regulate, subject to the President's approval, all domestic transactions in gold, including its import and export; he is also authorized to deal in gold and foreign exchange. Action under these authorities (such as was initiated on August 15, 1971) can result in altering the foreign exchange value of the dollar (as agreed with other leading governments on December 18, 1971, or taken by the Secretary on February 12, 1973 without formal agreement with other governments). In consequence, changes in holdings of national monetary reserves may acquire a larger (or smaller) leverage than before, when permitted by the Treasury and the Federal Reserve in turn to affect the economy's money stock.

mechanical services also contribute to the close working relations between the two agencies. In the first place, they comprise the servicing of the Treasury's cash balance account with the Reserve Banks on which the disbursement checks of the Federal Government are drawn and into which the Government's revenues, initially accumulated in Treasury deposit accounts (tax and loan accounts) with banks, are systematically transferred. A second category of such services embraces tasks incidental to debt management operations, including publicizing the terms of Treasury financings, receiving subscriptions and making allotments among dealers and other purchasers of new issues, delivering new securities to and receiving payment from purchasers, handling the exchange of securities in refundings, redeeming maturing securities, and paying interest coupons on outstanding issues as they become due. A third category of fiscal agency services consists of the Treasury's own market transactions in U.S. Government securities and in foreign currencies; these are executed for the Treasury, at its direction, by the Federal Reserve Bank of New York.

The Treasury's administration of the nation's monetary reserves and the conduct of its various financings for the Federal Government are of vital interest to the Federal Reserve authorities. Conversely, the Federal Reserve's monetary operations profoundly affect conditions in the credit market and are thus of vital interest to Treasury officials. Hence, the two agencies must maintain a close liaison, exchanging technical and other information and thereby establishing a common base of knowledge from which each agency can reach its own policy and operational decisions.

INDEPENDENCE OF THE FEDERAL RESERVE

Under the Constitution of the United States, Congress is specifically assigned the power "to coin money and determine the value thereof." To delegate this power, Congress founded the Federal Reserve System and endowed it with status as a special agency of the Federal Government *independent of* its executive branch. Congress requires the Board of Governors to report directly to it on the performance of the Federal Reserve System in executing national monetary authority and in ensuring the quality and orderly expansion of bank credit. Eventually Congress assumed a responsibility, manifest in recent decades, for active oversight of its overall performance and asserted a primary concern for any extension in the scope of its activities or basic change in its organization.

By originally giving the Federal Reserve System this special status as an "independent agency" and by subsequently making more positive its direct responsibility to Congress in the execution of its duties, Congress in fact transformed the Federal Reserve's role into one of trusteeship in administering the economy's credit and monetary affairs. Under such an assignment, the term "independence" means unequivocally *independence within and not of* the governmental structure. And such "independence" is not to be thought of as unlimited but only as latitude for the Federal Reserve to arrive at its own collective decisions independently within the sphere of responsibility delegated to it by Congress.

As an instrumentality of the Federal Government, therefore, the Federal Reserve System can never do less than cooperate, as fully as its trusteeship accountability to Congress and the public permits, in carrying out the economic policies determined by the incumbent administration to be in the national interest. When national policies that have a bearing on credit and monetary affairs are being formulated, the views of the Federal Reserve are usually sought by both the Executive Office of the President and Congress in regard to such technical criticism and advisory suggestion as it may be in a position to provide; in turn, the views of these sources of national authority are taken into account by the Federal Reserve when it is obliged to accommodate adaptations in national policies. On occasions when other government authorities seek the Federal Reserve's views, they naturally want only its advisory help in arriving at their own judgments.

2 | The Banking System and the Credit Market

THE FEDERAL RESERVE SYSTEM'S major policy instruments affect the credit and monetary conditions of the economy primarily by influencing the ability of commercial banks as a group to supply funds to the credit market. The credit market comprises three sectors: (1) a sector where credits are extended by direct negotiation between lender and borrower; (2) the money market which deals in marketable credit claims of short maturity (that is, close to cash in hand); and (3) a sector loosely called in the United States the capital market, where credit claims are longer term and partly marketable through intermediation of investment bankers, securities dealers, and brokers.

Accordingly, the process by which the Federal Reserve's policy instruments do their work is influenced by the necessity of adapting them to the existing banking organization, on which central banking leverage is applied directly and indirectly. This process is also greatly influenced by the nature and size of the economy's credit market as well as by the central role of the money market sector in liquefying marketable credit claims of short maturity.

THE COMMERCIAL BANKING SYSTEM

An outstanding feature of the financial structure in the United States is the number of institutions comprising the commercial banking system. Nearly 14,000 banking institutions are engaged in providing payments (check deposit) services to their customers (Table 2), of which about 5,700 are members of the Federal Reserve System and the rest are nonmembers. Although the proportion of member commercial banks is strikingly small, the functioning of all commercial banks is assisted by the Federal Reserve's operations. Of the three Federal Reserve instruments of monetary policy, only the discount facility and the variable reserve requirement are primarily confined in their direct incidence to the reserve positions of member banks; open market operations directly affect the cash reserve holdings of both member and nonmember banks as a group. The reserve funds provided or withdrawn as a result of open market operations, whatever their immediate incidence, are distributed within a relatively short time among all banks by means of the credit and equity markets, by the stream of payments for tangible goods and personal services transacted in the economy, and by the action of the public in allocating its money and quasi-money between bank deposits (both demand and time) and currency.

General characteristics

At the end of 1972, the member banks accounted for over 80 per cent of all commercial bank deposits, including interbank deposits (Table 2 and Chart 4), and for about the same percentage of privately held bank demand or checking deposits, net of interbank deposits and cash collection claims.[1] Of the nearly 5,700 member banks, just over four fifths (that is, national banks incorporated under federal charter) are required by law to be members; the remainder, which operate under state charter, are members by choice—provided that they meet the qualifications required by the Federal Reserve. Though the national banks hold the lion's share of member bank deposits, they are generally smaller in size than the state-chartered members.

For reserve requirement purposes, the member banks are divided into two groups—reserve city banks and country banks. The reserve city member banks, designated as such primarily because of their size, are typically located in leading commercial and industrial centers.

---

[1] The demand deposits of state and local governments are conventionally classed as privately held deposits. This deposit figure, net of the items listed, is traditionally used along with the total of the currency in actual circulation to reckon the narrowly defined domestic money stock.

Table 2. Banks and Competing Thrift Deposit Institutions
in the United States, Mid-1972

| | Number | Deposits | | |
| | of | Total[1] | Demand[2] | Time |
Kind of Institution	Institutions	*(billion U.S. dollars)*		
Commercial banks				
Member bank	5,714	433.6	207.6	226.0
Nonmember bank	8,161	119.1	48.5	70.6
Total	13,875	552.7	256.1	296.6
Classes of member bank				
National	4,606	322.3	151.3	171.0
State	1,105	111.3	56.3	55.0
Total	5,711	433.6	207.6	226.0
Reserve city	178	243.2	137.2	118.7
Country	5,536	190.4	70.4	107.3
Total	5,714	433.6	207.6	226.0
Classes of nonmember bank				
Insured	7,955	116.0	46.9	69.1
Noninsured	206	3.1	1.8	1.3
Total	8,161	119.1	48.7	70.4
Competing thrift deposit institutions				
Mutual savings banks				
Insured	325	75.9[2]	0.8[2]	75.1[2]
Noninsured	163	11.1[2]	—	11.1
Total	488	87.1	0.8[2]	86.2
Savings and loan associations				
Insured	4,271	184.9[2]	—	184.9
Noninsured	1,173[3]	7.7[2]	—	7.7
Total	5,444[3]	192.6	—	192.6
Credit unions	23,333[3]	19.9[3]	—	19.9[3]

Sources: *Federal Reserve Bulletin,* September 1972, pp. A 20-22 for commercial banks and p. A 39 for mutual savings banks (also February 1972, p. A 98 for the latter); and *Federal Home Loan Bank Board Journal (Special Issue: 1971 Annual Report),* April 1972, pp. 33 and 84 for savings and loan associations.

[1] Including interbank deposits.

[2] Approximate, based on the year-end 1971 distribution of deposits between insured and noninsured savings banks, as reported by the year-end call report issued by the Federal Deposit Insurance Corporation, and between insured and noninsured savings and loan associations, as reported by the Federal Home Loan Bank Board in the *Federal Home Loan Bank Board Journal,* Table S.1.2.

[3] Total number of savings and loan associations and credit unions from Table 4; figures for noninsured associations by deduction.

Chart 4. Change in the U.S. Commercial Banking Structure,
1950, 1960, and Mid-1972

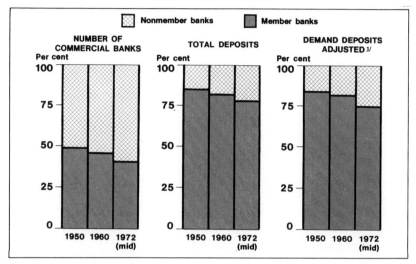

[1] Total demand deposits other than U.S. Government and interbank deposits less cash items
in process of collection. This quantity plus currency in public circulation equals the narrowly
defined money stock (M_1).

Although they are few in number—178 banks in all—they held nearly
three fifths of total member bank deposits at mid-1972, each having
on the average about $1.3 billion in deposits.[2] In contrast, there were
at that time over 5,500 member banks classified as country banks.
These banks were widely distributed, mainly in rural areas and suburban centers, and their average deposits were minuscule compared
with those of the reserve city banks.

Both reserve city and country member banks are required to keep
the same minimum ratio of cash reserves to time deposits—3 per cent
for savings deposits and 5 per cent for other time deposits. For
demand deposits, on the other hand, the required reserve ratio is
determined on a graduated basis, with higher ratios applicable to

---

[2] Up to late 1972, smaller banks in reserve city centers could be classified as
country banks, if such classification could be justified by their size and the
character of their business. Action by the Federal Reserve Board of Governors,
effective November 9, 1972, made size (as measured by volume of demand
deposits) the single criterion for classifying them as either reserve city or country
banks (see Chapter 6).

successively higher deposit brackets. Against these demand deposits reserve city banks presently incur an effective average reserve ratio of somewhat over 16 per cent, compared with a country bank average ratio of approximately 11 per cent. The Board of Governors is empowered both to impose its reserve requirements on a graduated basis and to vary the effective ratios within statutory limits (see Chapter 6).

All member banks are obliged by law to insure their deposit accounts up to a stated limit, currently $20,000 per deposit account, with the Federal Deposit Insurance Corporation. Nonmember commercial banks and mutual savings banks are eligible for the same amount of insurance on their deposit accounts, if they apply to the Corporation and are found by its examiners to be in satisfactory condition. In mid-1971 all but 182 of the 8,000 nonmember commercial banks and about a third of the approximately 500 mutual savings banks offered their customers government-insured deposit accounts.[3]

Concentration of banking resources. A sizable share of all U.S. commercial banking resources is concentrated in a relatively small

---

[3] Similar insurance is available to qualifying savings and loan associations from the Federal Savings and Loan Insurance Corporation, a division of the Federal Home Loan Bank Board, and to federally chartered and other qualifying credit unions from the National Credit Union Administration. The 5,400 savings and loan associations (of which 4,300 are insured institutions) and the 500 or so mutual savings banks compete actively with commercial banks in providing savings and time account services to the public. Many of them aspire also to compete with commercial banks by offering the public a checking account service. Reflecting this developing sentiment, a recent *Report of the President's Commission on Financial Structure and Regulation* (1971), pp. 33, 40, and 87-88, recommended that qualifying savings and loan associations and mutual savings banks be permitted to offer insured checking account services to nonbusiness customers in competition with banks.

In the State of Massachusetts, where deposit accounts of mutual savings banks may be insured under state authority, a Supreme Court decision of 1972 has made it practicable for any local mutual savings bank—and presumably any local non-federally insured savings and loan association—to render customers a service equivalent to a checking account service through the device of a so-called NOW (negotiable order of withdrawal) account, which allows the holder to write a freely negotiable order instructing his savings institution to withdraw funds from his account and pay them to a third party. The personal thrift accounts of the mutual savings banks and savings and loan associations in Massachusetts amount to over 5 per cent of the national dollar value of savings accounts outside of commercial banks.

number of institutions. The dominant position of the 178 reserve city banks has already been noted. The 10 largest member banks account for approximately 25 per cent of U.S. commercial banking resources, the 100 largest for roughly 50 per cent, and the 1,000 largest for almost 75 per cent. Virtually all of these large banks are multiple-office banks, with branch offices mainly in the same urban center or metropolitan area; only a score or so of the states permit statewide branch banking.

In addition, several hundred unit banks operate under centralized ownership control through regional holding companies, which may own both federally chartered and state-chartered unit banks (and thus both member and nonmember banks). At the end of 1971, there were some 197 multiple-unit bank holding companies, each controlling two or more banks. Together they had a majority ownership interest in nearly 1,300 banks, accounting for 27 per cent of total U.S. banking resources, but an additional number of unit banks (as many as 1,500) were affiliated with and partially owned, though not fully controlled, by bank holding companies.[4] Banking concentration by means of holding company families received fresh impetus with the broad amendment by Congress in 1970 of the Federal Government's bank holding company law; the number of banking units affiliated with bank holding companies (fully or partially controlled) increased from 723 at the end of 1969 to 2,820 at the end of 1972, according to the records of the Association of Bank Holding Companies.[5] Typically, the principal or largest bank in the multiple-unit holding company, usually a city bank, holds the interbank balances of the other units and provides centralized investment direction, securities custody, refinancing services, and management supervision or counsel.

Correspondent banking. Unit banks not in holding company groups obtain comparable mechanical and advisory services from big city banks which act as their correspondents. These services are rendered either at actual cost or at a nominal charge in return for keeping an interbank balance with the city bank. For refinancing, the city bank offers in advance bank loan participation and credit line commitments commensurate with the size of the unit bank and its interbank balance.

---

[4] See *American Banker,* February 13, 1973, pp. 1 and 126.
[5] *Ibid.*

The city bank further serves gratis as intermediary for its correspondents in obtaining an interest return on any of their surplus reserve balances by absorbing these Federal Reserve Bank funds (conventionally shortened to Federal funds) or serves as agent in placing such funds in the interbank market (hereafter referred to as the Federal funds market) on an overnight or temporary basis. It pays the correspondents the prevailing market rate for the use or placement of these funds. Thus a city bank at times can cover a sizable share (over 100 per cent in the case of a few city banks when credit conditions are generally easy) of its own reserve needs from Federal funds borrowed from correspondents on an overnight or very short-term basis.[6]

The many nonmember banks

The existence of many thousands of banks outside the supervision and operational sphere of the cental bank is a distinguishing characteristic of U.S. banking. These nonmember banks have voluntarily forgone ordinary access to the lending facilities of the Federal Reserve System.[7] For them, even contingency access to the Federal Reserve Bank discount facility through a member bank could be difficult under tight credit conditions, because the statutes preclude any member bank from channeling funds borrowed from a Federal Reserve Bank to a nonmember bank without express permission from the Board of Governors.[8] In terms of survival as profit-making institutions, nonmembers have thus committed themselves to relying primarily on their own management and resourcefulness. However, if a nonmember bank becomes insolvent and it is insured, its depositors may share

---

[6] The practice of lending Federal funds for more than one day has been reported in the financial press to have grown markedly in recent years.

[7] Nonmember banks may, however, obtain Federal Reserve Bank advances against U.S. Government obligations at a penalty rate above the discount rate, currently a penalty of 1¾ percentage points. In view of this high rate and the regulatory policy applicable to them, such advances essentially fall into an "access of last resort" category.

[8] Section 19, article 5, of the Federal Reserve Act. See also the Board of Governors of the Federal Reserve System, *Reappraisal of the Federal Reserve Discount Mechanism*, Vol. I (1971), pp. 20-21. In other words, only if the city bank correspondent of a nonmember bank were free of discount debt to its Federal Reserve Bank could it extend credit to the nonmember without risk of supervisory objection in tight credit conditions.

partial to full protection of their deposits, depending on the amount held, through the Federal Deposit Insurance Corporation.

These numerous nonmember banks are mainly small banks—typically, much smaller than the country member banks [9]—and are widely dispersed in local and suburban communities over the entire country. Compared with membership in the Federal Reserve System, nonmember status affords a bank both advantages and disadvantages, which have to be weighed constantly in deciding a bank's best interest.

Lower reserve requirements. A major advantage of nonmember bank status is that the cash reserve requirements imposed are less onerous than those imposed on member banks. For example, over half of the states specify that the reserves of their chartered banks shall be held in vault cash and deposits with other banks in financial centers, but they require percentage levels lower than those for member banks. Also, their nonmember banks are permitted to count as reserves the checks in process of collection (bank float), along with their vault cash and deposits in larger city banks.[10] Another advantage is that the nonmember banks in these states can place their deposited reserve balances with any city bank that offers the best package of compensating services.

---

[9] Nonmember banks with under $50 million in volume of deposits average about half as much in deposits as member banks falling within the same size class—$9 million as compared with $18 million at mid-1972.

[10] The Federal Reserve Bank of Boston has estimated that these uncollected items or balances of nonmember banks equal 8 per cent of their total demand deposits. The reserve funds represented by such balances are still lodged in the banks upon which the checks or other items are payable, and they are counted in the reserve funds of these banks. When also counted as reserve funds by the nonmember banks holding them for collection, they acquire the character of fictional or phantom reserve assets.

A member bank, in contrast, may only deduct uncollected items from its reported demand deposits (other than interbank) to arrive at an adjusted figure for demand deposits to which it can apply the applicable demand deposit reserve ratio in order to determine its required reserve against its net checking account balances. At mid-1972 (week ending July 12) the member bank reserve ratio against net demand and time deposits together stood at 8.5 per cent. If member banks could have added their uncollected balances to their reserves held (rather than deducting them from gross demand deposits) and could count this total in relation to their total demand and time balances, the resulting effective reserve ratio would have been about double that permitted by existing regulations (relevant data drawn from Table A 11, *Federal Reserve Bulletin*, September 1972).

In all but one of the other states (Illinois, which has no reserve requirement), nonmembers are subject to higher formal percentage reserve requirements than either nonmember banks in the cash reserve states or member banks. In these latter states, however, part of the reserve requirements may be met in holdings of federal, state, and local government securities, thus allowing lower gross cash requirement levels than for member banks. Their nonmember banks may also be permitted to count bank float as reserve cash and are generally privileged to hold other cash reserves (in excess of vault cash and bank float) as deposits in city banks.

In addition, some 25 states provide that their bank supervisors may at their discretion vary the nonmember bank reserve requirement within a specified range. While it has been customary for these supervisors to vary the ratios of required reserves, either their discretionary latitude or the specifications for the requirements of their banks have been such that they have been able to maintain the required cash reserve component at a definite competitive advantage over that imposed by the Federal Reserve System on its member banks.[11]

Other factors favoring nonmember status. There are further advantages favoring nonmember bank status. State law may be more lenient than federal law in regard to the range and conduct of authorized financial activities, and the inspection standards of state supervisory authorities and their periodic reporting tasks may be less burdensome than those required of member banks. In addition, some important mechanical services provided to members by Federal Reserve Banks may be provided almost as well, it is claimed, by the big city banks in which correspondent nonmembers hold the main part of their cash reserve balances. As mentioned above, moreover, the private city banks universally emphasize to nonmember correspondents the value both of their continuing investment and management advisory services and of their loan participation and credit line commitment

---

[11] It can be argued that the authority of state bank supervisors to vary the reserve requirement of their nonmember banks makes these supervisors—as a group, if not individually—a kind of monetary authority that is complementary, though subordinate, to the Federal Reserve System. On the basis of aggregate demand deposit statistics for nonmember banks versus those for member banks, however, it is difficult to find empirical support for the effectiveness of any state supervisory actions to change nonmember reserve requirements.

services, which the Federal Reserve Banks are not in a position to provide.

Two factors deter many smaller banks from voluntary membership in the Federal Reserve System. One is the availability of federal deposit insurance to qualifying nonmember banks. This raises the question of whether, if depositors are protected, it is in the interest of stock owners of nonmember banks to incur the banking expenses involved in membership. The other factor, confirmed by postwar banking experience, is the availability over time of a supply of Reserve Bank credit sufficient to sustain vigorous growth of the entire commercial banking system and, on occasion, to avert or cushion a national liquidity emergency. If the role of the Federal Reserve is to provide sufficient reserve funds to support a normal expansion of the banking system and to assure bank reserve availability in liquidity emergencies, any smaller nonmember bank may justifiably question whether the operational advantages of membership warrant its individual participation.

Concern over nonmember banking. For many years, the Federal Reserve has provided operational incentives for banks to become members by supplying gratis or at actual cost many services helpful to banks, especially smaller ones.[12] After 1960, however, Federal Reserve efforts to encourage growth in membership were not success-

---

12 The particularly relevant services are: (1) providing free to members (and qualifying nonmembers) a national computerized network for collecting at par out-of-town checks and automatically crediting the face value of checks cleared to a member's reserve account (or to a nonmember's clearing account) after a maximum of two days for collection time (after one day for country banks, as new computerized check clearance procedures introduced in the fall of 1972 become effective); (2) absorbing all costs of coin and currency shipment between a Federal Reserve Bank and a member; (3) collecting noncash items at actual service expense; (4) placing with dealers, if desired, member banks' buy and sell orders for U.S. Government and federal agency securities; (5) providing a free wire transfer service between major cities for transfers of $1,000 and over, a service of special value to smaller banks in transferring funds to and from the Federal funds market; (6) providing to members free safekeeping and servicing of any U.S. Government or federal agency or municipal securities, a facility enabling collateral advances to members without physical transfer of securities; and (7) providing a computerized book entry system for member bank ownership, custody, and transfer of U.S. Government or federal agency securities, thus obviating the individual handling of them. Besides these mechanical services, the Federal Reserve Banks will make available to smaller member banks, on request, supervisory suggestion or counsel as to management or audit control.

ful, and membership actually declined, while the total number of banks in the national economy increased. The falloff in membership reflected partly withdrawals of some member banks and partly the disinclination of newly incorporated nonmembers to assume the responsibilities of membership.

The Federal Reserve authorities are naturally disturbed by such extended membership attrition.[13] But they are more disturbed by an accompanying downward trend in the relative share of bank deposits (excluding interbank deposits) accounted for by member banks. Over the 1960s, the share of member bank adjusted demand and time deposits declined from about 83 to 76 per cent of the total for all commercial banks. Not only were the number of nonmember banks and their combined holdings of checking deposits growing faster than those of member banks, but Federal Reserve actions designed to temper sharply the growth in demand deposits, when taken in 1966 and 1969, had little apparent effect in slowing the growth in demand deposits of the nonmember banks.

As the adverse trend in membership developed, the Federal Reserve gave increasingly intensive thought as to how to redesign its operational practices to check it. By the early 1970s, it had proposed reforms in its discount facility (Chapter 5) and in its reserve requirements and check clearance services (Chapter 6) that would make membership more competitive with nonmembership in both an

---

[13] Over the 1960s, membership attrition for bank operating cost and net profit advantage mainly affected smaller banks. The Federal Reserve System's concern heightened in 1972 and 1973, however, when seven long-time member banks of some size—over $100 million in deposit liabilities and averaging nearly $250 million—withdrew from membership for this reason. The System's concern was also being influenced by the rapid organization of smaller banks into banking families through the device of bank holding company ownership or affiliation, because the small member banks that joined such families subsequently converted into nonmember status. In a recent decision permitting acquisition of a nonmember bank (Hamilton Bancshares, Inc., of Tennessee), the Board of Governors took the occasion to observe that large banks and families of banks should not shirk their public responsibilities "to be a part of and support the policies of the Nation's central bank"; otherwise, "the task of implementing monetary policy becomes more and more difficult and one-sided in its impact on the banking system as a whole." See *Federal Register*, Vol. XXXVII, No. 7 (January 11, 1973), pp. 1307-1308.

Arthur F. Burns, Chairman of the Board of Governors, later stated that the problem of nonmembership of banks was both one of equity and sharing the burdens of monetary controls and one of increasing "the precision and certainty with which the supply of credit and money can be controlled." (*New York Times*, April 27, 1973.)

accounting and opportunity cost assessment of banking operations for smaller banks.

THE U.S. CREDIT MARKET

Special financial factors affecting the conduct of central banking in the United States are the sheer size of the credit market and the diversity of the debt claims with which it deals. This is made clear in Tables 3 and 4. Table 3 gives a cross-section view by type of claims outstanding at each year-end for 1968-71. Table 4 groups identifiable investor participation by the amount of credit claims held at the end of 1968 and 1971.

Market features

Total debt claims of differing type, maturity, and quality at the outset of the 1970s aggregated nearly $1,700 billion, more than one and a half times the gross national product in current dollars. Part of these claims originate in direct negotiation between borrower and lender—in some instances with participation of several lenders and in others with ownership later transferred by negotiation from initial to other lenders. Additional claims originate in public offerings, regionally or nationally distributed, utilizing the services of investment bankers and security dealers and brokers. These may subsequently be resold in the active secondary trading sectors of the market; indeed, the market's annual trading volume in outstanding debt claims can be estimated to reach well over $1,000 billion already or several times the annual value of the trading in equity securities on the New York stock exchanges. Besides refinancing billions of dollars of maturing claims annually, the credit market in recent years has generated new debt claims at an annual rate ranging from $100 billion to $150 billion.

Participants in the credit market as lenders or investors (Table 4) include the nearly 14,000 member and nonmember commercial banks, the 35,000 nonbank thrift institutions, the cluster of several thousand investment bankers, securities dealers, brokers, specialists, and financial agents, the several credit agencies of the Federal Government, and many others—corporate and individual, domestic and foreign. The monetary system, comprising the Federal Reserve Banks and the commercial banks, accounts for about a third of the total investor portfolio of debt claims and the thrift institutions for about another third, with the remainder distributed among other holders. Foreign investors are estimated to account for only 3 per cent of the total.

**Table 3. Major Types of Debt Claims Utilized in the U.S.
Credit Market, End of Year, 1968-71**

(billion U.S. dollars)

Type of Debt Claim	1968	1969	1970	1971
Short-term claims primarily				
Negotiable certificates of deposit	23.5	10.9	26.1	34.0
Security credit (call loans)	27.5	22.8	22.3	24.0
Short-term securities	147.0	162.3	173.3	174.8
U.S. Government direct marketable [1]	119.4	128.4	133.8	130.4
Federal agency issues [2]	19.4	23.2	24.9	25.2
State and local government issues	8.1	10.7	14.6	19.2
Commercial paper	20.5	31.7	31.8	30.8
Bankers' acceptances	4.4	5.5	7.1	7.9
Long-term claims primarily				
Capital market claims				
U.S. Government bonds	173.3	165.7	180.4	213.0
Savings bonds	51.5	51.1	51.4	53.8
Other direct issues	108.3	98.4	105.6	132.7
Federal agency issues [2]	13.5	16.2	23.5	26.5
State and local government obligations	116.3	121.7	131.7	147.3
U.S. corporate bonds	156.5	170.3	193.1	216.9
Foreign bonds	11.7	11.7	13.2	14.2
Mortgage claims	397.5	425.3	451.7	499.9
Residential	298.6	319.0	337.9	374.7
Other	98.9	106.3	112.6	125.2
Other claims				
Bank loans [3]	139.0	158.6	162.9	177.2
Business	103.7	118.4	121.7	128.2
Finance	11.1	13.7	13.1	14.5
Households	17.5	20.4	21.9	25.8
Foreign	6.8	6.2	6.2	8.8
Consumer credit	113.2	122.5	126.8	137.2
U.S. Government loans [4]	51.0	59.2	63.9	64.3
Other [5]	25.5	33.2	37.7	40.6
Total [6]	1,355.9	1,467.7	1,573.6	1,724.1

Source: Data furnished by the Flow of Funds and Savings Section, Division of Research and Statistics, Board of Governors, Federal Reserve System.

[1] Consists of issues due in less than one year, plus part of those due in less than two years.

[2] Issues by U.S. Government agencies other than the Treasury—for example, issues by federally sponsored credit agencies not in the federal budget. Short-term securities include loan participation certificates issued by the Commodity Credit Corporation, Export-Import Bank, and Federal National Mortgage Association.

[3] Includes loans from bank affiliates.

[4] Includes loans from federally sponsored credit agencies.

[5] Finance company loans to business, mutual savings bank loans to noncorporate business, hypothecated deposits, and policy loans to households.

[6] Excludes negotiable certificates of deposit and security credit shown above, as well as corporate stocks.

Table 4. Participation in the U.S. Credit Market by Investor Category and Type of Deposit, End of Year, 1968 and 1971

	1968			1971		
		Total Assets			Total Assets	
	Number of Institu-	(billion U.S.	(per	Number of Institu-	(billion U.S.	(per
Investor Group	tions	dollars)	cent)	tions	dollars)	cent)
Central banks						
Federal Reserve Banks	12	53.0	3.9	12	71.0	4.1
Commercial banks	13,679	389.0	28.8	13,783	484.7	28.1
Federal Reserve member banks	5,977	314.6	23.2	5,727	379.1	22.0
Insured nonmember banks	7,504	72.1	5.3	7,875	103.0	6.0
Other banks	198	2.3	0.2	181	2.5	0.2
Bank affiliates	—	—	—	132[1]	2.8	0.2
Edge Act corporations and agencies of foreign banks	—	3.3	0.2	135	5.1	0.3
Banks in U.S. territorial possessions	—	1.0	0.1	44	1.6	0.1
Nonbank thrift institutions						
Mutual savings banks	502	66.9	4.9	489	82.9	4.8
Savings and loan associations	5,947	143.2	10.6	5,544	193.6	11.2
Credit unions	23,480	10.9	0.8	23,333	17.4	1.0
Life insurance companies	1,775	160.5	11.9	1,800[1]	182.2	10.6
Private pension plans	1,969	33.0	2.4	1,969	35.4	2.1
State and local government retirement funds	2,165	39.9	2.9	2,165	51.1	2.0
Other financial intermediaries						
Other insurance companies	1,205	25.4	1.9	1,212[1]	32.7	1.9
Finance companies	4,293	46.8	3.5	4,000[1]	60.4	3.5
Investment companies (open-end)	600	5.8	0.4	829[1]	7.1	0.4
Security brokers and dealers	4,355	2.5	0.2	5,077[1]	3.8	0.2
U.S. Government sponsored agencies[2]	5	26.5	2.0	5[1]	48.2	2.8
Other investors						
U.S. Government (lending program)	1	51.2	3.8	1	58.2	3.4
Foreign investors	—	16.0	1.2	—	52.1	3.0
Domestic nonfinancial investors	—	278.2	20.6	—	332.6	19.3
Total assets		1,353.1	100.0		1,722.9	100.0[3]

	1968		1971	
	(billion U.S.	(per	(billion U.S.	(per
Type of Deposit	dollars)	cent)	dollars)	cent)
Monetary demand deposits	170.9	45.6	198.8	42.0
Thrift and other time deposits	203.7	54.4	274.4	58.0
Total commercial bank deposits	374.5	100.0	473.2	100.0

Source: Data furnished by the Flow of Funds and Savings Section, Division of Research and Statistics, Board of Governors, Federal Reserve System.

[1] End of 1970.

[2] Includes Federal Home Loan Banks, Federal Land Banks, Banks for Cooperatives, Federal Intermediate Credit Banks, and Federal National Mortgage Association, which were all privately owned in 1968 and 1971.

[3] Percentages may not add to totals because of rounding.

Note: Assets included in Table 4 consist of holdings of credit market debt instruments as shown in the Federal Reserve flow-of-funds accounts. Credit market instruments are defined as all governmental, corporate, and foreign securities; mortgages; consumer credit; business bank loans; commercial paper; government loans; and minor forms of other loans. The figures exclude holdings of corporate stocks, security credit, trade credit, and institutional deposits. However, they include holdings of credit market debt claims issued by financial businesses as well as by nonfinancial borrowers.

The credit market is basically a composite of local markets, but these are connected or interlinked regionally and nationally by: (1) the activities of banks in urban centers and of nonbank financial institutions of regional or national scope; (2) the functioning of market dealers, brokers, and market specialists in offices throughout the United States; and (3) the participation of business corporations whose scale of operations is regional, national, or even multinational (or effectively made so through a complex of operational or inter-corporate relationships). Funds in excess of local demand are channeled into regional markets to satisfy a demand of larger size; if they then encounter excess supply, they flow on into the market's national center (New York City), where the volume of transactions is much larger and more sensitive to credit cost. Similarly, when the demand for loans exceeds the local supply, the demand spills over to the regional markets; when these markets get overcrowded with loan seekers or when the loans demanded are too big to be handled by the regional markets, qualified borrowers shift demands to the national market.

Through the transactions, communication, and service facilities of the credit market, demand and supply in local and regional markets are quickly balanced within a narrow range of interest rates, and these rates in turn are equated with those in the national market. In the process of equalizing the interest on transactions of similar size, differences may remain that are attributable to the presence or absence of collateral security, the credit standing of the borrower, the negotiability of the credit claim, the duration of the debt incurred, or the lender's willingness to loan.

The end result of this market interrelationship is a national structure of prices for money (that is, interest rates) that move over a period of time in a systematic relationship according to the size of transactions and other important characteristics. This relationship varies at different times as interest differentials widen or narrow within and between markets, but any changes in the grouping of these rates will find their rationale mainly in terms of alterations in market conditions and in terms of variations in the market's forward expectations (especially concerning inflation).

The banking system as an influence

Additional perspective on the U.S. credit market can be gained by viewing it in terms of net major sources of supply of and demand for its funds during four recent years. Table 5 makes clear the great influence on the functioning of the market and on the formation of the pattern and average of interest rates exerted by the total U.S. monetary sector (the Federal Reserve Banks and all commercial banks combined). In the years 1968, 1970, and 1971 when rather vigorous monetary expansion occurred, the monetary sector accounted for a share of the market's funds approaching or exceeding two fifths of the total, whereas in 1969 when monetary expansion was under vigorous restraint, its share of funds fell to less than half of the shares in 1968, 1970, and 1971.

**Table 5. Sources of Supply and Demand Funds
in the U.S. Credit Market, 1968-71**

Supply and Demand Funds	1968	1969	1970	1971	1968	1969	1970	1971
	(billion U.S. dollars)				(per cent of total)			
Funds Supplied, by Investor Category								
The monetary sector	43.8	17.8	39.9	59.1	44.8	19.2	39.1	37.8
Federal Reserve Banks	3.7	4.2	5.0	8.8	3.8	4.5	4.9	5.6
Commercial banks [1]	40.1	13.6	34.9	50.3	41.0	14.7	34.2	32.2
Institutional investors	34.1	29.1	41.0	71.1	34.9	31.4	40.2	45.5
Nonbank thrift institutions [2]	14.8	10.3	15.1	42.1	15.1	11.1	14.8	26.9
Insurance	22.0	22.1	27.2	30.2	22.5	23.9	26.7	19.3
Finance companies	−2.7	−3.3	−1.3	−1.2	−2.8	−3.6	−1.3	−0.7
Other private domestic investors	10.1	34.1	8.4	−11.0	10.3	36.9	8.2	−7.0
Government investors	7.3	10.2	1.7	9.9	7.5	11.0	1.7	6.3
U.S. Government and sponsored agencies	4.7	3.1	4.0	2.2	4.8	3.3	3.9	1.4
State and local governments	2.6	7.1	2.3	7.7	2.7	7.7	−2.2	3.9
Foreign investors	2.5	1.3	10.9	27.2	2.5	1.4	10.7	17.4
Total supply [3]	97.8	92.5	101.9	156.3	100.0	100.0	100.0	100.0
Funds Demanded, by Borrower Category								
Government borrowers	23.8	5.9	27.0	46.1	24.3	6.4	26.5	29.5
U.S. Government and sponsored agencies	13.4	−2.8	13.1	25.5	13.7	−3.0	12.9	16.3
State and local governments	10.4	8.7	13.9	20.6	10.6	9.4	13.6	13.2
Business borrowers	39.1	50.8	49.5	63.0	40.0	54.9	48.6	40.3
Corporate enterprise	30.7	40.2	39.8	48.6	31.4	43.4	39.1	31.1
Noncorporate enterprise	5.7	7.4	6.4	10.3	5.8	8.0	6.3	6.6
Farm enterprise	2.7	3.2	3.2	4.1	2.8	3.5	3.1	2.6
Household borrowers	31.9	32.6	22.3	41.6	32.6	35.2	21.9	26.6
Foreign borrowers	3.1	3.3	3.0	5.6	3.2	3.6	2.9	3.6
Total demand [3]	97.8	92.5	101.9	156.3	100.0	100.0	100.0	100.0

Source: Data furnished by the Flow of Funds and Savings Section, Division of Research and Statistics, Board of Governors, Federal Reserve System.
[1] Includes funds supplied by unconsolidated bank affiliates, Edge Act corporations, U.S. agencies of foreign banks, and banks in U.S. territorial possessions.
[2] Includes mutual savings banks, savings and loan associations, and credit unions.
[3] Figures may not add to totals because of rounding.

Since the credit market's demand for funds continued strong in the year of firm restraint (1969), its response to the contraction in funds advanced by the monetary sector was a rise in all market interest rates to the highest level recorded in a century. These high interest rates in turn resulted—with surprisingly short lag—in a dramatic increase in the share of the market's funds supplied directly by nonfinancial domestic investors. This increase nearly compensated for the contraction in shares provided by the monetary sector and enabled almost as much credit demand (94 per cent) to be satisfied in 1969 as in 1968 when interest rates were appreciably lower and in 1970 when they were rapidly declining.[14]

Of the two components of the monetary sector (the central bank and the private commercial banks), the private banks accounted for the larger and more variable share of the market's funds. This should be expected, since part of the funds that the central banking system provides through market processes go into the reserves of the commercial banks and there form the base on which those banks as a group generate multiple funds to supply the market. In addition to having this elasticity, the commercial banks are thrift or store-of-value (savings and time deposit) institutions. On these deposits they have much lower reserve requirements than on checking deposits, and when the availability of reserves is easy, this helps to make their group reserves stretch further as a support for their deposit expansion.

By combining demand and time deposits, and in some instances a trust business, the commercial banks can be less specialized in the types and maturity of market claims they acquire for their own accounts, custody accounts, or trust accounts than can other financial intermediaries engaged predominantly in time account, insurance, or pension fund activities. Therefore, the banks participate in some measure as lender or investor in virtually all types of credit market claims. When central banking action puts them into a position of aggressive expansion, this aggressiveness in acquiring debt claims soon affects all sectors of the market. A counter process is set in

---

[14] In 1970 and 1971, the aggregate credit supply was strikingly enlarged by dollar funds acquired by foreign monetary authorities in exchange operations to support the international value of their currencies. As they were accumulated, these funds were promptly invested largely in short-term market obligations of the U.S. Treasury or in special nonmarketable Treasury issues exceeding one year in maturity and available to foreign central bank investors.

operation when central banking action limits or reduces the financing of commercial bank expansion.

THE MONEY MARKET

The existence within the credit market of a large and fluid sector known as the money market is of such special relevance to the functioning of the U.S. banking system that it may be regarded as another major factor affecting the whole central banking operation. The role of the money market is to provide ready, low-cost transfer of ownership to negotiable credit claims that are low risk and near maturity, that is, have the attribute of high cash liquidity (Table 6).

Principal features

The money market is primarily a wholesale market and is therefore chiefly accessible to investors able to advance funds or to borrowers able to raise funds through individual transactions of large size. To its investors, this market offers a wide range of claims. To borrowers of its funds, it provides both a secondary trading facility through which a holder may redeem claims through prompt and low-cost sale to other investors and a mechanism by which any new liquid claims that borrowers desire to issue may be quickly distributed to investors in the market. While the money market embraces only approximately a seventh of the entire credit market's aggregate of outstanding claims, it accounts for the great bulk of its annual trading volume.

The money market, like the rest of the credit market, centers in New York City. Its activities, however, are more concentrated at the center than those of the broader credit market, partly because its typical transactions are of large size. The main service intermediaries of the central money market are the securities trading departments of the very large New York City banks, the securities dealers specializing in U.S. Government and federal agency securities as well as several types of private money market paper, the large commercial paper houses, and a small group of very large finance companies. However, the large banks and related intermediaries in major cities other than New York City are active market transactors and, in trading together as well as with the New York market, they form important local and regional submarkets. Efficient communication and information services, as well as numerous long-established interregional trading channels, link these submarkets in a nationally integrated network of liquidity facilities.

The money market is continuously in close communication with foreign financial markets, reflecting its large volume of transactions with foreign private bank and nonbank holders and foreign central banks. Private dollar funds owned abroad are held in short-term investment custody by, or on deposit with, large U.S. banks; the appreciably larger volume of foreign central bank funds is now held,

Table 6. Major U.S. Money Market Claims Outstanding, End of Year, 1968-71

(billion U.S. dollars)

Type of Money Market Claim	1968	1969	1970	1971
Claims used by banks primarily				
Federal funds claims [1]	5.6	8.6	13.5	17.4
Euro-dollar claims [2]	6.0	12.8	5.7	0.9
Loans to brokers and dealers [3]	7.7	6.7	8.6	9.3
Generally available market claims				
Short-term securities [4]	147.0	162.3	173.3	174.8
Treasury bills	74.0	79.8	87.2	97.5
Other (under 1 year)	72.9	82.5	86.1	77.3
U.S. coupon issues	45.4	48.6	46.6	32.9
Federal agency securities	19.4	23.2	24.9	25.2
Municipal securities	8.1	10.7	14.6	19.2
Negotiable certificates of deposit (over $100,000) [5]	23.5	10.9	26.1	34.0
Commercial paper [6]	20.5	31.7	31.8	30.8
Bankers' acceptances [6]	4.4	5.5	7.1	7.9
Gross total [7]	214.7	238.5	266.1	275.1

Source: Data furnished by the Flow of Funds and Savings Section, Division of Research and Statistics, Board of Governors, Federal Reserve System.
[1] Federal funds sold to commercial banks as reported in the call reports for all commercial banks.
[2] Liabilities of U.S. banks to foreign branches.
[3] Commercial bank security loans to brokers and dealers (call loans).
[4] Treasury bills as reported in the Treasury survey of ownership regularly published in the Treasury *Bulletin;* U.S. coupon issues represent flow of funds total of short-term marketable securities, less Treasury bills (including some debts with maturity of more than one but less than two years); federal agency securities include some loan participation certificates; municipal securities, as reported in the U.S. Bureau of the Census, *Governmental Finances* (published annually for fiscal years), interpolated to end of calendar year, on the basis of Federal Reserve information on net issues.
[5] As reported by banks reporting weekly.
[6] Data from monthly survey published by Federal Reserve Bank of New York.
[7] Totals are gross rather than net, because the issuance of some claims may finance dealer inventory or other temporary holdings of alternative market claims, such as bank negotiable certificates of deposit and bank broker and dealer loans.

for the most part, in the form of money market claims through agency services performed by the Federal Reserve Bank of New York. International linkage is also strengthened by the intermediary activities of branches and offices of U.S. banks abroad, by the activities on behalf of head offices and customers of U.S. agencies and branches of foreign banks, and by the participation in the market of numerous corporations and traders that are established in many countries, with various international financial or trading interests.

Large financial and nonfinancial domestic corporations are among the major investors in the money market. The market provides them with liquid paper in which funds in excess of immediate operating needs can, in the interim, earn interest while awaiting longer-term use.[15] With rising levels of interest rates over the past decade, corporations, especially larger ones, have intensified the stringency of their internal cash management and, for this purpose, have widely resorted to computer technology to strengthen their accounting and investment controls. Together, these adaptations have worked to expand greatly corporate participation in money market investment; at the close of 1971, for example, nonfinancial business corporations held just over two thirds of their liquid funds in money market claims, compared with less than half a decade earlier.

The role of the banks. The active use by commercial banks of the U.S. money market reflects several influences arising out of their liabilities to the public. Each individual bank, whether a member or nonmember of the Federal Reserve System, needs to keep a part of its assets invested in claims readily shiftable to other bank and nonbank holders in order to meet short-term declines in deposits, both expected (mostly seasonal) and unexpected; and this need is greater for nonmember banks, which are restricted in access to Reserve Bank discount facilities. When gaining deposit funds, moreover, every bank needs to have readily available money market claims that can be purchased at low credit appraisal and transaction cost (fee or commission); these can serve as high-quality earning assets temporarily, pending more permanent placement in bank loan or investment paper of higher appraisal and transaction cost.

---

[15] For example, distribution as dividends, interest payments on corporate debt, expenditure on real investment, or financial investment in the long-term claims or equity issues of other corporations.

Both member and nonmember banks need, or may find highly useful at times, an interbank market through which they may borrow cash or lend excess reserves or operating balances (Federal funds) very temporarily (overnight or for a few days), pending other more costly portfolio adaptations.[16] In fact, many smaller banks rely on the Federal funds market for the regular use of some of their secondary reserves (liquid assets).

Special role of large city banks. The very large banks situated in leading financial centers have special uses for the money market's facilities. They function primarily as intermediaries for the Federal funds supplied by outside banks to the interbank market, and they must stand ready to lend funds through it, should demand rise sharply, or to absorb residual funds not demanded from it. They are thus exposed to both a sudden efflux and a sudden influx of bank reserves.

In addition, the big city banks act as bankers for the large regional, national, and multinational industrial and trading corporations. They hold the operating balances of the large majority of nonmember banks and most of the nationally known nonbank financial institutions. In this special role, they confront at any time a large backlog of loan commitments of uncertain takedown as well as uncertain demands for temporary financing of liquidity needs from each of these customer groups. Therefore, they must constantly maintain both an open bidding position for money market funds and an ample portfolio of its claims to adapt to the variable asset and liability shifts caused by the flow of these funds.

In a year of acute stringency in the whole credit market such as 1969, the exigent pressures upon these city banks not only induced them to bid vigorously for Federal funds but also to resort to such competitive expedients as aggressive borrowing from the Euro-dollar market, sale of assets to nonbank investors under repurchase arrangements, borrowing through subsidiaries and affiliates from the commercial paper market, and discounting with the Federal Reserve Banks as much as permissible (Chapter 6).

---

[16] Resort of nonmember banks to the Federal funds market, while much less frequent than that of member banks, has been growing in recent years. In the Dallas Federal Reserve District, some 28 per cent of its nearly 700 nonmember banks were sellers of Federal funds during 1969 (a year of credit restraint), and 43 per cent during 1970 (a year of monetary expansion). In 1969, 4 per cent were purchasers of funds and in 1970, 2 per cent. See the Federal Reserve Bank of Dallas, *Business Review*, March 1972, pp. 1-8.

Reserve Bank practice in member bank discounting. The active participation of member banks in the money market reflects in part the attitude of the Federal Reserve System toward their borrowing from the Reserve Banks. Under existing discount practice as prescribed in the regulations of the Board of Governors, member bank access to the discount or lending facility is normally a privilege to be used as a temporary supplement to a bank's other adjustments of assets in meeting adverse swings in deposit liabilities or sudden shifts in loan demands.

The member banks, accordingly, cannot regard borrowed Reserve Bank funds as a continuously and generously available supplement to their own resources. Rather, they are expected to maintain an appropriate margin of asset holdings in money market claims or to borrow excess reserve funds of other banks through the interbank or Federal funds sector of the money market to ease the adjustment to short-term changes in deposits and loan demands. The counterpart of this official constraint on member bank use of Reserve Bank credit is that when member bank reserves and deposits are otherwise growing at a vigorous pace—especially in the early stages of such growth—the member banks are expected to keep the frequency and volume of their Reserve Bank debt in moderation and to use some of the accruing deposit funds to enlarge their portfolios of money market claims.

Service to the Treasury and Federal Reserve

There are two other main participants in the money market—the U.S. Government and its domestic monetary authority, the Federal Reserve System. The U.S. Government is the major borrower from the money market, accounting for 60 per cent of its generally available claims, and the direct borrowings of the federal agencies (guaranteed as to principal and interest by the Federal Government) may bring the total up to 70 per cent or more. Treasury bills of three to twelve months' maturity constitute most of the direct claims against the Federal Government in the money market; the remainder consists of coupon issues with an unexpired maturity of less than one year.

In part, the predominant role of short-term debt of the Federal Government in the money market reflects the curb on the issuance of long-term U.S. Government bonds because of the 4¼ per cent statutory interest ceiling on Treasury bond offerings until 1971 (a rate below that prevailing in the market on long-term Treasury bonds since mid-1965),[17] and because of a long-standing congressional prejudice against sales of new U.S. bonds at a discount. It has also resulted from the strong expansion over the past decade in the demand for liquid claims in the money market. Short-dated Treasury paper, being free of credit risk, is an ideal interest-earning liquidity asset for money market investors. Consequently, these claims are the most actively traded in the market. All of these factors encourage heavy Treasury reliance on the issue of money market paper.

The continuously active secondary trading facility in short-term government claims serves efficiently the dual investor-seller role of the Federal Reserve System in its open market operations. Having ready access to an actively traded market for riskless liquid assets, the Federal Reserve can freely engage in large outright transactions to buy or sell as dictated by policy. Since these transactions would generally account for only a moderate fraction of that sector's total transactions, they would have little effect on market prices. This characteristic of the money market also encourages Federal Reserve repurchase and matched sale-purchase transactions (discussed in Chapter 3), which mainly facilitate an orderly market.

THE MONEY MARKET AND MONETARY POLICY

The U.S. money market is a sensitive and often volatile segment of the credit market. It is important for central banking because it is the first to feel and to react to the environmental or monetary policy developments affecting the liquidity of the commercial banks or of the nonbank private sector. Accordingly, any shift in Federal Reserve monetary policy, which must be implemented through actions affecting the reserve position of the banks, is registered almost at once in the performance of the money market.

To illustrate this process, assume that U.S. monetary policy shifts from constraint on the expansion of aggregate monetary demand to stimulation of its current growth. Such a shift is typically manifested by larger outright net purchase transactions by the Federal Reserve, primarily in the short-term government security sector of the money market. The larger net purchases of short-term securities, with the

---

[17] In the spring of 1971, however, Congress authorized the issuance of up to $10 billion of new Treasury bonds at rates exceeding this ceiling.

proceeds first accruing to the money market banks but soon being distributed among many money market participants, add to the cash reserves of numerous banks throughout the United States. Thus, the banks as a group can supply additional funds to the money market, accelerate their own lending and investment activities, and generate an increased volume of deposits against newly acquired loan and investment assets.

Effect on bank policies

To acquire earning assets of high quality outside the central money market at a low appraisal and transaction cost, the banks for an initial period actively turn to the money market as lenders to the Federal funds sector, and they also become active net purchasers of other money market claims in competition with money market banks investing the Federal funds that flow to them. The observable market response will be a decline, perhaps sharp, in the interest return from placement of Federal funds as well as from other money market claims. In this development, the nonbank investors, who are sellers of market claims, will benefit from capital gains. As the added bank reserves become more widely distributed through money market transactions among a still larger number of outside banks, this downward adjustment of market rates will receive added support from bank loan and investment expansion by these outside banks, in this way diffusing further the easier credit and monetary conditions through the financial mechanism.

Initially, monetary response will tend to be a spreading increase in the cash balances of investors for reinvesting and a greater ease for borrowers in issuing new claims to the markets. This will be followed by a gradual increase in bank lending to those taking the initiative in investing or spending with borrowed bank funds and, *pari passu*, by a gradual rise in the average cash balance holding of businesses and consumers. Should the shift in monetary policy be from stimulus of monetary expansion to its restraint, the sequence would generally be the reverse.

As the impact of bank participation in the credit market extends through the various sectors, the entire range of these submarkets will, with short lag, feel the direct and expected effects of a modified flow of commercial bank credit transactions in response to altered monetary policy. Both long-term and short-term interest rates in all sectors will come under downward or upward pressure simply because the shift in bank demand exerts a sufficiently strong marginal effect on the demand for, and supply of, credit in the subsectors. The effect on interest rates will be greatest in the money market, as its various issues of paper are almost interchangeable for meeting the liquidity needs of investors and have advantages in transactions cost and fluctuation in market value over longer-dated claims. Accordingly, the interest rates of the money market tend over a period of time to move as a closely knit band, varying systematically according to the credit risk and marketability of each type of market claim (see Chapter 5, Chart 6).

The market's performance

In the present-day pattern of central banking in the United States, the Federal Reserve System relies on the money market as the central mechanism through which any change in the availability of commercial banking reserves (initiated at the Federal Reserve's discretion) is distributed among many banks. Once the availability of bank reserves has been altered, the money market further helps to translate the change in bank reserves into a multiple increase (or decrease) in the overall supply of credit, the extent of the increase (decrease) depending on the prevailing compulsory bank reserve ratios.

In other words, the U.S. money market works to help to accelerate or decelerate credit and monetary expansion, as determined by official monetary policy. In this way, it amplifies initial impulses set in motion by such policy and assists in their conversion into more powerful impulses which affect credit developments broadly through the economy as well as the cash balance positions of businesses, governmental units, and individuals. Thus, a changed climate of supply, availability, and cost of credit, as well as a larger or smaller average of cash balances, permeates the economy and works to expand or curb the financing of current investment and expenditure.

The Federal Reserve System has traditionally placed special emphasis on the money market's sustained orderliness and efficiency. Its justification for doing so has been twofold: (1) the vital function that the domestic money market performs in the U.S. monetary process; and (2) the dependence in the present-day context of many large financial and business units upon it to provide ready market redeemability for their interest-yielding liquid claims (see Chapter 3).

This emphasis alone does not make the market's performance a primary aim or target of the Federal Reserve's monetary operations, although such policy risk is always present. There have been periods in the past when to professional and academic observers the dominant target was to ensure that the component elements of the money market fluctuated within a narrow range. Without questioning the evidence of history, the Federal Reserve officially stresses that such emphasis basically recognizes that in the modern setting the task of pursuing its broader economic responsibilities while relying mainly on open market operations would be more unpredictable and difficult if the money market's attributes of efficiency and orderliness should deteriorate significantly (Chapter 3).

3 Open Market Operations

OPEN MARKET PURCHASES of eligible financial claims at the initiative of a central bank create new reserve cash for the commercial banks, and open market sales of such claims absorb reserve cash from them.

The United States is one of three countries in which open market operations have developed into a major instrument of central banking monetary policy.[1] It is perhaps the only country at the present time where they have become the *dominant* instrument for implementing monetary policy.

Certain conditions must be met before open market operations can serve as the major policy instrument. First, there must be a large and continuously active market in which the central bank can conduct transactions in eligible claims without the risk of sharply affecting their market activity and prices.[2] Second, the central bank's discount

---

[1] The other two countries are the United Kingdom and Canada. The open market operations that their central banks conduct differ in important aspects from those of the Federal Reserve System for historical and institutional reasons.

[2] In other words, a market having the characteristics of (a) "depth," in the sense that securities dealers hold many orders that will be made effective by small fluctuations above and below prevailing market prices; (b) "breadth," in the sense that the volume of orders is large and from many investors; and (c) "resiliency," in the sense that sharp and unexpected fluctuations in prices will

mechanism must be designed in such a way that the volume of credit (discounts and advances) that it makes available to meet the requests of private banks can be effectively coordinated with its own transactions in the open market. This condition has a crucial bearing both on the practice the central bank follows in relating its discount rate to market interest rates and on any standard constraints it imposes on direct access to its credit by the private banks. Third, open market operations must be able to serve as a continuously available and flexible instrument for exerting a steady or a progressive degree of either restraint or stimulus, as dictated mainly by domestic and partly by international financial conditions, without marked capricious or perverse effect on the performance either of the credit market itself or of the banking system as a whole.

PROCEDURES IN OPEN MARKET OPERATIONS

Open market operations in the Federal Reserve System are the province of the Federal Open Market Committee and are conducted exclusively under that Committee's direction and supervision, as provided by law. The Committee's agent is the Federal Reserve Bank of New York, which conducts all its transactions for the joint account of the twelve Federal Reserve Banks. It allocates among them the daily net portfolio change on the basis of their relative share of the total outstanding note liabilities of the Federal Reserve Banks.

A senior officer of the Reserve Bank of New York carries out the transactions of the Federal Open Market Committee. Designated by the Committee to serve as Manager of the System Open Market Account, he is appointed by the Reserve Bank of New York to serve concurrently as its Senior Vice-President in charge of the Bank's Securities Function. Although he is thus an officer of two statutory bodies, as Account Manager of the Federal Open Market Committee he is immediately and solely accountable to the Committee for ordering on its behalf any open market transactions for the account of the Federal Reserve System.

Scope of authorized transactions

The Committee's transactions in the open market are executed by

---

cause a prompt flow of new orders into the market from many investors. See the "Report of the Ad Hoc Subcommittee of the Federal Open Market Committee" (November 1952) in the *Hearings of the Joint Economic Committee, 83rd Congress, 2nd Session,* December 6-7, 1954, pp. 257-307, specifically p. 265.

its Account Manager through the mediation of approximately 24 securities dealers—with a few more nonbank than member bank dealers—who are prepared to do business in U.S. Government securities and also in federal agency securities (hereafter referred to as agency securities) as principals with banks, other financial institutions, and indeed any sizable investor. In the language of the financial community, they function as primary marketmakers. In this role, they regularly bid firm prices against customer offers to sell, and they quote firm prices when customers seek to purchase. While their bid and offer prices are constantly changing throughout a trading day, they will take purchases from customers into their own inventory if such purchases are not matched by concurrent sales and will meet sales to customers from their own inventory or through concurrent market purchases.

The Account Manager transacts orders with dealers who have a well-established record of financial responsibility and a reputation for integrity and efficient performance in serving buyers and sellers of federal securities. Besides these primary dealers, others (including banks) engaging as intermediaries in the market for federal securities act mainly as agents for customers, often on the basis of a commission or other compensation rather than as principals for their own account. As brokers, they do not make a practice of carrying open positions and usually clear through the group of primary dealers any net transactions remaining at the close of a business day.

Each dealer with whom the Manager does business must be willing to: (1) report to the Reserve Bank of New York each day the volume, by maturity, of his buying and selling transactions for that day; (2) supply the Manager's trading desk with his buying and selling quotations throughout each market day; (3) report his borrowing position by major sources to the Reserve Bank of New York daily; and (4) submit his firm's statement of financial position and net earnings to the Bank at scheduled intervals.

The Manager's open market transactions comprise three types: (1) outright transactions in authorized securities; (2) purchases of such securities from nonbank dealers under agreement to resell them to the same dealer within an agreed period of up to 15 days (repurchase transactions); and (3) sales of authorized securities to either bank or nonbank dealers under agreement with the Federal Reserve System to repurchase identical securities within a period of one to seven days (matched sale-purchase transactions).[3] Insofar as practicable, the Committee's transactions are based on competitive dealer pricing. As specified by statute, the Committee's authorized securities include all direct and fully guaranteed obligations of the U.S. Government; the direct and fully guaranteed obligations of federal agencies; and short-term bankers' acceptances of prime quality not exceeding six months in maturity.[4]

Because the market for U.S. Government securities is the most active and continuous of the three market sectors, most of the Federal Open Market Committee's outright, repurchase, and matched sale-purchase transactions are conveniently made in these securities. Transactions in agency securities were first authorized in late 1966, but until late 1971 were limited to repurchases with dealers, as issues by individual agencies were neither of large size nor consistently traded in the market in sufficient volume to permit sizable Federal Reserve transactions on both sides of the market. Wider investor interest and greater activity in the agency market led the Committee in late 1971 to authorize outright purchases and sales on a gradually increasing scale with a view to helping to "widen the base of its open market operations and . . . [add] . . . breadth to the market for agency securities."[5] Both

---

[3] In addition, he may make accommodation loans of U.S. Government obligations for up to five days (subject to renewal) to both dealers and banks participating in the computerized clearing arrangements of the Federal Reserve System for U.S. Government securities transactions. Such loans, however, are not cash loans and have no effect on bank reserves. Their only purpose is to improve the functioning of the market by avoiding failures of dealers to deliver securities sold on customary schedule.

[4] The open market operations of the Federal Open Market Committee embrace marketable convertible currencies as well as the marketable securities of the U.S. Government and its agencies. As the Committee's operations in key foreign currency markets are different in orientation and purpose from those in the domestic securities market and are conducted in close collaboration with the U.S. Treasury, they are described separately (see Chapter 4).

[5] In November 1966, when it was decided to limit operations in federal agency securities to repurchases, the outstanding volume of such securities totaled about $14 billion; in August 1971 when outright purchases and sales were also authorized, their volume approximated $45 billion and has since grown further. The Committee has limited purchases to issues of $300 million and over, maturing in five years or less, and to issues of $200 million, maturing in over five years. Also, it has limited Federal Reserve holdings of the securities issued by any one agency at one time to 20 per cent of the outstanding amount of that issue, and holdings of all securities issued by any one agency to 10 per cent of the aggregate outstanding amount of all such issues.

outright and repurchase transactions are made in bankers' acceptances. Such repurchase transactions are discontinuous and in limited amounts, because the Federal Reserve System's portfolio holdings of acceptances may not at any one time exceed $125 million or 10 per cent of the acceptances outstanding in the market, whichever is smaller.[6]

Steps in policy making

The Federal Open Market Committee meets at the offices of the Board of Governors in Washington about once a month, but interim meetings may be called by its chairman either on his own initiative or at the request of the Committee's Account Manager. Urgent matters may sometimes be taken up through meetings held by closed-circuit telephone hookup. At each regularly scheduled meeting, the Committee's principal business is the formulation of its current economic policy directive (to be made public after a lag of 90 days and to be accompanied by a summary of the background discussion).[7] In accordance with the practice adopted by the Committee in early 1972, each formal directive now consists of four paragraphs.[8]

The Committee's first concern in formulating the directive is with the economy—production, employment, prices, and balance of payments; hence, the initial paragraph summarizes the latest movement shown by the major economic indices. The second paragraph describes the most recent trends in the financial variables that the Committee relies on for guidance in conducting its open market operations. In this way, it formally recognizes the effects, both immediate and delayed, of current financial conditions on the economy.

---

[6] An arbitrary limit set by the Federal Open Market Committee in the mid-1950s and to date unchanged.

[7] Each directive is also formally published after its public release 90 days later in the next issue of the *Federal Reserve Bulletin* and, after the close of each year, in the *Annual Report* of the Board of Governors, in both cases under the title: "Record of Policy Actions of the Federal Open Market Committee."

[8] The Committee's economic policy directive formerly contained only two paragraphs, the first of which combined the substance of the first three paragraphs of the present format, while the second set forth the operational directive to the Manager. This latest adaptation aims at achieving a better form of presentation as well as greater latitude in emphasizing key developments influencing a decision to change policy.

In the light of the economic and financial indicators incorporated in the first and second paragraphs, as well as the Committee's forward projections for the economy (made clear in its policy record), the Committee's objectives for monetary policy are then stated in the third paragraph. The Committee's statement of policy aims usually remains unchanged for an extended period. However, should it need amendment at any meeting in the light of experience and of recent and projected economic performance, it would be modified to indicate any change (trade-off) in emphasis. Modification is effected with utmost care, for it may imply some shift in guidance that the Committee will set for the Account Manager's market operations in order to attain the different policy emphasis. In addition, the Committee always has in mind the paragraph's relevance for guiding collateral bodies within the Federal Reserve System in the use of instruments for which they have statutory authority.

Market strategy for the Manager

The Committee's concluding task is to express in the fourth paragraph a market strategy for its Account Manager in terms of the money and credit variables and a pattern of money market—and more broadly credit market—performance that he is to use as guides or interim targets relating to policy goals. In order to shape an appropriate guidance strategy, the Committee reviews past, current, and prospective relationships among key economic and financial variables. Sometimes this assessment may place special emphasis on very recent developments affecting the economy, the money and credit markets, the monetary aggregates, and interest rate levels, while on other occasions it may emphasize a longer perspective.

Over successive meetings, the Committee strives to arrive at a consensus about its forward operations that reflects group judgment as to whether the monetary developments and prospects in the economy are consonant with, or deviate from, the objectives that the Committee had accepted earlier. If inconsistencies have developed, some changes will be necessary in the Committee's operational tactic, and perhaps also in policy objectives. When consensus is finally reached, the Committee will concern itself with the possibility of undue volatility in money market conditions, indicating generally a range of rate fluctuation for Federal funds that it considers reasonable in relation to prospective money market pressures and to which it desires its Manager to adhere for the time being.[9]

The Committee's paragraph of formal instruction to the Account Manager is normally quite compact, yet sufficiently explicit (given preceding committee discussion) to make clear the monetary and credit elements that he should take into consideration (and is accountable to the Committee for considering) in his day-to-day transactions. The instruction will usually refer to any forthcoming Treasury financing so that the Manager can modify his strategy in the market while the financing is being absorbed. As his purchases in most months will exceed his sales, he may also at times be authorized to emphasize the purchase of longer-term securities when providing the reserve funds to the banks, in order to dampen rising trends in long-term interest rates or to relieve the short-term sector of any downward pressures that might result from concentrating his purchases there.

The Committee's interest in the Account Manager's market transactions does not end with its formulation of operating instructions at the committee meeting. Between scheduled meetings, the Manager's operating strategy and plans are monitored daily by telephone communication between him and the Committee's senior staff at the Board of Governors; participation regularly includes one Reserve Bank president as a member of the Committee, often the president of the Reserve Bank of New York, who is Vice-Chairman of the Committee, and perhaps one or more Board members who are statutory committee members. While the Manager's orderly money market operations (discussed below) and his policy operations, as well as the interrelations between them, may come into question in the course of this daily monitoring, the discussion for the most part assumes that he will always attempt to offset seasonal and irregular factors. In addition, the Committee requires the Manager to submit detailed written reports on his transactions to its members regularly before each meeting.

---

[9] To member banks, the Federal funds rate is a measure of the opportunity cost of marginal reserve funds in relation to their profit margin. To other participants in financial markets, it is an early indicator of the Committee's willingness to supply the banking system as a whole with nonborrowed reserves. Since it is a highly sensitive and volatile rate, readily visible to all concerned, its behavior enables financial markets to become quickly aware of any shift in the policy thrust of Federal Reserve open market operations. See Alan R. Holmes, "Open Market Operations and the Monetary and Credit Aggregates—1971," *Federal Reserve Bulletin*, April 1972, pp. 340-62, especially p. 342.

THE ACCOUNT MANAGER'S TRANSACTIONS

The Account Manager's transactions reach sizable totals each year (Table 7). For example, his gross market transactions—outright (but excluding cash redemptions), repurchase, and matched sale-purchase—for the five years 1967-71 averaged $93 billion annually. If matched sale-purchase transactions were excluded as being technical market accommodations, the annual average would come to $65 billion; and if both repurchases and matched sale-purchases were excluded for this reason, the volume of his outright transactions would average about $12 billion annually for the same years. As the federal securities market features wide participation by investors and large activity, the Manager's daily volume of outright transactions alone averaged only about 3 per cent of the gross volume of outright transactions handled by market dealers in this period.[10] Most of the Manager's outright transactions (nearly 95 per cent in the 1961-72 period) are in short-term securities—preponderantly in U.S. Treasury bills (Chart 5).

The nerve center for the Manager's operations is the trading desk of the Securities Department of the Federal Reserve Bank of New York. The staff of this desk keeps in close contact with each of the principal dealers in the markets for securities of the U.S. Government and its direct agencies; collects information continuously from dealers on their bid and ask quotations by maturity sector throughout each trading day; keeps posted on market performance for reference in assessing activity and price changes on any given day; and, on the basis of daily reports from each dealer on his sources for financing and periodic reports on his financial position, keeps a close watch for any threats to the liquidity and solvency of any individual dealer.

Committee transactions in securities

The dealers in federal securities, though small in number, are highly competitive, each seeking to obtain as large a share as he can of the business each day, including transactions originated by the Account Manager. To ensure that every dealer has an opportunity to compete on an equal footing, the Manager advises all dealers simultaneously of a major projected Federal Reserve transaction in

---

[10] Obviously, the inclusion of the Manager's technical transactions in this comparison would raise this volume to over 15 per cent, but these are properly excluded as transient market accommodations.

Table 7. Open Market Transactions of the Federal Reserve System in U.S. Government Securities, 1961-71

(million U.S. dollars)

Year	Net Change in System Open Market Account Holdings	Outright Transactions			Repurchase Transactions		Matched Sale-Purchases[1]	
		Gross Purchases	Gross Sales	Cash Redemptions	Gross Purchases	Gross Sales	Sales	Purchases
1961	1,497	9,105	6,057	1,310	4,620	4,861	—	—
1962	1,939	9,829	6,721	1,353	6,115	5,932	—	—
1963	2,773	8,789	4,533	1,152	8,895	9,226	—	—
1964	3,451	10,454	5,437	2,093	9,286	8,760	—	—
1965	3,724	9,888	4,227	1,690	14,923	15,171	—	—
1966	3,514	9,051	8,642	2,176	9,756	9,420	4,056	4,056
1967	4,830	8,548	2,746	3,739	16,793	17,287	1,300	1,300
1968	3,824	7,050	3,462	1,477	15,862	15,994	16,400	16,400
1969	4,217	5,188	1,752	1,848	23,790	23,790	22,487	22,487
1970	4,988	10,294	1,782	2,160	33,859	33,859	12,177	12,177
1971	8,076	12,344[2]	3,841	1,064	44,741	43,519	15,906	15,906
Total	42,833	100,540	49,200	20,062	188,640	187,819	72,326	72,326
Average	3,894	9,140	4,473	1,824	17,149	17,074	12,054[3]	12,054[3]

Sources: Board of Governors, Federal Reserve System, *Annual Reports*, 1961-71; and data furnished by the Government Finance Section, Division of Research and Statistics, Board of Governors, Federal Reserve System.

[1] First authorized in 1966.
[2] Includes $485 million in gross purchases of federal agency securities, which were first authorized for outright purchase in 1971.
[3] Six-year average.

Chart 5. Total Outright Transactions of the Federal Open Market Committee in the Market for U.S. Government Securities, 1961-72

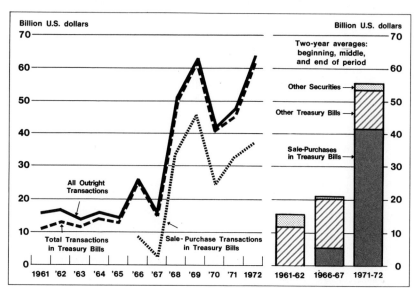

[1] Includes sale-purchases but excludes repurchases. Sale-purchase transactions, first authorized in 1966, have since grown appreciably and largely account for the subsequent sharp rise in the Committee's outright transactions. Their inclusion reflects technical differences between repurchases and sale-purchases; however, both types are commonly used in orderly market operations.

short-term U.S. Government or federal agency securities and he asks them for bids or offers. After reviewing their firm quotations, he makes a choice of dealers on the basis of amounts bid for or offered at best and next-best prices until his order is covered. If the transaction is relatively small and not suited to full market auction (as, for example, some transactions for customer account), he will seek bids or offers from three or more dealers, executing the transaction at the best bids or offers that will cover his order.

As far as possible, practices for short-term securities are applied to longer-term securities. However, trading activity in these securities is normally smaller than in bills, the inventories carried by dealers are usually much smaller, and the spread between bids and offers made by dealers is wider and more sensitive to the size of transactions. Therefore, in his purchases of longer-term securities, the Account Manager has to guard against orders that dwarf the usual size of transactions in the market, thereby causing dealers either to be reluctant to make offers or to be encouraged to raise their offer prices beyond those in effect before the market had been notified of the projected transaction. Accordingly, transactions are scaled to the Manager's best estimate of what can be done under existing conditions. Having made this judgment, his standard practice is to seek offers for a consistent amount of notes or bonds within specified maturity classes from dealers whose inventory reports, submitted to the Reserve Bank of New York after the previous day's closing, showed such security holdings. Upon receipt of these offers, he promptly allots his transaction among them according to the amounts that they have individually offered and at the best prices they have quoted, until he covers his transaction.

For many years the Account Manager has avoided sale offers of longer coupon issues, because they have too often had unsettling effects on prices of these securities and have raised questions among the dealers about the Federal Reserve's purpose in selling them (rather than short-term securities) and about the possibility of further selling orders. Moreover, since the Federal Reserve System has had ample holdings of Treasury bills and coupon securities of short-term maturity for selling as occasion demands, the Manager could easily wait until the maturity of longer-term issues held in portfolio shortened.

Two-way transactions

The Account Manager's repurchase transactions supply dealers with temporary financing, whereas his matched sale-purchase transactions temporarily absorb their working funds.[11] Both types thus attain their objective of affecting the reserve position of money market banks.

The Manager employs a specially tailored technique for each type of transaction. He announces the availability of repurchases to all primary dealers; however, bank dealers who have the discount facility of a Federal Reserve Bank available are not eligible for repurchases. He may use either the competitive or the quasi-competitive method of executing the transaction. The competitive method, introduced in April 1972, is his present standard procedure, but the quasi-competitive method is still an alternative when authorized by the Federal Open Market Committee.

---

[11] As noted earlier, the authorized maturity limit is up to 15 days for his repurchases and up to 7 days for matched sale-purchases.

Using the competitive technique, the Manager announces the availability of a specified amount of repurchase funds to all dealers at some point in a trading day. Nonbank dealers who need such financing submit bids within a stated time for the amount of sales they will make for the period he offers, and they quote the rates they are willing to pay the Federal Reserve. The Manager's final task is to allot his offer of purchase among the dealers bidding the interest rates closest to established rates on competitive financing from market sources. The successful bidders must agree to repurchase the securities that the Manager acquires in the transaction at least by the forward date he specifies, that is, a date within his authorized maturity limit for repurchases. Thus, the funds supplied by his repurchase transactions on a given date must be withdrawn from the market by the forward date specified by him. At times, when the Manager wishes to inject temporarily a larger amount of reserves than nonbank dealer borrowing needs will permit, he may invite nonbank dealers to seek out collateral from banks and other customers who wish to obtain repurchase accommodation.

If the Account Manager were to follow the superseded quasi-competitive technique, when announcing the availability of repurchase funds to dealers, he would indicate the discount rate applying to his transactions.[12] Nonbank dealers with pressing inventory problems would respond to his offer, because his accommodation rate would be attractive in comparison to the rate then charged on funds from other sources for financing. Once in possession of dealer responses, the Manager would allocate the amount of repurchases sought among the dealers in accordance with a formula based on their past price quotation and transaction performance with the trading desk. The securities acquired by the Federal Reserve under these arrangements would be subject to their repurchase by the dealer on or before an agreed date, at the latter's option.

The quasi-competitive method of arranging Federal Reserve repurchase transactions had two disadvantages: (1) since the Account Manager had some leeway in designating his rate for repurchase accommodation, the announcement of his offers of accommodation

---

[12] The Federal Open Market Committee gave the Account Manager authority to choose as his lower limit (1) the prevailing discount rate, (2) a rate between the discount rate and last auction rate on three-month Treasury bills (if below the discount rate), or (3) the last such auction rate.

was sometimes interpreted by participants in the securities market as being a portent of policy change, thereby affecting the market's performance;[13] (2) the Manager was not always able to ensure that the repurchase rate he set was close to the current cost of funds available from private sources. Although these disadvantages were by no means crucial, there was ample justification for adoption of a more economically defensible procedure.

The Account Manager offers matched sale-purchase arrangements with very short maturities to all dealers whenever he judges the reserve position of member banks to be temporarily in sufficient excess over their total required reserves to exert an undue downward pressure on money market interest rates.[14] In these situations, he offers to sell one or a number of Treasury bill issues to any dealer, bank or nonbank, at the going price under dealer agreement to resell the bills to him at a specified firm price a few days later. The dealers are given one-half hour to determine the amount of the Manager's offer they are willing to take and to specify the price at which they will resell.[15] When all dealer responses are in, the Manager selects for commitment the dealers whose composite bid and resale quotations will yield the best prices. When the Manager repurchases the bills at maturity of the transaction, the reserve funds absorbed by the initial sale are automatically returned to the market.

---

[13] Late in 1971, the Committee permitted its Account Manager temporarily to breach its earlier lower limit on his repurchase rate in order to "supply reserves on a flexible temporary basis, in anticipation of possible large-scale sales of U.S. Treasury bills [then held] by foreign central banks, and in the light of prevailing costs of funds to dealers and . . . [the difficulty of arranging] . . . repurchase agreements . . . under existing rate limitations." At the Committee's first meeting in 1972, this phrasing was amended to add, as a concluding clause, ". . . while taking account of international developments." The unexpected effects on the market of these special actions prompted the Committee to re-examine the Manager's repurchase practices in mid-1972, resulting in abandonment of the quasi-competitive method. See the Committee's record of policy actions in the *Annual Report* of the Board of Governors, 1971, pp. 201-202, and in the *Federal Reserve Bulletin*, April, May, and July 1972, pp. 396-97, 461-62, and 641-42, respectively.

[14] As mentioned in Chapter 2, when banks outside New York are experiencing a general increase in their reserve positions, many will immediately channel the increase back into the reserves of the money market banks through the Federal funds market.

[15] In many cases, the dealer serves as middleman for the transaction, placing the securities with a bank having a temporary reserve surplus.

Transactions for Treasury and foreign central banks

The Senior Vice-President in charge of the Securities Function of the Federal Reserve Bank of New York serves not only as Manager of the System Open Market Account but also as fiscal agent in securities transactions for the U.S. Treasury. In the latter capacity, he advises the Treasury on the scheduling and terms of its financings. In addition, he executes for the Treasury all market transactions in securities for the Federal Government's trust accounts that the Treasury administers, market transactions authorized by the Treasury for these accounts or its stabilization fund to temper adverse tendencies in the market, and any market transactions the Treasury may direct to facilitate dealer underwriting and distribution of its new or refunding issues. In some years, the total transactions of the Reserve Bank of New York in federal securities for the Treasury account may reach a sizable volume, though in no year have they rivaled those executed for the Federal Open Market Committee.

Individual Treasury orders, whatever their size, entail debits or credits to the Treasury's deposit balance at the Reserve Banks; transactions to buy for Treasury account add to bank reserves while orders to sell reduce them; thus these operations must be viewed by the Manager in the context of his wider responsibilities of open market intervention. In conducting the Treasury's transactions, the Reserve Bank of New York follows the same practices of receiving competitive bids or offers from dealers as it does for the Federal Reserve System. However, the trading desk typically identifies customer orders as such to the dealers to differentiate them from those for the Federal Reserve account.

The Federal Reserve Bank of New York is prepared, of course, to undertake all orders for U.S. Government securities placed by foreign central banks and international financial institutions that have a correspondent account. These orders are received by the Bank's Foreign Department and are promptly channeled to its Securities Department for execution. At times the orders may be filled directly as received from the holdings of the Federal Reserve, but more often they are transacted with dealers through the market—in either case, at the best prices quoted at the time.[16] When such orders are large,

---

[16] On one recent occasion in June 1972, the Federal Open Market Committee instructed its Manager for the immediate future to execute foreign central banks' orders for Treasury bills as far as practicable by sales from the portfolio of the

they are consummated through market auction to ensure competitive bidding and pricing, in some cases being combined with transactions of the Federal Reserve being handled on the same day. Over a relatively short period, aggregate foreign orders executed by the trading desk can be sizable. For example, over the years 1971-72, which were characterized by an unusually large U.S. balance of payments deficit, purchase orders to increase foreign correspondent holdings of marketable U.S. Government securities totaled about $23 billion.[17]

Manager's role in market surveillance

The two official participants in the market for federal securities—the Treasury and the Federal Reserve System—have a special concern that the market's functioning be above criticism or reproach, not only in underwriting Treasury financing and in executing their respective official transactions but also in handling any investor's transactions. The immediate contact of the two official agencies with the market is the Senior Vice-President in charge of the Securities Function of the Federal Reserve Bank of New York, who is also Manager of the System Open Market Account. They look to his constant surveillance over market practices to assure their appropriateness and desirability. In recent years, the two agencies have affirmed his responsibility for positive surveillance by establishing a Treasury-Federal Reserve staff group to work with him in a continuing study of the market's operations and practices and in an assessment of the adequacy and effectiveness of the reporting required of dealers.

ORDERLY MARKET INTERVENTIONS

The Federal Open Market Committee's primary concern is with the Federal Reserve System's general monetary policy and interim open market operations appropriate to it. The Account Manager's actual market interventions between meetings, however, chiefly serve to

---

Federal Reserve System in order to avoid significant declines in bill rates. Just before this, foreign central banks had been acquiring large amounts of dollars while maintaining exchange rates for their currencies within the margins agreed with the International Monetary Fund.

[17] The aggregate of marketable U.S. Government securities, held in custody for foreign account by the Reserve Banks, totaled $35 billion at the end of 1972. In addition, they held nearly $16 billion of nonmarketable Treasury bonds and notes in custody for foreign official correspondents.

maintain an orderly market, that is, to cope with the interplay of monetary factors that can give rise to wide day-to-day and week-to-week variations in the money market. For example, his gross repurchase and matched sale-purchase transactions in the market clearly have these aims, as they only temporarily alter basic supply or demand in the market. Over the five years 1967-71, such transactions averaged more than seven eighths of his reported market transactions. His outright (nonmatched) transactions were only one eighth of this annual average, and less than half were needed to sustain the growth that occurred in the Federal Reserve's total open market portfolio.

Market factors in operations

The Account Manager in his orderly market operations must take account daily of the following seven organic market factors, the first four of domestic and the remaining three of international origin.

(1) Reserve Bank float or credit in connection with their service to member banks in clearing out-of-town checks under a two-day collection allowance;[18]

(2) The Treasury's cash balance at the Federal Reserve Banks, against which all U.S. Government checks are drawn;

(3) Other authorized deposits with the Federal Reserve Banks, that is, deposits of nonmember banks maintaining check-clearing accounts with them and deposit balances of federal agencies and international institutions;

(4) The volume of currency in public circulation;

(5) The Federal Reserve System's international monetary reserves, represented by its gold and special drawing right (SDR) certificate

---

[18] In 1970-72, Federal Reserve Bank float for check-clearing averaged $3 billion a day and showed a week-to-week fluctuation in daily averages ranging from $2 billion to $4 billion. After adjustment to a November 1972 change in the regulation of the Board of Governors covering Federal Reserve check clearance and collection crediting (discussed in Chapter 6), the average level of float was expected to decline significantly (by as much as $1 billion). Moreover, as a result of recent innovations in computerized intercity check-clearing and wire-transfer facilities as well as of the development of a computerized system of book entry for the safekeeping and ownership transfer of U.S. Government securities held by member banks for their own or custody account, the average volume and range of fluctuation of check-clearing float should gradually decline further. Other developments in computerized book entry that are still being explored may eventually cause some additional decline to take place over a longer period.

accounts with the Treasury, through which international transfers of gold and SDRs are monetized or demonetized;

(6) The deposit balances that foreign monetary authorities, mainly central banks, hold with the Federal Reserve Banks, either for current operating purposes (central bank stabilization of the exchange value of their currencies) or awaiting investment in the U.S. money market or in Treasury nonmarketable obligations; and

(7) The Federal Reserve System's own foreign currency balances, acquired in defensive foreign exchange transactions and also by credits from foreign central banks, to cushion volatile capital flows internationally and to maintain orderly dollar exchange market conditions.[19]

Conduct of orderly market operations

These seven monetary factors can be a large element in the Account Manager's market operations on a quarterly as well as an annual basis, as shown in Table 8 [20] for 1970, a year in which the Federal Reserve policy shifted from strong restraint to active stimulation of bank credit and monetary expansion, while the entire credit market's performance was marked by continuing uncertainties and historically high, though declining, interest rates. As quarterly averages smooth out interim fluctuations, it is evident that transitory shifts in these factors (individually and collectively) could in the short run have large and undesirable effects on the reserve positions of member banks. Consequently, the Federal Open Market Committee has long regarded the offset or cushioning of market instabilities stemming from these shifts to be orderly market operations for maintaining trading in short-term federal securities as a pivotal activity within the money market. Accordingly, a discretionary responsibility for them has in effect been delegated to its Manager.

To facilitate market intervention of the Account Manager for this purpose, his staff maintains detailed records of factors having a sys-

---

[19] This item largely dropped out of the list of inherent monetary factors during the period from August 15, 1971, when convertibility of the U.S. dollar into gold was suspended, to July 19, 1972, when Treasury-Federal Reserve foreign currency operations were resumed for purposes of helping to maintain orderly conditions in the dollar exchange market. After six months, disequilibrium in dollar payments abroad again occasioned their suspension, but at mid-1973 operations were once more resumed. See Chapter 4.

[20] Two of the less variable factors listed above (3 and 6) are combined in Table 8 as "Other deposits and liabilities net."

tematic seasonal and growth pattern. Each business day the Manager has before him projections of the expected change in these monetary factors, and he looks to their interplay in judging the net impact on member bank reserves and the need for compensating transactions. For factors subject to irregular seasonality or to sudden random change, he must make ad hoc appraisal and judgment on the basis of their estimated net effects on key money market variables and must look to movement of the Federal funds and other sensitive money rates

Table 8. Factors Affecting Member Bank Reserves, 1970

(million U.S. dollars; end of period)

Factors	1970	1970 I	II	III	IV
Endogenous monetary factors					
Federal Reserve float	+667	−1,312	+516	−617	+2,080
Treasury accounts (Treasury currency and other cash holdings and Treasury deposits at Reserve Banks)	+773	+314	+227	+192	+40
Other deposits and (other) liabilities net	−272	−211	−108	+36	+11
Currency outside banks	−3,122	+839	−1,591	+245	−2,615
Gold, SDRs, and foreign accounts at Reserve Banks	+1,151	+1,416	+30	−258	−37
Defensive market transactions in foreign currencies net (including change in other Federal Reserve assets)	−1,383	−391	−665	−112	−391
Total endogenous factors	−2,186	+655	−1,591	−514	−912
Federal Reserve monetary operations for domestic aims					
Open market operations in authorized securities	+4,185	−1,695	+1,443	+2,499	+1,938
Member bank borrowings	−834	−168	−49	−226	−391
Total System monetary operations	+3,351	−1,863	+1,394	+2,273	+1,547
Member bank reserves	+1,165	−1,208	−197	+1,759	+635

Source: Data derived from quarterly averages of daily figures supplied by the Banking Section, Division of Research and Statistics, Board of Governors, Federal Reserve System.

to gauge the validation of this assessment. If his assessment has not been confirmed, he may need to take further counteraction.

Interaction of market and policy operations

Inevitably, fluctuations in the net market factors may occur when overt market intervention would be desirable to meet policy objectives, so that the Account Manager may deliberately allow the fluctuation of market factors to accomplish the same result as deliberate policy intervention. Thus, the release or absorption of bank reserve funds through market factors may implement policy in the short run just as much as actual market intervention. In practice, however, the Manager's orderly market and policy-directed transactions will be closely knit from day to day, and only he can ascertain from the flow of banking figures over ensuing weeks whether his joint orderly market and policy operations at a particular time have been in keeping with his last strategy directive from the Committee.

While the Federal Open Market Committee wants to be kept informed about the rationale underlying the trading desk's daily transactions, it is more concerned with their ultimate results than whether they are "orderly market" or "policy oriented." In other words, the Committee wants to know how the total bank reserves, after seasonal adjustment, have moved over a specified time; whether the overall availability of reserve funds to the banks has been consistent with the Committee's plan; whether banks have been promptly and actively responding to the cumulative changes in their reserve positions by expanding or limiting their lending and investment; and whether the performance of the money and credit markets has been compatible with the Committee's operating strategy and policy objectives.

Justification of orderly market transactions

The Federal Open Market Committee's orderly market transactions take place almost solely in the money sector of the market in U.S. Government and federal agency securities. The Committee's justification for the scale of these operations may be explained in a general way.[21] First, the money market reflects the changing demands of the

---

[21] See the Committee's official explanation published by the Board of Governors: "Monetary Aggregates and Money Market Conditions in Open Market Policy," *Federal Reserve Bulletin*, February 1971, pp. 79-104, with special reference to pp. 92-94 (reprinted in the Board's booklet, *Open Market Policies and Operating Procedures—Staff Studies*, July 1971, pp. 194-218, specifically pp. 206-208).

private sector of the economy for liquidity, and it is the Federal Reserve's responsibility to keep the market orderly to facilitate these changes.

Second, the market is subject to temporary instabilities—large seasonal and sometimes unpredictable short-term shifts in the demand for money and credit—which are self-corrective. Consequently, it is desirable to avoid sharp short-term fluctuations in money market conditions that could be disruptive to broader credit market conditions, particularly if large enough to cause any sizable number of commercial banks to make abrupt adjustments in their holdings of marketable financial claims. Hence, the Federal Reserve System should offset or cushion the effects of these temporary instabilities on the reserve positions of member banks and thus obviate potential widespread banking adjustments.

Third, if the Federal Reserve should permit a sudden and large transitional shift in money market conditions, market participants might erroneously interpret the market's instability as a harbinger of a more lasting change in credit conditions, and the public at large might be misguided as to prospects for the economy. Until longer-term change in credit demand or supply is more evident, precautionary action by the Federal Reserve to temper abrupt money market instability may be justified.

Finally, more current and continuous information is available on the money market (showing its use of funds from the banking system, trading volume, interest rates, and other aspects) than for any other market sector.

These reasons for orderly market transactions do not mean that the Committee feels justified in pursuing market orderliness to such an extreme that it may fully offset unstable market factors. Experience over the past decade has taught the Committee that "orderliness" too narrowly conceived can lead to virtual "stabilization" of prices and of yields on securities, especially those of short-term maturity. It also can practically eliminate market uncertainty about any larger range of fluctuation, thereby impairing investor responsiveness if such a larger fluctuation should occur. As the next section explains, the Committee in very recent years has made clear its awareness of these dangers and has sought (though not always with full success) to keep its range of market orderliness consonant with other aims of current open market operations.

COMMITTEE GUIDANCE OF POLICY OPERATIONS

Over the first half of the 1960s, the Federal Open Market Committee focused particularly on "money market conditions" as its operational target, specifying the Account Manager's task in terms of maintaining, easing, or tightening prevailing money market conditions, especially interest rates. Although the Committee never officially defined "money market conditions," [22] it left its intentions to be inferred from the Manager's practices in market transactions.

"Money market conditions" guideline

The market gradually understood that the Committee's definition of "money market conditions" was neither mystifying nor all-embracing. Rather, it referred to the performance of interrelated strategic money market variables that the Account Manager could assess either currently or after very short lag. The Committee's market indicators comprised the ranges within which the interest rates on Federal funds and on Treasury bills were free to move; the trend of total bank reserves; the recent movement of total borrowings and excess reserves of member banks, as well as of their net borrowed or free reserve position; and current tendencies in the distribution of nonborrowed and borrowed reserves between banks in the money market and other banks.

From evolving practice in open market intervention, it was clear that the Committee might give different emphasis to individual indicators (for example, to money market rates vis-à-vis borrowing by member banks and related marginal reserve variables) and that even interrelated variables could show quite divergent movements over short periods. The Account Manager, however, was obliged to heed the Committee's instruction as to the "money market conditions" it desired and, if these variables moved too divergently, he was to try to put them back into a relationship which would accord with his instruction.

No matter how the Committee might qualify the importance of selected money market variables, it usually specified for them a relatively limited range of fluctuation. The practical outcome of the

---

[22] A decade later, however, the term was at least semiofficially explained in a study by Stephen H. Axilrod, "The FOMC Directive as Structured in the Late 1960s: Theory and Appraisal," in the Board's booklet (*ibid.*, pp. 5-6 and pp. 14-17).

Account Manager's operations under this pattern of instruction was inevitably one of eventually accommodating whatever demands for credit and money the economy at large was then generating.[23] Consequently, the Committee's reliance on "money market conditions" as the Manager's guideline gave it no very firm control over the quantity of credit the Federal Reserve itself supplied, no satisfactory influence over the course of credit market interest rates appropriate to normal forces of supply and demand, and no means of effectively regulating growth in the reserve positions of commercial banks. However, this practice did assure the financial and business community that any undue contraction in bank reserves and in public holdings of bank deposits would be prevented, even if it was by Federal Reserve open market purchases that increased total bank reserves and risked subsequent unplanned (and potentially inflationary) expansion of bank credit.

One monetary aggregate for guidance

Concerned that monetary growth over the early 1960s had been excessive and had unduly provoked public criticism of Federal Reserve policy, the Committee at mid-1966 decided to modify its method of guiding open market operations. Accordingly, it instructed the Account Manager to continue to look to "money market conditions" for primary guidance but to modify his operations "provided that" a single monetary aggregate—total bank credit [24]—would deviate from the course the Committee had projected for it. His action should be reasonably compatible with the conditions in the money market and the economy that the Committee desired his operations to foster.

While thus modifying its instructions to the Manager, the Committee failed to direct him explicitly as to how far total bank credit should be

---

[23] *Ibid.*, p. 6.

[24] However, a measure of total bank credit embracing all commercial banks is reported only twice each year, although interim estimates are available monthly. The Committee found that member bank deposits, a continuously available series, reported daily, showed similar secular movement and that total member bank credit and total member bank deposits showed closely coincidental short-term fluctuation. It concluded that the member bank deposit series could be accepted as a satisfactory *proxy* for total bank credit, in spite of some likely divergences over the short run and some gradual divergence over the long run from the relatively faster deposit and bank credit growth of nonmembers.

permitted to deviate from the Committee's target before he modified his operations to remedy the situation. Further, the Committee gave no definite instruction as to how much change in money market conditions it would tolerate if the Manager took such action. Partly because of these vital omissions, partly because the Committee's target was seldom set with precision, and perhaps also because the Committee was unwilling to authorize "large" changes in money market conditions at the Manager's initiative, he could only proceed after delay in the light of clear evidence. Hence, he seldom implemented this instruction and, when he did, his actions were seldom forceful.[25]

Use of this proviso clause in the Committee's directives to the Manager did not last long. After three years of highly unstable performance of total bank credit combined with gradual acceleration of inflationary trends, it became evident that open market operations guided by money market conditions with such a proviso represented little advance toward closer Federal Reserve control over the nation's money creation and credit market process for the purpose of economic stabilization.

To regain a firmer control and to dampen inflationary trends, the Committee concluded that it had to tolerate money market conditions in 1969 (and persisting into 1970) that were marked by unprecedentedly high levels of market interest rates and severe tightness of credit availability throughout U.S. financial markets. It also had to press steps by the Board of Governors to restrain city banks from over-exploiting nondeposit sources of lendable funds, a practice that developed during this period (Chapter 6). In these circumstances, the Committee felt obliged to re-examine its guidance procedures and to amend them in ways that it considered more workable and more acceptable in the public interest.

New pattern for instructing the Manager

Early in 1970 the Federal Open Market Committee decided that its instructional guidance to the Account Manager would in the future be formulated by reference to a desired forward course for four major

---

[25] It can be argued, however, that even these modest implementations were helpful to the Federal Open Market Committee (with its frequent meetings) in identifying turning points in money and broader credit market pressures.

monetary aggregates:[26] (1) the active or narrowly defined money stock, that is, adjusted demand deposits of all commercial banks plus currency in circulation outside the banks (a variable conventionally identified as M_1); (2) the active or narrowly defined money stock, together with time deposits other than negotiable certificates of deposit of $100,000 and more at major city banks [27] (identified as M_2); (3) total credit of member banks (represented by their total adjusted deposits)[28] as an appropriate proxy for total commercial bank credit; and (4) total member bank reserves, the Federal Reserve's primary leverage base in influencing the other three.

The key new element of this revised pattern of instruction was that the Committee henceforth would rely on formally derived staff projections for the four variables that extended forward several months instead of relying on ad hoc group judgment based on very recent trends. Initially, the Committee stated that it would attach a roughly equal weight to each variable. After brief experience, however, the Committee indicated that it would trade off its projections of these interdependent aggregates for what it believed to be desirable conditions of credit availability and interest rates in the credit market and particularly in the money market—depending on the interplay of transitory economic forces and tendencies. As amended in this way, the new plan of instruction became a joint guidance strategy.

Apparently, the Committee intended that the Account Manager should keep immediate money market conditions reasonably aligned with the targeted magnitude of the four guidance variables. Should the latter diverge from the Committee's projections (given the relative

---

[26] A semi-official explanation of the Committee's intent under the new plan is set forth in the Federal Reserve article, "Monetary Aggregates and Money Market Conditions in Open Market Policy," and reprinted in the Board of Governors' booklet, *Open Market Policies and Operating Procedures,* both cited above (see footnote 21). All of the studies in the booklet help in understanding the background for adoption of the new guidance plan.

[27] Serving a money market function primarily and, after issue, involving no direct customer-bank relationship until maturity.

[28] In order that member bank deposits might serve as a satisfactory current proxy for total bank credit, it became necessary, as member banks exploited nondeposit sources of funds during 1969-70, to revise the proxy to include them. The proxy presently used, therefore, adds to member bank deposits funds borrowed from the Euro-dollar market and (through bank affiliates) the commercial paper markets.

weight attached to each), the Manager could either adapt his market operations to bring about any change in money market conditions and the member bank reserve position that would be necessary to put the other guidance variables back on target, or—if this seemed outside the scope of his instruction—refer the problem back to the Committee for additional guidance. The Committee's new instructional format thus combined two time horizons in its own planning and in the manager's operations: (1) a short-term horizon with its focus on the money market and its interest rates; and (2) a longer-term horizon, extending forward three to six months, with its focus on targeted paths for the monetary aggregates.

After experimenting with the new pattern of operational instruction for two years, during which there was greater irregularity in performance of monetary aggregates than the Committee desired, a consensus was reached early in 1972 that the member bank reserve aggregate (modified as "reserves to support private nonbank deposits")[29] should be shifted from a longer-run target to a guidance element that would be coordinate with money market conditions in the Committee's short-run strategy. In this way, the Manager's response to unanticipated trends in the monetary aggregates might be more explicitly, even though tentatively, prescribed, thus facilitating (1) a closer adherence of the aggregates to their projected paths and (2) after a period of experience, a better adaptation by money market participants (especially banks) to any wider range of short-run variability in money market interest rates and other conditions that the Committee might then permit.

The Committee, however, apparently still had in mind some limit to such variability, desiring that its Manager avoid abnormally large fluctuations in money rates and conditions caused by temporary shifts in liquidity demands or by a temporary maldistribution of bank reserves nationally. The reason for this was that any large fluctuation in market conditions might be interpreted by market participants as signaling a change in Federal Reserve policy or would otherwise heighten the market's uncertainties. Thus, the Manager had to keep continually alert to this concern of the Committee.

---

[29] Technically defined as reserves required against private demand deposits, total savings and other time deposits, nondeposit funds subject to reserve requirements, and excess reserves.

In changing its guidance pattern to achieve a more effective operational instruction, the Federal Open Market Committee was manifestly seeking a tighter and more responsive control over the cyclical fluctuation and longer-term trend of Federal Reserve credit, together with that of the commercial banks, while continuing to exercise an influence over the short-run level and longer-run course of interest rates, mainly those in the money market. Such joint control was believed to be consistent with the alternative theories on how monetary policy could best meet stabilization goals[30]—that is, it took into account both the mechanics of the monetary aggregates and the vital role of interest rates in the decision making with respect to private credit usage—and thus entailed a balanced application of both theories. Therefore, the 1972 adaptation could accommodate longer-term policy aims and also allow the Committee to sanction short-run operations in order to cushion erratic shifts in demands for desired liquidity, in demands for money to spend, or in maldistribution of bank reserves between regions.

Its practical purpose, as officially stated, was to conduct the Federal Reserve open market operation with greater assurance that "undesired shortfalls or excesses in demands for goods and services, and hence in demands for credit and for money balances, would not lead more or less automatically to too little or too much expansion in bank reserves, bank credit, and money."[31] The ultimate and express aim of the Committee was the orderly and stable development of both the financial markets and the underlying economy by combining in committee operations long-run targets and short-run flexibility.[32]

DIFFICULTIES WITH THE OPEN MARKET INSTRUMENT

In choosing open market operations in the early 1950s as their dominant policy instrument, the Federal Reserve authorities were influenced mainly by five considerations: (1) the immediate and powerful leverage of such operations on the banks' reserve position; (2) their continuing instant availability for keeping the money and security markets orderly or, more specifically, for coping with both

---

[30] Committee statement on "Monetary Aggregates and Money Market Conditions in Open Market Policy," *op. cit.*, pp. 86-87.

[31] *Ibid.*, p. 87.

[32] *Ibid.*

inherent market factors and unusual transient developments affecting the banks' reserve position; (3) their flexibility in dealing with cyclical instabilities in credit and money flows; (4) their ready reversibility in the event that financial forces affecting monetary policy and action had been misjudged; and (5) their usefulness in facilitating government financing when no important compromise of monetary objectives was involved. While these are all fundamental points, Federal Reserve experience in applying the open market instrument has brought to light a number of problems of interest to central bankers generally.

The agent's instruction and money creation

In administering an open market operation for policy purposes, for example, a principal difficulty is that of deciding on a definite instruction to the agent-broker who executes a central bank's market transactions. Because such transactions directly affect the demand for or supply of debt claims in money and securities markets—thereby affecting the level and variability of interest rates, perhaps even stabilizing interest cost to borrowers from the money market—there are constant private and public pressures on the policy-making authority to maintain stable short-run costs of credit as a dominant aim of market interventions in order to limit uncertainties within the financial markets. If too persistently pursued, operations based primarily on short-run credit costs will lead to neglect of the longer-run quantitative effects of official transactions on the process of money creation and on its end products—the major monetary aggregates and the general availability of credit to borrowers—in relation to economic activity.

Because these longer-run effects seem to be a fundamental focus for a central bank, a dilemma confronts open market policy. At one extreme, open market operations may give priority to the lowest attainable short-run credit costs and to the corresponding money market conditions as the chief target for official transactions. Consequently, this priority must lead to the banking system's ready response to the demands of the economy for credit and money in the near term, leaving the monetary aggregates to perform abnormally. At the other extreme, the growth trend of one or more major monetary aggregates may be the priority target for open market operations. If so, a much longer perspective must govern official transactions in the short run, and the central bank authorities must accept a wider short-run variation in market interest rates and related conditions—at times accentuated by unexpected event or shock.

One way out of this dilemma in the present state of central bank expertise is for the bank to resort to a joint strategy of perspectives and targets in policy making. This is the choice of the Federal Reserve authorities under their new guidance plan for market operations. How well such an instructional strategy will meet U.S. central banking objectives over a period of years remains to be demonstrated.[33] It would seem to be the only practicable adaptation, however, that could reasonably reconcile, on the one hand, competing theories of how monetary policy should function under present conditions and, on the other hand, the shorter-run and longer-term responsibilities of a central bank for keeping credit and monetary conditions consistent with the orderly functioning of the financial markets. Regarding this second point, long experience has repeatedly shown the modern financial market mechanism to be highly sensitive to current economic and political developments—including central banking actions or avoidance of action.

Risks in orderly market operations

Inherent monetary factors affecting money creation, which are a potential source of seasonal or transient instability in the securities markets, need careful identification and measurement. In many instances, their net effect on the banks' reserve position should be tempered (or even offset) by the open market agent at his discretion. However, such cushioning interventions by the agent may be dependent not only on the interplay of these factors of market instability but also on the range of fluctuations, particularly of short-term interest rates, that higher central bank authority has instructed him to consider as a special criterion of money market orderliness.

Should his policy instruction be to keep changes in market conditions "within a fairly narrow range," the agent's market operations to offset instabilities beyond that range could come into conflict with his instruction relating to other operational targets such as the desired performance of key monetary aggregates. To adhere to his "orderly market instruction," the agent might either provide or absorb more bank reserves than would be needed for attainment of these longer-range targets. If demand or supply pressures to tighten or ease market conditions were strong, his transactions to keep them within a narrow

---

[33] The difficulties of such a strategy for the central bank's market agent during a single year are brought out by Alan R. Holmes, *op. cit.* (see footnote 9).

range would have to exceed those dictated by the balance of technical market variables alone.

Furthermore, the longer the instruction to the agent remains in force, the larger would be his cumulative market transactions to keep market fluctuations within the range specified. Such growth in orderly market transactions could prove detrimental to the central bank's open market operation: (1) if it impaired the self-reliance of market dealers in financing their securities positions; (2) if the money market also became overdependent on the central bank's market transactions; and (3) if the central bank's releases of reserve funds to the commercial banks should surpass or fail to reach the amounts needed to realize its longer-range operational targets.

Should these effects actually develop over an extended period when credit demand is strongly expanding, additional adverse complexities could arise. Interest rates in the longer-term sectors would rise, widening the spread between them and those in the money market. With expanding reserve positions keeping the latter rates within a narrow range, there would be a continuing availability of credit at commercial banks to meet the credit needs of private borrowers. In these circumstances "narrow money market orderliness," if pursued too long, could seriously handicap the conduct of monetary policy directed to the stabilization goals that central bankers usually regard as desirable.

Limits to active open market operations

Open market operations, like discount rate action, can be used only within limits to implement a restrictive or a stimulative monetary policy. In periods of restraint—adopted, say, to combat excessive boom accompanied by inflationary tendencies—too tight a reserve availability brought about by official market operations might precipitate acute banking tensions, combined with a sharp advance in market interest rates and an abrupt decline in security prices.

Such an extreme development could threaten the solvency of some financial institutions, have severe, adverse effects on the net worth of individual investors, and give rise to recessionary and deflationary trends. Should there then be widespread defaults on outstanding loans of solvent banks, the uncertainties that ensued could severely dampen the banks' sensitivity to a later reversal of monetary policy toward stimulation of banking expansion with the result that the bank reserves supplied generously by open market operations could pile up in excess, thus negating somewhat the shift in monetary policy to bring about economic revival or at least delaying the intended effect.

In a longer period of recovery less traumatic to the banking community, open market purchases too vigorously pursued to counter cyclical recession may also result in some piling up of a sizable transitional surfeit of excess reserves in commercial banks. If resumption of productive activity in the economy then generates a sudden increased demand for bank credit, the response of the banks could produce an undesirably rapid monetary expansion. In view of the excess reserves in the banks, open market operations would need to absorb a good share of that excess, but such action may affect financial markets unfavorably and further endanger economic recovery.

Risks in facilitating government financing

The central bank's responsibility for facilitating the market financing of national budgetary deficits may also affect open market operations. If the treasury (or ministry of finance) in any country uses the central bank's agent-broker for its market transactions in any underwriting period, it may cause him a potential "conflict of interest." If the central bank's responsibility extends to actual underwriting of such financing, the central bank may risk money creation during the financing period in excess of that required for purely monetary policy objectives, and such excess money may be hard to extinguish later. If the central bank is permitted to use the money-creating powers of the whole banking system in full support of government deficit financing, the central bank jeopardizes its own stabilizing influence on the domestic value of the national currency. The central bank's traditional independence within the government structure has evolved largely to guard against this danger.

Difficulties from central banking structure

The central bank's organizational structure leads to other difficulties for open market operations. Authority is obviously at its administrative center. In a decentralized organization such as the Federal Reserve System, it has been expedient to place the responsibility for open market operations in a committee of "large size," with a membership or participation of top officials representing all organizational units that share responsibility for market operations.[34] Given the Federal Reserve System's statutory structure and organization, the Federal Open Market Committee must: (1) delegate the execution of its market transactions to the Reserve Bank at the credit market's center; (2) permit its agent-broker to serve a dual Federal Reserve-Treasury role; (3) utilize a staff that has other assignments and is drawn from various geographic areas; and (4) function without its own direct budget control.

There is considerable criticism of this decentralized arrangement, but the Federal Reserve has made it work without serious impediments to efficiency in decision making. In a less complex central banking structure, the administration of open market operations would be centralized under a less cumbersome authority, and the central bank's agent would be held directly accountable to this authority. The critical risk in such tighter integration of open market operations with the policy-making responsibility lies, of course, in entangling the policy function too closely in daily operations. This could distort the perspective of the central bank's policy authority on the underlying economic forces subtly changing its policy problem as well as on the options open to it for using other available instruments as alternatives or supplements to open market action.

Coordination with other instruments

A further difficulty is coordination of the open market operation with other monetary instruments of central banking. When the open market instrument serves as the dominant means of implementing monetary policy, coordination of the other instruments with open market operations is the prime difficulty. As instrument coordination is discussed in Chapter 8, it is sufficient to state here that a central

---

[34] G. L. Bach's authoritative study of the decision-making process in U.S. monetary and fiscal policy proposes that the Federal Open Market Committee be abolished and that final authority over all monetary policy instruments be placed in a Board of Governors of five members. In determining Federal Reserve policy and its implementation, the Board would be required to consult regularly with the twelve Reserve Bank presidents. See G. L. Bach, *Making Monetary and Fiscal Policy* (The Brookings Institution, Washington, 1971), p. 247. However, it is difficult to imagine any important policy-making gain in substituting regular meetings of 17 officials for the meetings of 19 officials now being held under the present Board of Governors-Federal Open Market Committee regime.

bank has only one overall policy at any specified time, though it has several operational means for carrying out that policy.

Hence, it must use all instruments available in whatever coordinated sequence and strength may be expedient—or even necessary—to achieve the objectives given first priority. A central bank's success in coordination is always largely determined by the amount of support that its monetary policy receives from the fiscal and other economic policies of the central government.

PUBLIC DISCLOSURE OF MARKET OPERATIONS

As a central bank's open market operations at any given time are either absorbing financial claims of the debt market or supplying them to it and affecting—directly and indirectly—market interest yields, the financial community can always be expected to follow them closely. Because open market operations create or extinguish money and influence the supply of credit through transactions in a privately organized market, the financial community at large constantly needs to be assured that such operations are properly conducted.

Therefore, it is always important for the central bank to issue publicly, and with short lag, either its formal record of decisions and actions in open market transactions or an authoritative explanation of the objectives prompting them. Such authoritative background becomes more important as the size of the open market operations becomes larger in relation to the private market's total activity. The basic need in the modern context is that the central bank support its credibility with the public by the fullest disclosure feasible of the conduct as well as the objectives of its monetary policy.

4

Open Market Operations in Foreign Currencies

SINCE EARLY 1962 (but with periods of interruption as described below), the open market operations of the Federal Reserve System have also included international transactions in designated convertible currencies.[1] These transactions are undertaken in collaboration with the U.S. Treasury to maintain orderly trading conditions for the dollar in international exchange markets. They are restricted mainly to periods when (1) the foreign exchange markets are characterized by fluctuating two-way transfers of funds to settle intercountry trade and financial commitments or to take advantage of investment opportunities; or (2) disequilibria in intercountry money flows are brought about by temporary influences.

Over the past two decades, central banks of other convertible currency countries have widely used the U.S. dollar to intervene in exchange markets for the purpose of sustaining orderly trading conditions for their own currencies in periods of temporary imbalances in payments flows. Such official interventions have therefore given

---

[1] These included the Austrian schilling, Belgian franc, Canadian dollar, Danish krone, French franc, deutsche mark, Italian lira, Japanese yen, Mexican peso, Netherlands guilder, Norwegian krone, Swedish krona, Swiss franc, and pound sterling.

rise to closer cooperation among the central banks concerned with the day-to-day administration of exchange markets. During the same period, there has been a closer interlinking of world financial markets as a result of growth in world trade, improved world communications and transport facilities, and the rapid expansion of multinational banking and commercial or industrial enterprise. These developments have heightened market sensitivity to imbalances in money flows between countries, with the result that market forces may quickly generate such a volume of transfers internationally that they exhaust the capabilities of official intervention and eventually produce crises requiring exchange realignments. In recent years, successive market crises of this type have prompted officials in the various countries, through their participation in the International Monetary Fund, to undertake reform of the international payments system.

ADMINISTRATIVE ARRANGEMENTS

In the same way as for its operations in U.S. Government securities, the Federal Open Market Committee designates the Federal Reserve Bank of New York to serve as its agent in executing foreign currency transactions on behalf of the System Open Market Account. Since the foreign exchange market is also centered in New York City, but has many technical features distinguishing it from the securities market, the Committee regularly selects the senior officer of the Federal Reserve Bank of New York in general charge of its Foreign Department as its Special Manager for conducting these operations. Each year the Committee adopts a formal directive that sets forth the Committee's operational objectives and provides explicit guidelines for the Special Manager to follow in any foreign currency transactions in which he may engage for the System Open Market Account. This directive is revised annually in the light of the Committee's experience in dealing with foreign currencies during the preceding year.

In the initial arrangements for these operations, the Special Manager was given two interrelated functions: (1) intervention in the spot and forward exchange markets for the dollar and authorized foreign currencies when such action is consistent with committee guidelines; and (2) maintenance of a network of advance arrangements for reciprocal currency exchange with foreign central banks.

INTEREST OF THE U.S. TREASURY

Since the U.S. Secretary of the Treasury is charged by statute with direct responsibility for stabilizing the exchange value of the dollar through the Treasury Stabilization Fund or through such agencies as he may designate, he had to approve the inauguration of foreign currency operations by the Federal Open Market Committee. He concurred in the Committee's program with the understanding that it would be "supplemental to and in collaboration with . . . [foreign exchange operations] . . . of the Treasury" and that he would be kept informed of Federal Reserve activities in the exchange market.[2]

The arrangement has involved little extra burden in communication between the two agencies, because the Chairman of the Board of Governors is in frequent consultation with the Secretary of the Treasury. Furthermore, since the Senior Vice-President of the Reserve Bank of New York in charge of its Foreign Department (the Committee's designated Special Manager) is also the Treasury's agent in foreign currency transactions either on behalf of the Treasury Stabilization Fund or for governmental expenditure abroad, he is in a strategic position to coordinate any market transaction in the System Open Market Account with those being ordered at the same time by the Treasury.

While the Special Manager was gaining experience in coordinating his market operations between the Federal Reserve and the Treasury, he made a practice of advising both the staff of the Federal Open Market Committee and the staff of the Treasury in charge of transactions for its Stabilization Fund whenever he felt that official interventions in the foreign exchange market might be appropriate and desirable. After consultation in this manner, any transactions that he directed could be either for the account of one agency only or for the joint account of both agencies. The compelling arguments for this practice are that: (1) the two agencies have a common interest in a stable international value for the dollar and in protecting the monetary reserve position of the United States; (2) their collaborative relations can avert any problem of allotting the Special Manager's transactions between them; (3) it is advantageous to both agencies for the market to feel that either or both could take an interest as

---

2 Board of Governors, Federal Reserve System, *Annual Report,* 1962, pp. 54-63, specifically p. 55.

principals in the Special Manager's transactions; and (4) only the Federal Reserve has the financial resources to carry out large-scale foreign exchange transactions.

EXCHANGE MARKET INTERVENTIONS

Authorized exchange market interventions by the Special Manager differ both technically and basically from those engaged in by the Account Manager for the Federal Open Market Committee on the U.S. Government securities market. For one thing, they occur intermittently rather than almost daily. Also, they are ordinarily fairly small in size and only become large in periods when the conditions in the exchange market are markedly disturbed. Lastly, even though these official interventions unavoidably release reserve funds to the member bank reserve position or withdraw funds from it, they are never intended to affect the domestic reserve position of member banks. However, if this effect does occur, it is at once known to the Committee's Account Manager and he either takes appropriate ad hoc action in the securities market to counteract the effect or allows it to have an operational impact on member bank reserves.

The Special Manager's interventions in the U.S. foreign exchange market arise out of his day-to-day function of exercising constant oversight of that market and of facilitating its orderliness by outright intervention when necessary. If he considers that market intervention is needed on any occasion, his objectives would be to temper or cushion unusual instabilities, to maintain orderly conditions in the market in accordance with the Articles and Decisions of the International Monetary Fund (but see Effect of Suspension of Dollar Convertibility, below), and thereby to regulate at least the timing of accumulations of dollar liabilities to foreign central banks temporarily invested in short-term to medium-term U.S. Government securities, and possibly minimize their amount.

More specifically, his interventions are intended to facilitate market absorption of abrupt changes in supply of or demand for dollars caused by speculative or other transitory factors and not reflecting transfer payments for merchandise trade, services, and foreign investment. In addition, this defensive role may require the Special Manager to respond to any disequilibrium between spot and forward exchange rates that would encourage undesirable short-term capital movements through interest rate differentials. Whenever he needs a supply of foreign currency with which to engage in spot exchange interventions or to cover any forward exchange risks undertaken, the Special Manager may resort to the Federal Reserve's network of reciprocal currency exchanges or credits (see The Swap Network, below), with concurrence of a network bank. Up to mid-August 1971, he could also use these credit facilities to cover the exchange risk for any partner bank in the network unwilling to accumulate dollars in excess of the amount it considered necessary to maintain orderly conditions in the market for its own currency.

In the early stages of U.S. official intervention in the foreign exchange market, there was always some risk that purchase or sale of a particular country's currency would unintentionally frustrate an opposite intervention by the central bank of that country. Over a period of time, however, there developed an effective mechanism of daily communication between central banks for the interchange of intelligence about supply and demand tendencies in their respective foreign currency markets and about any official interventions that might be or actually were being contemplated. In periods of unsettled market conditions, such interchanges might take place several times during a business day. From long-established practice, U.S. official intervention in the market for any foreign currency is always avoided if it is not considered helpful by the central bank concerned.

Whenever a correspondent foreign central bank desires its currency to be supported on the New York foreign exchange market, the Special Manager stands prepared to intervene in the market on behalf of the foreign central bank, serving as a transactions agent in accordance with its instruction. When his interventions are for Treasury, Federal Reserve, or their joint account, however, they are conducted only on the U.S. market. Market interrelationships soon convey to markets abroad any special message intended from his interventions.

THE SWAP NETWORK

Upon initiating foreign currency operations in early 1962, the Federal Open Market Committee authorized the establishment of a network of reciprocal commitments to exchange or swap currency holdings with selected central banks and directed its Special Manager to negotiate the necessary commitments. The purpose of the network is to provide a facility for supporting orderly market conditions (ready market convertibility) for currencies of the participating central banks. The partners in the network at the end of May 1973 numbered 14 central banks (see Table 9) whose currencies were recognized as convertible by the International Monetary Fund under Article VIII of its Articles of Agreement and were authorized by the Committee to serve as the medium for the Special Manager's transactions. An additional partner is the Bank for International Settlements, which invests the deposits held in it by central banks in the short-term liquid paper available in major international money markets.

This network of advance commitments between the Federal Reserve System and foreign central banks enables either of the parties to a commitment to swap or draw on request an equivalent value of a partner bank's currency for its own currency up to a prearranged maximum amount. Repayment of a swap drawing is typically called for at the end of three months at the same rate of exchange as the original drawing rate. However, these cross credits can readily be renewed for an additional three months, and further renewals may extend the date of repayment (reversal) for as long as one year—or even beyond one year with special approval. Ordinarily, each advance commitment has a one-year duration, but extension is automatic unless one party withdraws from it on or before the terminal date. During any period that a swap drawing is outstanding, either party to it is free to use in foreign exchange operations the currency credited to its account by the other partner. Unless the currency thus credited is used in foreign exchange operations, it is invested in a time deposit or other liquid asset claim, each partner receiving the same rate of interest on invested proceeds of the swap currency.

When the convertibility of the dollar into gold was suspended on August 15, 1971 (see Effect of Suspension of Dollar Convertibility, below), the currency exchanges which the United States was entitled to have outstanding aggregated $11.7 billion (see Table 9). From the inception of the currency swap facility on March 1, 1962 to that date, there had been a total of $27 billion of swap drawings either by the Federal Reserve System or by its several network partners. A little short of three fifths of this amount had been at partner initiative and just over two fifths at Federal Reserve initiative. Approximately three fourths of the nearly $16 billion of partner drawings were intended to help defend the exchange values of their currencies against volatile international capital flows; the remaining share had mainly the joint purpose of providing partners with exchange risk cover against dollar accumulations considered excessive and of deferring for a period their redemption into other reserve assets. Of the approximately $11 billion of drawings at Federal Reserve initiative, almost two thirds were intended to avert or at least delay gold conversions by partners; a little over one third was intended to defend the dollar against volatile capital flows.

On August 15, 1971, when the convertibility of the dollar into gold was suspended, no swap partner was indebted to the Federal Reserve System on drawing account, but the Federal Reserve System was indebted for a total of $3 billion for drawings on partners. About half of this indebtedness had been repaid by the time of the announcement of the second devaluation of the dollar on February 12, 1973,[3] and the U.S. position remained unchanged as of May 31, 1973.

EFFECT OF SUSPENSION OF DOLLAR CONVERTIBILITY

Early in the 1970s two phases of acute disequilibria occurred in the U.S. dollar market. The first, which developed over the late spring and summer months of 1971, culminated in an order by the President of the United States on August 15, 1971 suspending temporarily the convertibility of the dollar into gold and other monetary reserve assets, "except in amounts and conditions determined to be in the interest of monetary stability and in the best interest of the United States."[4] This action also temporarily suspended the Federal Reserve's open market operations in authorized foreign currencies, but did not impose any restrictions on payments and transfers for current international transactions.

Four months later on December 18, 1971 the major trading countries "reached agreement on a pattern of exchange relationships among their currencies." This became known as the Smithsonian Agreement.[5] Their decisions were to be announced later by individual

---

[3] See Charles H. Coombs, "Treasury and Federal Reserve Foreign Currency Operation," *Monthly Bulletin of the Federal Reserve Bank of New York*, March 1973, p. 49.

[4] From the address by President Nixon to the nation on radio and television on August 15, 1971.

[5] These countries, which participate as members of the Group of Ten in the IMF's General Arrangements to Borrow, are: Belgium, Canada, France, Germany, Italy, Japan, the Netherlands, Sweden, the United Kingdom, and the United States. Their *Press Communiqué* was issued on December 18, 1971 at the close of the two-day ministerial meeting held at the Smithsonian Institution in Washington

Table 9. Federal Reserve Network of Reciprocal Currency Arrangements:
Total Swap Drawings, March 1, 1962 to August 15, 1971, and
Amount of Arrangements on August 15, 1971 and July 11, 1973

(million U.S. dollar equivalents)

| Bank | Amount of Swap Drawings, March 1962 to August 1971 | | | Amount of Arrangement | |
	At Federal Reserve Initiative	At Foreign Central Bank Initiative	Total	Aug. 15, 1971	July 11, 1973
Austrian National Bank	50	100	150	200	250
National Bank of Belgium	1,889	769	2,658	600	1,000
Bank of Canada	20	518	538	1,000	2,000
National Bank of Denmark	—	615	615	200	250
Bank of England	835	8,675	9,510	2,000	2,000
Bank of France	72	1,155	1,227	1,000	2,000
Deutsche Bundesbank	1,368	—	1,368	1,000	2,000
Bank of Italy	1,400	1,450	2,850	1,250	2,000
Bank of Japan	—	80	80	1,000	2,000
Bank of Mexico	—	—	—	130	180
Netherlands Bank	1,475	247	1,722	300	500
Bank of Norway	—	—	—	200	250
Sveriges Riksbank	—	—	—	250	300
Swiss National Bank	3,173	—	3,173	1,000	1,400
Bank for International Settlements	925	2,268	3,193	1,600	1,850
Total	11,207	15,877	27,084	11,730	17,980

Sources: Data for 1962-69 furnished by the Division of International Finance, Board of Governors, Federal Reserve System; data for 1970-71 taken from the semiannual reports on "Treasury and Federal Reserve Foreign Exchange Operations," *Federal Reserve Bulletin,* March and September; and data for 1973 from *Federal Reserve Bulletin,* July 1973.

governments in the form of par values or central rates. The United States specifically agreed to propose to Congress a suitable means for devaluing the dollar in terms of gold to $38.00 per ounce (from $35.00). It was also agreed that, pending agreement on monetary reforms, provision would be made for margins of exchange rate fluctuations 2¼ per cent above and below the new exchange rates.[6]

under the chairmanship of the U.S. Secretary of the Treasury. The Managing Director of the Fund also participated.

[6] IMF Executive Board Decision No. 3463-(71/126), December 18, 1971, provided for a temporary regime under which a Fund member might permit the exchange rates for its currency to move within margins of 2¼ per cent on either side of the parity relationship based on par values or central rates. (See International Monetary Fund, *Annual Report, 1972,* p. 39.)

The new par value for the U.S. dollar of $38.00 per troy ounce of fine gold, representing a devaluation of 8 per cent, became effective on May 8, 1972. After several months of testing the new exchange rates in world markets, the Federal Open Market Committee on July 19, 1972 again conducted market transactions in selected currencies, with the primary objective of demonstrating renewal of active Federal Reserve cooperation with leading central banks abroad in maintaining orderly market conditions of their exchanges vis-à-vis the dollar.

Toward the end of 1972, it became evident that disturbingly large disequilibria were continuing in money flows between the United States and important surplus countries (especially Japan and certain European countries) and that it would take longer than had been expected to correct the U.S. international payments deficits. Individual European central banks began to take positive action to cope with domestic inflationary trends which were then showing clear signs of acceleration. Intensified activity in foreign exchange markets indicated a heightening uncertainty as to the durability of the Smithsonian Agreement—that is, the exchange rate realignment agreed to in late 1971. Before long, foreign exchange markets became increasingly turbulent, with a greater payment flow against the dollar, and key central banks continued to buy up dollars to defend their economies against money inflows. By late January and early February of 1973, the international exchange markets had generally become unbalanced under the pressure of massive money flows from dollars into the few currencies that the market believed could still offer a relatively open haven for speculative and protectively motivated transfers of funds.

When it became clear that these disruptive conditions undermined continued adherence by major countries to the Smithsonian realignment of currency relationships, the Secretary of the Treasury, speaking on behalf of the President of the United States, announced on February 12, 1973 a devaluation of the dollar by 10 per cent below the level agreed to in December 1971, bringing its cumulative devaluation to somewhat less than 18 per cent.[7] In itself, this action involved no obligation for the U.S. Government to intervene in the foreign exchange markets. These markets, however, were at once thrown

---

[7] At the end of July 1973, Congress had before it, favorably recommended, a bill to reduce the value of the dollar from SDR 0.9211 to SDR 0.8290.

into such disorder that central banks of countries with convertible currencies abandoned their foreign currency interventions for the time being, closed their official exchange markets, and allowed their exchange rates to float in response to market forces.

To relieve the crisis in the exchange markets, the central banks initiated emergency international discussions in Paris and in Brussels to work out a common operational approach. On March 16, 1973 finance ministers and central bank governors of 13 countries met in Paris, together with representatives of the international organizations that were particularly concerned.[8] Each participating country stated that it would "be prepared to intervene at its initiative in its own market, when necessary and desirable, acting in a flexible manner in the light of market conditions and in close consultation with the authorities whose currency may be bought or sold." Furthermore, it was agreed that "such intervention will be financed, when necessary, through use of mutual credit facilities," and that "to ensure adequate resources for such operations, it is envisaged that some of the existing swap facilities will be enlarged." [9]

Official foreign exchange trading was resumed on March 19, and by that time important measures relating to foreign exchange had been taken. The German authorities had announced a new central rate expressed in SDRs which represented a 3 per cent revaluation over the previous central rate. Six members[10] of the European Economic Community (EEC), joined later by Norway and Sweden, had decided to maintain the maximum margin of 2¼ per cent for rates in exchange transactions between their currencies and the currencies of each of the other countries, but would no longer undertake to maintain margins against the U.S. dollar. The other EEC members (Ireland, Italy, and

---

[8] *Press Communiqué* of the Ministerial Meeting of the Group of Ten and the European Economic Community, Paris, March 16, 1973. Finance ministers and central bank governors of Denmark, Ireland, and Luxembourg attended as members of the EEC. The President of the Swiss National Bank had observer status. Representatives of international agencies, attending mainly as observers, included the Managing Director of the IMF, the Chairman of the Committee of the Board of Governors of the IMF on Reform of the International Monetary System and Related Issues (the so-called Committee of 20), the Vice-President of the Commission of the European Community, the Secretary-General of the Organization for Economic Cooperation and Development, and the General Manager of the Bank for International Settlements.

[9] *Ibid.*

[10] Belgium, Denmark, France, Germany, Luxembourg, and the Netherlands.

the United Kingdom) continued to permit their currencies to float, as did Canada and Japan.

Against this background, the March 16th agreement could hardly be interpreted to imply the beginning of broad intervention in exchange markets on the part of the European central banks to stabilize the exchange value of their currencies in terms of the dollar. Rather, the dollar would remain floating unless stabilized in relation to their currencies by action on the part of U.S. monetary authorities. This, however, the U.S. authorities were not prepared immediately to undertake. After further weeks of moderate fluctuation in the exchange value of the dollar, a fresh depreciating trend set in, accompanied by wide press attention to the dollar's eroding value. In these circumstances, the Federal Reserve began negotiations in June to fortify its swap network with central banks of other countries. On July 11, 1973, the Board of Governors announced that these negotiations had resulted in an increase in Federal Reserve's swap lines with 13 foreign central banks and the Bank for International Settlements in the amount of $6,250 million, bringing its total network credit lines to $17,980 million (Table 9). Drawings made upon the enlarged credit lines for Federal Reserve exchange market interventions, it was intimated, would be reported at intervals by the Federal Reserve Bank of New York.

5 | Discount Operations

DISCOUNT OPERATIONS of the Federal Reserve System are a companion instrument to its open market operations in regulating the member banks' reserve position and influencing credit and monetary conditions in the United States. They differ from open market operations in that the central bank credit made available through them originates in member bank responses to Federal Reserve action rather than in transactions directly undertaken in financial markets by the Federal Reserve authorities.

Under the law, each member bank is granted the privilege either of obtaining advances from its Reserve Bank against designated collateral or of reselling to (discounting with) its Reserve Bank any customer loan paper that meets statutory and regulatory standards of eligibility. The term discounting covers both means of member bank access to central bank credit. However, all Reserve Bank discounting is now in the form of collateral advances, mostly against U.S. Government securities.

The member bank privilege of borrowing from or discounting with its Reserve Bank is subject to two constraints. First, any member bank choosing to borrow Reserve Bank credit must be willing to incur the interest (discount) charge that its Reserve Bank imposes for the time being on its credit extensions to individual members. Second, it must conform to the rules (that is, the regulations deriving from statute) that determine the eligibility of the assets proffered to obtain Reserve Bank credit and the propriety of a member's borrowing initiative. Of these constraints on the availability of central bank credit to member bank borrowers, the Federal Reserve authorities place greater emphasis on the second.

GENERAL FEATURES

If a member bank seeks an advance from a Reserve Bank at its basic discount rate, it must offer as collateral either U.S. Government securities, securities of federal agencies, or customer notes and private money market paper that meet standards of eligibility laid down by the Federal Reserve Board of Governors; if, however, the member is prepared to pay an interest charge ½ percentage point above the regular discount rate, the acceptable collateral may be other investments or customer paper satisfactory to its Reserve Bank. The paper tendered for purchase by a Reserve Bank, on the other hand, must have its origin in agricultural, industrial, or commercial transactions, conform to the Board's eligibility rules, and bear the endorsement of the discounting bank.

In administering its discount facility, the Federal Reserve is governed by a statute which requires that, within each Federal Reserve district, the discount rate must be uniform for each class of paper presented for Reserve Bank purchase or as collateral security; it must also be uniform as between the two classes of member banks to which a Reserve Bank may extend credit, so that there will be no discrimination in access to central bank credit among member banks in the same district. Federal Reserve practice in accommodating statute in these matters has long been to apply a single basic discount rate both to purchases of eligible paper and to advances against prime collateral. On purchases of eligible paper from member banks, however, each Reserve Bank charges its rate at the time of discount, and its charge will be unaffected if the Bank's announced discount rate is changed before the paper's final maturity. On advances, in contrast, any newly established discount rate applies to outstanding advances as well as to new borrowing, and the interest is debited to the borrower's reserve account at the time of repayment.

Despite well-established intradistrict rate uniformities, the statute permits differences to emerge and continue in the discount rates charged borrowing members by each of the twelve Reserve Banks,

In recent years, however, internal procedures have been developed within the Federal Reserve System under which the separate Reserve Bank discount rates soon become unified into a single national rate for all member banks.

Since formal administrative rules as well as the discount rate work to constrain exercise of the member bank discount privilege, the Federal Reserve authorities do not consider it a necessary practice for the System's national discount rate to be regularly established at a "penalty" level in the credit market—that is, a level which would act as a positive cost deterrent to member bank discounting.[1] The authorities generally position the discount rate, therefore, within the cluster of rates on money market claims (see Chart 6, page 109).

The administrative rules governing the appropriateness of a member bank's discounting with a Federal Reserve Bank, as laid down in Regulation A of the Board of Governors, stipulate that the Reserve Bank discount facility is to be used by member banks primarily for meeting their short-term adjustment needs for reserve funds. Discounts or advances consequently are to be limited to short maturities, implying that discount credit is not to be relied upon as a substitute for bank capital nor employed as common practice by any member for an extended period. In addition, a member bank's use of funds obtained from the Federal Reserve discount facility should be consistent with the aims of the System; in particular, its use should neither affect adversely the maintenance of sound credit conditions, "either of the institution or the economy generally," nor permit a borrowing member to extend to customers an undue amount of credit to finance speculative trading in securities, commodities, or real estate. Furthermore, a member bank's borrowing should not have the specific purpose of obtaining a tax advantage, of profiting from interest differentials, nor of relending the borrowed funds in the Federal funds market.[2]

The effectiveness of the Federal Reserve discount instrument, therefore, hinges more on its regulatory rules than on the cost to member banks of using the discount facility. This reliance on rules has three

---

[1] Reasonably defined as a rate level higher than the highest rate on prime private paper in the money market and also than the prevailing rate charged by large banks on customer loans of the highest quality.

[2] These three proscriptions, deriving explicitly or implicitly from statute, are not formally set forth in the latest, streamlined version of Regulation A (effective April 19, 1973), although they were expressly stated in the superseded version (see section on Reform of the Discount Mechanism later in this chapter).

interrelated consequences of critical importance to the Federal Reserve's use of the discount instrument along with and in support of the open market instrument. First, the limitations on discount credit oblige member banks to use it sparingly, thus keeping member bank discounting to a nominal volume in periods when the Federal Reserve's open market policy accommodates or stimulates bank credit expansion. Second, the discount facility cannot serve as a wide-open "escape hatch" for member banks whenever the Federal Reserve cuts back the amount of reserve funds supplied to them by its open market operations. Third, the volume of member bank discounting moves inversely with the aggressiveness of open market operations—increasing when Federal Reserve policy restricts the availability of bank reserves and declining when policy is overtly stimulative. Thus, although the volume of member bank discounting is an indicator to the financial community of the trend in Federal Reserve monetary policy, a marked increase (or decrease) in such discounting will only delay somewhat, and not necessarily offset to any critical extent, the intended impact of open market operations.

FIXING THE DISCOUNT RATE

The initiative for fixing each Federal Reserve Bank's basic rate, as noted in Chapter 1, rests with its directorate, which is obliged by law to fix a rate every 14 days or more often if the Federal Reserve Board of Governors finds it necessary. However, the rate fixed by the Bank directorate cannot be announced and made effective until the Board of Governors has "reviewed and determined" its appropriateness. Practical considerations will dictate that any new rate proposed to the Board be reasonably related to the discount rates being charged member banks in other Federal Reserve districts.

Meaning of "review and determine"

The statutory authority of the Board of Governors to "review and determine" Reserve Bank discount rates has some ambiguity. Over the years, however, it has been established—on the basis of legislative intent, interpretation by the Attorney General of the United States, judicial interpretation, and precedent—that such authority embodies full power to (1) disapprove a proposed rate change it considers inappropriate; (2) suggest an alternate rate change; or (3) determine and order the discount rate to be charged.

This established legal interpretation has clearly made the fixing of Reserve Bank discount rates a joint responsibility of the Reserve Bank directorates and the Federal Reserve Board of Governors, with final authority residing in the Board. In practice, the Board has more often than not approved the recommended rates. On one notable occasion in 1927, however, the Board set an important precedent in determining the rate to be charged by one of the Reserve Banks. In recent years, moreover, the Board has disapproved several recommendations of the directorates as inappropriate under the circumstances.

Coordination of Reserve Bank rates

Although the decentralized structure of the Federal Reserve System permits differentials among Reserve Bank discount rates, certain factors tend to make these differences short-lived. First, the local and regional credit markets are closely intermeshed into a national market (Chapter 2). Consequently, if a Reserve Bank outside the central money market seeks to maintain a discount rate below that of other Reserve Banks, banking funds soon flow from its district into money market investment, where interest rates reflect the higher discount rates of the other Reserve Banks. Such investment begins with Federal fund claims but speedily encompasses the range of money market paper.

On the other hand, a Reserve Bank charging a higher discount rate than the other Reserve Banks finds its members drawing funds through the money market from other districts where the rates are lower; also, such a Bank exposes itself to complaints of member banks that they are burdened with the expense of a borrowing cost not incurred by members in other districts. In both of these instances, Reserve Bank discount officers of districts most affected by the interdistrict flows activated by these interest differentials may find their administration of member bank discounting either very difficult or virtually ineffective.

Second, the use of the Federal Reserve's several policy instruments is coordinated through the meetings of the Federal Open Market Committee (Chapter 1). Discussions and determinations of overall monetary policy at the Committee's monthly meetings, attended by all of the Reserve Bank presidents, give them guidance on the desirability of a change in the discount rate in the near future and enable them to make closely concurrent recommendations for such a change to their respective directorates. When the desirability of such a change in rate has been indicated, the Board of Governors may delay use of its authority to "review and determine" until several directorates have already made their recommendations.[3]

Third, the Federal Reserve authorities recognize the present-day need for all Reserve Bank rate changes to be consistent with national monetary policy, as formulated and expressed at short intervals by the Federal Open Market Committee in its directives for open market policy. If any Reserve Bank should lag unduly in aligning its rate with the rates that the other Reserve Banks have recommended and got approved, that Bank would risk having its rate "determined" by the Board of Governors to make it identical with the other rates.

Nevertheless, discount rate differentials among Federal Reserve districts do develop for short periods because (1) meetings of Reserve Bank directorates are on varying calendar schedules; (2) individual Bank presidents may hold differing views on the desirability of a rate change; and (3) a Reserve Bank directorate, on first recommendation from its president for a rate change, may not reach the same judgment as to its desirability in terms of its responsibility for "accommodating commerce, industry, and agriculture" as did participants in the meeting of the Federal Open Market Committee or as did some other directorates. But experience over recent years in discount rate administration shows that rates among the twelve Reserve Banks usually become uniform within a week or two (and rarely over three weeks) after the first approval by the Board of Governors of a rate change initiated by one or more Reserve Banks. Therefore, it is proper to view the present process as ending in a single national Reserve Bank discount rate rather than in a cluster of interrelated rates.

ADMINISTRATIVE RULES IN DISCOUNTING

The directorate of each Federal Reserve Bank is responsible for overseeing all credit extensions to its own member banks and for

---

[3] When current credit market developments and the Federal Reserve's policy course both point to a need for a discount rate change, individual Reserve Bank presidents may express their views at meetings of the Federal Open Market Committee on the need for the change for the benefit of the Board members and other presidents present. In view of the Board's responsibility for later action, however, Board members avoid specific comment on any proposed rate change, unless such a change is consonant with their own views on prospective needs for additional Federal Reserve action to supplement the Board's open market operations.

ensuring that their use of the discount privilege accords with the law and the regulatory supervision of the Board of Governors, as stated in Regulation A.

Discounting procedures

As a matter of Reserve Bank lending practice, each new request for an advance to, or discount for, a member bank in good standing is promptly granted, demonstrating the ready accessibility to members of Federal Reserve credit for meeting short-term adjustment and contingency problems. To simplify the procedure for obtaining advances (beginning in 1971), any member bank, instead of submitting a note for each borrowing, may enter into a continuing borrowing agreement under which a relevant amount of the securities or other paper held in custody for it at its Reserve Bank may be transferred by the Reserve Bank to a collateral account against a particular borrowing and be held there until the borrowing is repaid. Members using the discount facility under a continuing borrowing agreement must keep themselves fully posted on the regulations applying to borrowings.

Each borrowing has a specified maturity, and either a repayment or request for an extension (renewal of an advance) is expected on that date. For advances against U.S. Government securities or eligible customer paper, the statute specifies a maximum maturity of 90 days, but the maximum maturity may extend as long as four months against other acceptable securities or customer paper (technically ineligible). For the latter advances, however, the discount rate must be ½ percentage point above the basic discount rate.[4] While these are maximum maturities permitted by law, member banks usually borrow for much shorter terms, following either a suggestion of their Reserve

---

[4] Many member banks no longer appear as hesitant as they formerly were to seek Reserve Bank advances secured by other than federal securities or eligible customer notes at ½ percentage point higher than the regular discount rate. In fact, some members have appreciably reduced the share of U.S. Government and federal agency securities in their portfolios (federally taxed as to income yielded) and increased the share of state and local government securities, which, though typically bearing lower market yields than U.S. Government securities, may provide the member a higher after-tax yield because of their exemption from federal income taxes. As with U.S. Government securities, member banks may keep these or other pledgeable collateral in custody safekeeping with their Reserve Bank, and, as needed, may have them removed from custody account for pledging as collateral against a borrowing from their Bank.

Bank, the spirit of Regulation A of the Board of Governors, or simply their own need or preference.

Surveillance of member bank borrowing

A closely uniform surveillance procedure is followed by each Reserve Bank to ensure that all indebted member banks adhere to Regulation A principles and that they retire their indebtedness as agreed. The Reserve Bank will directly discuss its discount relationship with a borrowing member bank—sometimes merely for information—in three cases: (1) when a member bank has been a borrower for a few days during each of several recent weekly reserve reporting periods, in effect making continuous use of Federal Reserve credit over the successive periods; (2) when a member bank, while an advance is outstanding, makes inappropriate use of the funds; and (3) when a member bank has borrowed to meet a special need such as an unexpected deposit loss or an obviously temporary increase in loan demand and then seeks renewal of its advances after the exceptional circumstances are over.

Follow-up on outstanding advances

Each Federal Reserve Bank follows up on outstanding member bank indebtedness as described below.

(1) In order to trace the borrowing bank's current operational pattern, the Reserve Bank officer in charge of the discount function requests his staff to examine past use of the discount facility and the recent movement of deposits, loans, and investments, as well as to review other information about its activities regularly reported to the Reserve Bank. The examination reveals whether the member has recently been a frequent or extended Reserve Bank debtor, borrowed to take advantage of interest differentials, or sold Federal funds (net) while borrowing; whether it has recently increased its loan and investment accounts unduly in relation to the growth of its deposits and reserves; and whether the borrowing is large in relation to the borrower's required reserves or is not immediately related to the bank's operating needs. With this information, the discount officer will be able to make an initial judgment as to the appropriateness of the amount and stated duration of the member's current borrowing.

(2) Any questions arising from these internal reviews about the legitimacy of the borrowing may be discussed with the indebted

member by letter, through a visit, or by telephone. Such contacts may lead to informal or direct suggestion for reducing the frequency or amount of a member's borrowing, or they may uncover special reasons for the borrowing, such as temporarily depressed economic conditions in the local area that would warrant continuing the discount accommodation.

(3) If this discussion does not resolve any remaining doubts about the appropriateness of the member's borrowing, a Reserve Bank officer discusses with a principal officer of the bank whether its continued use of the discount facility is consistent with the principles of Regulation A.

(4) If none of the above procedures corrects the borrowing bank's improper use of the discount facility, the Reserve Bank officer then requests it to submit a program that will avoid recurrent reserve period discounting or retire its outstanding indebtedness within a reasonable period.

(5) The member bank may finally be advised that, in the absence of any new circumstances affecting its position, the Reserve Bank will not be prepared to accommodate its request for another borrowing of reserve period credit or for a further extension of its outstanding indebtedness.

Uniformity and stability of surveillance

Since these follow-up procedures are adhered to as uniformly as practicable by the Reserve Banks, all members are subject to essentially the same debtor surveillance and risk of administrative discipline in their use of the Federal Reserve's discount facility. Moreover, since the procedures do not lend themselves to flexible variations with changes in credit and economic conditions, they remain stable regardless of adaptations in monetary policy.[5]

---

[5] In the mid-1950s when these procedures were adopted, the Federal Reserve authorities recognized the need both for their uniform application by each Reserve Bank and for their stability at all Reserve Banks as monetary conditions changed. Near the climax of the 1966 tight money period, however, the Board of Governors in September 1966 solicited member bank cooperation in restraining inflationary business borrowing of bank credit. The Board's communication to them suggested a more liberal treatment at the discount facility for cooperating banks than for those seeking to incur discount debt to support continued expansion of business loans. This compromise with the established practice for surveillance provoked a strongly critical retrospective study by the American Bankers Association.

For a number of years after the Federal Reserve Banks began standard administrative review of member bank discounting, the Federal Reserve authorities received many complaints from bankers that standards differed between districts. This kind of criticism eventually faded away, but member bankers remained skeptical about the consistency of such surveillance as economic and financial cycles occurred. Apparently, they based their skepticism on the inverse relation of the borrowing activity at the Reserve Bank discount facility to the Federal Reserve's monetary policy (whether it was restrictive, accommodative, or stimulative).

But this inverse relationship is not necessarily related to higher standards of administrative surveillance by Reserve Banks in periods of restrictive monetary policy. It results in such periods primarily because (1) more banks need to borrow temporarily from their Reserve Banks as the result of deposit declines, depressed portfolio values of investments, or a reduced availability of other funds from market sources at costs competitive with the discount rate; and (2) more borrowers remain in discount debt longer than they might under easier credit conditions.

To ascertain the risks to a member bank of being subjected to exceptional administrative pressure under different monetary conditions, the Federal Reserve System began in 1966 to compile records of member bank borrowing in any stage of follow-up surveillance (stages 2 through 5 above) during successive quarters. Up to mid-1972, these records made clear that in periods when Federal Reserve policy was decidedly accommodative or easy, the exposure of any borrowing bank to administrative review ranged from 1 out of 15 to 1 out of 25 borrowings. During periods of tight reserve availability, on the other hand, a bank's chances of such review might range from 1 out of 5 to 1 out of 8 borrowings, because of a need to borrow more frequently or for longer periods.

The actual incidence of firm administrative pressure on any given debtor bank in any period is, however, much lower than these figures suggest. For one thing, the initial steps in any follow-up review are largely informational and educational for both the Reserve Bank and the borrowing member; for another, the recording of instances of review over recent years does not distinguish between banks in early stages and in advanced stages of administrative pressure. In short, only a very few cases of review ever reach an advanced stage and fewer still reach forced termination of a borrowing.

Uncertainty about Reserve Bank lending

Under Federal Reserve law, member bank access to the Reserve Bank discount credit is a privilege and not a right of membership. Accordingly, if a member's request for access to Reserve Bank credit is judged "inconsistent with the maintenance of sound credit conditions," a Reserve Bank may refuse to accommodate it, even though the member bank can offer to sell or pledge eligible assets.[6] The Federal Reserve System has had to compromise with this statutory constraint on its credit extension procedures by granting immediately any reasonable request for an advance or a discount and then initiating an administrative review to ascertain the legitimacy of the credit extension.

Although this discounting procedure is practical and is necessary to meet the discounting standards which the Reserve Banks should uniformly observe, it has been a source of considerable irritation to member banks because of uncertainty about the amount and duration of permitted borrowing. As lenders in a competitive credit market, bankers feel obliged to advise any prospective borrower who has an established credit standing as to how much the bank is willing to lend and how long any given loan transaction may extend.

Since the creditworthiness of any member bank is known to its Reserve Bank at all times by means of bank examinations and current operating reports, the member banks believe that Reserve Bank credit practice should be equally certain to them as their own credit lines are to their business, industrial, and farm customers, even though Reserve Bank credit must be limited by regulatory standards. In addition, member banks point to the practice followed in some important countries in Europe of providing credit certainty to eligible banking institutions through known discount quotas at the established discount rate, while permitting borrowing over the quota at a penalty interest rate through special negotiation.

In view of the dissatisfaction of the member banks with the discount process, Federal Reserve officials have in recent years intensively studied methods of making the amount and duration of Reserve Bank lending more certain and liberal and have adopted a "fundamental reform" of the discount mechanism (summarized below in this chapter). One of its aims is to alleviate the dissatisfaction of the member

---

[6] Section 4, Article 8 of the Federal Reserve Act.

banks, especially of smaller ones, with this aspect of Reserve Bank discount service.

CHANGING THE DISCOUNT RATE

Certain technical aspects of the Federal Reserve discount mechanism influence the manner and frequency of changing its regular discount rate. An important part of the process is the Federal Reserve's long adherence to a rate relationship with money market interest rates now generally regarded as "normal."

Discount and other money market rates

Historically, the "normal" position of the discount rate vis-à-vis money market rates has been between the interest rate on Treasury bills of three months' maturity and the rate on prime commercial paper of four to six months' maturity (Chart 6). Treasury bills entail no credit risk to the investor; have the most actively traded and fluid secondary market; and are widely used by commercial banks and nonbank financial and nonfinancial institutions as secondary reserves (for short-term asset and liability adjustment). In contrast, commercial paper comprises unsecured promissory notes of well-known business and financial corporations; bears the highest credit risk of any type of money market claim; lacks a well-organized professional or secondary trading market (although one seems to be developing); and will most likely have to be held to maturity by investors.

Despite this accepted "norm" for the discount rate between Treasury bill and commercial paper rates, in some periods of Federal Reserve restraint on bank credit and monetary expansion, including perhaps successive discount rate increases, Federal Reserve authorities have finally permitted the Treasury bill rate as well as all other money market rates to rise above—even well above—the basic discount rate and to continue above it for some time. The authorities then risk the emergence of an interest rate incentive to member banks to use the discount facility to acquire funds that can be employed at a higher rate of return in the money market. During the second half of 1972, considerations of national anti-inflationary policy caused the Federal Reserve authorities to permit a temporary gap in the alignment of the discount rate with money market rates. As the rate spread progressively widened, more and more member banks resorted to borrowing

Chart 6. Selected Money Market Interest Rates, 1963 to August 1973

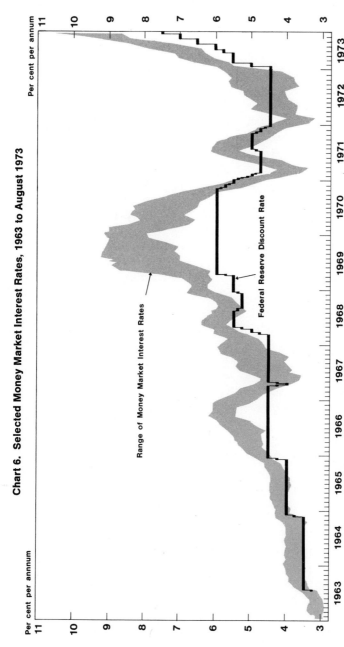

Per cent per annum

Per cent per annum

Range of Money Market Interest Rates

Federal Reserve Discount Rate

Note: The monthly average money market interest rates included in the range shown are: (1) the overnight Federal funds rate; (2) the market rate on 3-month Treasury bills; (3) the market rate on 90-day bankers' acceptances; (4) the offering rate on 6-month large denomination certificates of deposit issued by city banks (that is, the median of the monthly range of rates); and (5) the market rate on prime 4-month to 6-month commercial paper. Under conditions of relative ease in money market funds. Under conditions of market tightness, however, the Treasury bill rate will be lowest, with other rates clustering closely toward the upper limit and varying from month to month in relative position.

from their Reserve Banks—presumably because of relative cheapness of the funds thus borrowed. Whatever the reason, the total volume of their borrowing rose abnormally fast—from under $200 million at mid-1972 to nearly $1.8 billion at the beginning of 1973.[7]

Until this recent experience, however, the risk of undue discounting to take advantage of interest differentials had not proved serious because of the regulatory constraints on use of the discount facility by member banks. Moreover, the pattern in its use by many of the member banks had revealed their reluctance to make known to larger depositors that they were willing to rely on central bank discount credit (a priority liability) for other than transitory adjustment. Managements of many member banks also apparently believed that the discount facility was primarily a source for contingency borrowing or even one that should be used only as a "last resort" and therefore should be conserved.

While this longer experience confirmed the practicality of the Federal Reserve's customary and lagged positioning of its discount rate in relation to market rates, in recent years widespread change in member bank management practice has put in question the established discount rate pattern.[8] This newer practice has entailed (1) greater stress by larger and even medium-sized banks on aggressive lending and deposit expansion, with resultant effort to acquire supporting reserve funds and (2) increased reliance on short-term borrowing from market sources (for example, the Federal funds market) to keep reserve positions in required relation to deposit growth. Thus, subtle change in bank management practice had made many members more dependent on Reserve Bank discounting as a fall-back recourse, if Federal Reserve policy should shift abruptly toward strong restraint on banking expansion.

In the second half of 1972, therefore, the Federal Reserve authorities found eventual discount rate action a necessary response to the rapidly

---

[7] At this time, money market rates were more than 1 percentage point higher than the discount rate on overnight Federal funds and Treasury bills, and on prime commercial and industrial paper were nearly 1½ percentage points higher.

[8] Many academic economists, however, criticize Reserve Bank administration of borrowing by member banks as a counterweight to Federal Reserve practice in charging members a "nonpenalty" discount rate. They contend that it goes beyond prudent borrower surveillance and involves credit rationing, whereas in their view they believe that the allocation of central bank credit among its users in a market economy should be the primary—even exclusive—role of price (that is, the discount rate).

accruing resort by many members to the System's discount facility. At mid-January 1973, they raised the discount rate from 4½ to 5 per cent as an initial step in restoring it to a more appropriate relationship with market rates. Over the ensuing seven months, this step was followed by six increases, four of ½ percentage point each and two of ¼ percentage point each, to a record high of 7½ per cent at mid-August —a level, however, still below the cluster of money market rates.

Review of discount rate changes

Over the 22-year period of flexible U.S. monetary policy from 1951 through 1972, there were 39 changes in Federal Reserve discount rate (18 increases and 21 decreases), an average of less than two changes annually. Prior to 1970, the typical change was ¼ percentage point when the rate was below 3 per cent and ½ percentage point when it was above that level. The size of rate change up to 1970, however, represented mainly acceptance of a reasonable rule of thumb; beginning in 1970, the practice was shifted to a ¼ percentage point change, with a ½ percentage point change likely in tight money conditions.

Change in the discount rate following the restoration of Federal Reserve policy flexibility after World War II has generally come after a change in money market interest rates—sometimes within a few days or within a week or two. Since an upward or downward movement in market rates may persist for several months, corresponding changes in the discount rate may follow to keep it in general alignment with the rise or fall in rates on the money market. The typical lag in Federal Reserve action on the discount rate in relation to the movement of market interest rates reflects three main factors: (1) the strategy at that time in Federal Reserve open market operations; (2) the formal (and sometimes time-consuming) procedures which the Federal Reserve has had to follow in coordinating use of its major policy tools; and (3) the public relations weight attaching to an announcement of a discount rate change (a change in the discount rate is given wide coverage in the press and on some occasions the change may not appear to harmonize with overall government policy).

The first of these factors—the strategy of the Federal Reserve open market operation—merits special comment, since the open market operation is the leading instrument in implementing U.S. monetary policy. Also, since "money market conditions," as specified at each meeting of the Federal Open Market Committee, typically act as a collateral or short-run guidance target for open market operations under a "mixed" strategy, the Committee may instruct its Account Manager either to limit the range of fluctuations in money market interest rates or to take into account an imminent change in the Reserve Bank discount rate.

If the Manager is instructed to limit fluctuations in market conditions, he may be obliged to limit them when liquidity forces in the economy are bringing about changes in market levels. In this case, his limits on fluctuations could obscure the emerging need for a discount rate action. Eventually, the fundamental market forces may overwhelm the Manager's limit on one side or the other, impelling a discount rate response that lags behind the movement of short-term rates in the market. On the other hand, if he is instructed to take into account an imminent discount rate change, he is usually also instructed to ease or tighten money market conditions, with some resulting rise or decline in the average of market rates. In this case, his emphasis would quickly register in the reserve position of city banks and therefore in market rates on Federal funds, Treasury bills, and other money market paper, with the result that this movement would precede the discount rate change. Thus, a policy instruction might be the background for any observed close relationship between the discount rate and market rates and any movement of money rates ahead of discount rate change; that is to say, whatever rate pattern emerges, it undoubtedly reflects to some extent prior Federal Reserve policy.

Recent official reports and statements on the Federal Reserve discount rate practice indicate that changes may become more frequent to keep discount rates more closely and continuously aligned with money market rates;[9] hence, the rate change practice since 1969 (that is, ¼ percentage point change, unless tight money conditions prevail) may be accepted as the more likely future practice.[10] The present-day active communication with the Federal Reserve System on current

---

[9] Federal Reserve System Committee Report, *Reappraisal of the Federal Reserve Discount Mechanism* (July 1968), p. 20; also see Vol. 1 of a three-volume study published under the same title by the Board of Governors in August 1971 and June 1972, p. 22.

[10] This changing practice is reflected in the 7 rate changes for 1973 and the 6 rate changes for 1971; in the preceding 20 years there were 10 years of 0 or 1 rate change, 7 years of 2 or 3 changes, and only 3 years of 4 or 5 changes.

policy problems certainly makes feasible a practice of frequent rate changes. On the other hand, it is still questionable whether this practice can overcome the drawbacks, noted above, to flexible timing of discount rate changes, and exceptions are to be expected.[11]

Moreover, official statements have indicated that sometimes upward discount rate changes may encounter a ceiling, such as 6 per cent or higher. Also a further rise in Reserve Bank discount rates—even though appropriate to existing restrictive monetary policy—may be deterred by lack of public and political acceptability, by risks of unsettling effects on both domestic and international credit markets, by activating disadvantageous money flows between financial intermediaries and the securities markets, and in liquidity emergency, by an unduly strong and inelastic demand for Reserve Bank discount accommodation.[12] Also, the course of policy pursued in the most recent economic recession of 1970-71 indicated that the risk of activating disadvantageous international money flows from the United States to foreign financial markets might sometimes set a floor for the discount rate when domestic considerations favoring credit ease might justify a still lower rate.

Government interest in rate changes

Any change in the Reserve Bank discount rate traditionally benefits the financial markets and the public by acting as: (1) an indicator of domestic credit conditions; (2) official confirmation that the recent movement in market interest rates is more than a transient deviation; and (3) a forerunner of Federal Reserve monetary policy in the immediate months ahead. Changes thus not only receive wide attention in the press but are of special interest to officials of the Federal Government most concerned with its financial policy. To officials of

---

[11] The gap in discount rate action during the fall of 1972 illustrates the difficulties that can arise. In this period, the Federal Reserve authorities apparently desired to avoid any action of "high visibility to the public" that might lend support to prevalent expectation of higher market interest costs ahead and, therefore, prove detrimental to the Federal Government's efforts to contain the emergence of stronger inflationary pressures than were already present in the economy. As part of this program, an official Committee on Interest and Dividends, chaired by the Chairman of the Board of Governors, was charged with responsibility for measures to dampen upward tendencies in interest rates.

[12] Committee Report, *Reappraisal of the Federal Reserve Discount Mechanism,* *op. cit.*

the Treasury, in particular, any rate change invariably has a bearing on its debt management policy and forward financing schedule and further, has implications for flows of bank funds between international markets to which the Treasury must pay close attention in carrying out its responsibility for the international value of the dollar.

Accordingly, when a proposal for a discount rate change is received from a Reserve Bank directorate, that fact may be communicated informally to these government officials by the Chairman of the Board of Governors. Such communication gives them opportunity to express their views regarding the necessity or desirability of the suggested change before the Board of Governors undertakes to "review and determine" the specific recommendation to establish a higher or lower rate. While these informal consultations can be helpful to the Board, the Board alone is responsible under statute for the final decision to take a discount rate action.

One difficulty with this official exchange of "inside" information is that, as a discount rate change is a newsworthy item, there is a risk that any strong government opposition expressed in advance of it may become publicly disclosed. In the spring of 1956 and late fall 1965, objections of high government officials were voiced publicly, although the disclosure occurred after the Board of Governors had acted. There would appear to have been other occasions when the Board was prevailed upon to defer approval of a recommended discount rate change, either by the positive objection of key government officials or by the knowledge that vigorous government objection to the change would be likely in the particular financial stuation.

EMERGENCY DISCOUNTING

When a member bank must take immediate borrowing action because of local, regional, or national emergencies, special rules apply to discounting. On such occasions, a member bank may resort to its Reserve Bank discount facility at the prevailing discount rate; the original maturity of an advance may be tailored to the bank's need, and renewals may be readily granted until the member's financial crisis is sufficiently relieved. If a member bank's holding of U.S. Government obligations or eligible paper is insufficient to finance its emergency need, the discount facility is still available under statutory provision through an advance secured by any other collateral satisfactory to its Reserve Bank.[13] The rate charged on borrowing against such collateral must be ½ percentage point higher than the Reserve Bank's regular discount rate. Although the maturity may extend as long as four months, a shorter maturity is usually arranged immediately after the need for the borrowing is assessed by a Reserve Bank discount officer.

In coping with an acute credit emergency, upon authorization by five members of the Board of Governors the Reserve Banks may discount notes that are satisfactorily secured or endorsed for individuals, partnerships, and corporations unable to obtain adequate accommodation otherwise. Also, they may extend advances to such borrowers against federal obligations under special regulations of the Board; the rate on such advances is established in the same manner as the regular discount rate but at a higher level—at present, 2 percentage points above it.[14]

This provision for emergency advances technically permits nonmember banks to obtain Reserve Bank credit directly to meet exigent needs for outside funds. While such advances were approved on two occasions in the late 1960s,[15] the Federal Reserve authorities had expressed the view shortly beforehand that such advances to nonmembers should be closely limited as a matter of continuing policy. Since these banks had forgone Federal Reserve membership, thus avoiding the higher banking costs of members, and since they had relied mainly on deposit insurance for ultimate depositor protection,

[13] Section 10b of the Federal Reserve Act. The Board of Governors in recent years has sought legislation that would permit member banks to borrow against any collateral satisfactory to a Reserve Bank without paying the higher rate on "ineligible" collateral.

[14] No current rates have been established on emergency discount of notes so secured of individuals, partnerships, and corporations. When last established in 1935, the rate was 6 per cent—2 percentage points higher than that on advances to such borrowers secured by U.S. Government obligations.

[15] The Board of Governors authorized Reserve Bank advances to mutual savings banks, savings and loan associations, and other banks on three occasions—once during the "credit crunch" of 1966, a second time at the advanced stage of credit stringency of 1969, and a third time, a renewal of the 1969 action, in the spring of 1970. In the third instance, the Board permitted such advances only to those savings and loan associations that were nonmembers of the Federal Home Loan Bank System and, therefore, without access to the Home Loan Bank credit facilities. See the Board of Governors, *Annual Report,* 1966, 1969, and 1970, pp. 91-92, 92-93, and 67, respectively.

the Federal Reserve had come to the conclusion that it would accede to a nonmember bank request for an emergency discount accommodation only with approval of the responsible supervisory authority (the Federal Deposit Insurance Corporation or the state banking supervisor) and that it would retain the option of refusing such a request.[16] Federal Reserve authorities further emphasized that a nonmember bank granted emergency credit would be required to pursue a remedial program to be closely followed by its Reserve Bank.

In cases of emergency, specialized bank and nonbank financial institutions are more likely than ordinary businesses to need to apply for Reserve Bank discount credit. As emergency loans to them require the pledge of U.S. Government securities as collateral and as they are unlikely to hold these in sufficient volume for emergency borrowing needs, the Federal Reserve has accepted the expedient of channeling emergency credit to them through member banks cooperatively serving as conduits. In such lending, any Reserve Bank makes a collateralized advance to the cooperating member bank, which in turn extends a loan to a nonmember institution, either secured to the lending member's satisfaction or unsecured, charging interest at a rate acceptable both to the borrower and to the lending bank.[17]

Such indirect lending to specialized bank and nonbank financial institutions is not precluded by law, although it could not be done without express permission of the Board of Governors if the borrower were a nonmember bank. Conduit lending, confined to selected types of nonmember depository institutions (such as mutual savings banks, other banks with the Board's explicit permission, and noninsured savings and loan associations) was first permitted in the credit crunch of 1966. The permission was repeated in 1970 during the credit market's months of liquidity tension; and after the insolvency of a major railroad company in that year, member banks whose corporate customers had issued commercial paper were also encouraged to engage in conduit lending to those customers unable to refinance (roll over) their maturities through the market. While no conduit discounting was extended to member banks for relending to nonmember financial institutions in either 1966 or 1970, some $500 million of such credit

---

[16] Committee Report, *Reappraisal of the Federal Reserve Discount Mechanism,* *op. cit.,* p. 19 (or p. 21 of alternative source).

[17] Presumably at a higher rate for unsecured than for secured borrowing.

was extended to them for conduit lending to commercial paper obligors during the summer months of 1970.[18] The provision of such credit reflects the strong view of the Federal Reserve System regarding its role as an emergency lender to nonbank financial institutions. The Federal Reserve considers that it must serve in emergencies, to the extent permitted by interpreted statute, as "lender of last resort" to a wider spectrum of financial institutions than member banks, and that in widespread emergency it must serve the entire financial system in this way.[19] There can be little doubt that this position represented a consensus at the highest level among Federal Reserve policy-making officials.[20]

REFORM OF THE DISCOUNT MECHANISM

In the mid-1960s, the Federal Reserve System launched a high-level study and re-examination of its discount mechanism. The aims were to improve the mechanism's functioning as a companion tool of Federal Reserve open market operations, to serve member bank needs for direct credit accommodation in Federal Reserve funds, and to cushion member bank reserve adjustments to future changes in required reserve ratios. The ensuing report of the study group set forth recommendations for administration of a more flexible discount rate, as well as recommendations to make member bank access to Reserve Bank lending facilities "clearer cut and more liberal" with respect to the amount and the duration of discount credit to member banks.

In regard to discount credit, the study group presented three main recommendations.[21] The first would be a grant to each member bank of a "no-questions-asked" discount quota or basic borrowing privilege,

---

[18] Andrew F. Brimmer, "Member Bank Borrowing, Portfolio Strategy, and Management of Federal Reserve Discount Policy," a paper presented to the Forty-seventh Annual Meeting of the Western Economic Association, August 25, 1972, p. 26.

[19] Committee Report, *Reappraisal of the Federal Reserve Discount Mechanism*, *op. cit.*, pp. 16-19 (or pp. 18-21 of alternative source) and a review of that report in *Federal Reserve Bulletin*, July 1968, pp. 545 and 549-50.

[20] The Chairman of the Board of Governors at that time was ex officio member of the Committee on the Discount Mechanism, whose membership also included three other Board members and four Reserve Bank presidents. Governor George W. Mitchell was Chairman of the Committee.

[21] Committee Report, *Reappraisal of the Federal Reserve Discount Mechanism*, *op. cit.*, pp. 7-16; also Vol. 1, pp. 9-18 *op. cit.* (see footnote 9).

limited in extent and frequency of use to a short period. The second would be a privilege of short-term borrowing over the quota but subject to established procedures in Reserve Bank discount surveillance. The third would grant a privilege of longer-term seasonal borrowing, on condition that it would be negotiated in advance and that a bank's usual seasonal swing in deposits and loans would be large enough to warrant it.

These liberalizations in regard to discounting were subject to one important overall caveat: they were not to lift the Federal Reserve's long-standing restraint on continuous and permanent reliance by individual member banks on borrowed funds supplied by the Reserve Banks. In fact, the report explicitly reaffirmed the principle that the Reserve Bank lending authority, except for regional or local emergency, was designed to accommodate short-term adjustments in member bank assets or liabilities—the principle behind the Federal Reserve's reliance on a nonpenalty discount rate and essential to dependence on open market operations as a primary tool of action. However, the report recommended modifying the guidelines for appropriate member bank discounting by eliminating the guideline that excluded discounting to take advantage either of tax loopholes or interest rate differentials while retaining the rule against borrowing to relend Federal funds to other banks.

In making these proposals for discount liberalization, the study group was particularly concerned over the relatively slight use of Reserve Bank discount facilities by member banks and the small volume of discount credit outstanding for the 1960s. The highest monthly average volume of discount credit for the decade amounted to only $1.4 billion, or 2.3 per cent of the total Federal Reserve credit then outstanding, and this peak borrowing occurred in a year when monetary policy and credit conditions were unprecedentedly stringent.

Moreover, on average only a little over half of the small number of reserve city member banks and a little more than a tenth of the very much larger number of country member banks were Reserve Bank borrowers during any one calendar quarter in the 1960s, and the borrowings during that decade of both classes of member banks averaged under 2 per cent of the average required reserves of their class. These quarterly averages, of course, varied from year to year as credit conditions changed (Table 10 and Chart 7). Thus, in tight money years the percentage of the city banks borrowing in a quarter went as high as 71 per cent while that of the country banks went up only to 16 per cent, although in such years each group in its total borrowings averaged only as much as 4 per cent of its required reserves.

In the light of these averages, the Committee felt that the Federal Reserve's process of monetary regulation could hardly be put in serious jeopardy if these ratios were regularly to be appreciably higher. On the positive side, the study group believed that if many more members were to resort more frequently to their Reserve Bank discount facility and if a higher ratio of required reserves were typically to be borrowed, this might help to bring about more salutary relations between member banks and the Reserve Bank—especially in communications on discount activity as related to other monetary operations and to general monetary policy. Finally, the Committee felt that if smaller country banks could be induced to use the discount facility more in their shorter-run operations, this might help to check their withdrawal from membership in the Federal Reserve System and make membership more attractive to nonmembers—a structural problem that could be allevi-

Table 10. Annual Average Borrowing by Member Banks from Federal Reserve Banks, 1961-72[1]

| Year | Number of Member Banks | | Percentage of Member Banks Borrowing Per Quarter | | Borrowing as Percentage of Required Reserves of Each Class of Member Bank | |
	Reserve City Banks	Country Banks	Reserve City Banks	Country Banks	Reserve City Banks	Country Banks
1961	230	5,906	44.6	9.3	0.4	0.5
1962	225	5,840	45.2	8.2	0.6	0.5
1963	218	5,850	57.6	9.4	1.6	0.7
1964	209	5,972	58.8	9.4	1.7	1.0
1965	203	6,028	64.3	8.7	2.7	1.3
1966	193	5,991	70.3	13.2	2.8	2.8
1967	188	5,918	40.3	7.6	0.8	0.7
1968	183	5,838	59.6	10.7	2.1	2.3
1969	180	5,739	70.5	15.8	3.9	4.3
1970	178	5,623	51.2	11.2	3.3	2.0
1971	177	5,559	37.4	6.6	1.7	0.9
1972	177	5,530	35.0	5.8	1.0	0.9

Source: Data furnished by the Division of Federal Reserve Bank Operations, Board of Governors, Federal Reserve System.

[1] Beginning November 9, 1972, the classification "Reserve City" was changed to include only banks with net demand deposits over $400 million. For comparability in this table, data for the period November 9-December 31, 1972 were calculated on the basis of the classifications in effect on November 8, 1972.

Chart 7. Member Bank Borrowing from Reserve Banks, 1961-72

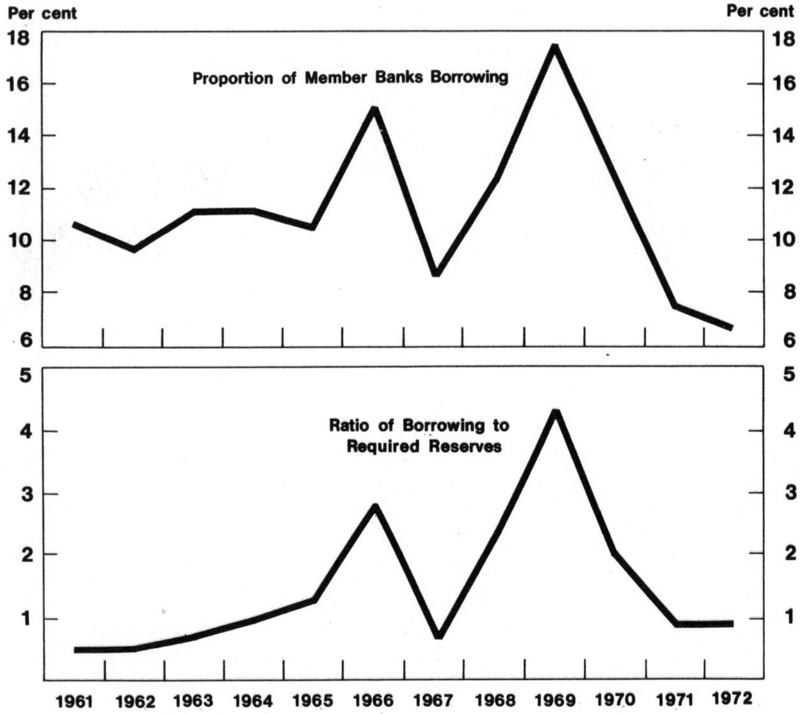

Source: Data computed from Table 10, page 119.

ated only by legislation or, if left in the hands of the authorities, by a many-sided administrative approach (Chapter 2).

After study and debate over a period of nearly five years about how best to reform the Federal Reserve System's discount facility, the Board of Governors in early spring 1973 issued a comprehensive revision of its Regulation A.[22] The revised regulation re-emphasizes that the usual availability of a Reserve Bank's discount credit to its member banks is on a short-term basis to meet their temporary or more persistent requirements for borrowed reserve funds pending an orderly adjustment of their assets and liabilities. Furthermore, it states explicitly that credit from the Federal Reserve System is not available as a substitute for bank capital over extended periods. In order to

---

[22] Effective April 19, 1973.

simplify Regulation A, the revision eliminates specific guidelines as to inappropriate discounting.

The new regulation does not contain the proposal of the high-level study group in 1968 for a grant to each member bank of a basic borrowing privilege (a no-questions-asked discount quota) because this is to be given further study, but it does accept as its main feature the study group's recommendation for a seasonal borrowing privilege to banks qualifying for it. This privilege is made available to members that have a recurring seasonal fluctuation in deposits and loans lasting at least eight weeks and exceeding 5 per cent of a member's average total deposits in the preceding calendar year. Such borrowing could be up to 90 days at first maturity, with renewal of the borrowing permitted for the duration of the "demonstrated" seasonal need. It is estimated that close to half of the 5,700 member banks—mainly banks with small deposits—might make seasonal calls for Reserve Bank credit with which to serve their communities and areas; thus, the total of such calls in any year could be substantial.

Another feature of the reform is a liberalization of eligible paper offered as collateral against a Reserve Bank advance to a member bank.[23] Finally, the new regulation affirms the readiness of Reserve Banks to supply credit to member banks confronting exceptionally adverse banking pressures locally or regionally, and it expresses the Federal Reserve System's responsibility to serve in national financial emergencies as lender of last resort to financial institutions other than member banks.

After the member banks fully adapt their operations to the modernized Regulation A, the volume of member bank reserve funds normally supplied to them by the Reserve Bank discount facility may be expected to exceed somewhat the volume typically outstanding over the past two decades. In addition, the Federal Reserve System would

---

[23] For example, the revised Regulation A removes a prohibition against a Reserve Bank's acceptance as collateral of paper drawn to finance any kind of fixed or permanent investment, providing that it has a remaining maturity of 90 days; by this change, notes of home mortgage lenders may serve as eligible collateral in Federal Reserve lending. Another important liberalization for commercial purposes is the inclusion in eligible paper of any note drawn by a member bank to finance the purchases of services. Against advances, these amendments only make such notes eligible as collateral at the basic discount rate; as mentioned earlier, however, they are already acceptable collateral for advances made at a charge ½ percentage point above the basic discount rate if a Reserve Bank regards them as satisfactory for that purpose.

expect its average volume at discount credit to undergo some secular growth as more and more banks resort to seasonal borrowing.

The net result would be an appropriate downward adjustment in the relative volume of Reserve Bank credit available through Federal Reserve open market operations, as well as an adjustment in the typical net free or borrowed reserve position of member banks as a group in periods of ease or restraint in monetary policy. However, the Federal Reserve System should be able to accommodate these operational adjustments without adverse effects upon its ability to regulate the basic reserve position of the commercial banking system.

6

The Variable Reserve Instrument

THE ORIGINAL FEDERAL RESERVE ACT prescribed required reserve percentages for several classes of member banks but did not provide for discretionary variation of the ratios. Amendment of the Act in 1933 authorized changes in them under emergency conditions, and further amendment in 1935 established the variable reserve requirement as a continuing instrument for implementing Federal Reserve monetary policy. Although both open market operations and the discount instrument are joint responsibilities of the Board of Governors and the Reserve Bank officials, the authority to fix and change the ratios of cash reserves to deposits that member banks must hold resides exclusively with the Board. These required reserves may be held in currency or deposit balances with the Reserve Banks.

AUTHORITY OF THE BOARD OF GOVERNORS

The Board of Governors exercises its authority over the required reserve position of member banks first by translating broad statutory provisions into specifications to which the member banks must adhere. The basic specifications to be designated by the Board are as follows:

(1) The liabilities of member banks that are to be classed as deposits subject to a reserve requirement.

(2) The deductions that any member bank is permitted to make from liabilities classed as deposits in arriving at a deposit figure against which reserves must be held.

(3) The centers selected to serve as "reserve cities" on the basis of criteria determined by the Board—such as the size of the center as measured by its resident population and its commercial and financial importance or centers having one or more banks of specified size— thus making either banks located in such centers or of that size (wherever located) subject to the reserve requirements against net demand and time deposits of banks classed as "reserve city banks."

(4) The individual banks or bank classes located in "reserve cities" that are eligible for the lower reserve ratios assigned to banks located outside these cities.

(5) Whether and how the reserve requirements of member banks shall be graduated.

(6) The period over which member banks determine and report their reserve positions in relation to the official reserve percentages (at present, one week ending on a Wednesday for all member banks).[1]

(7) The penalty that any member bank will incur from a deficiency in its daily average reserve balance below its required holding during a reserve period (traditionally set at 2 per cent above its Reserve Bank's discount rate).

---

[1] The weekly period for reserve reporting is the week ending the second preceding Wednesday. For that week, each member bank computes its reserve by applying the relevant percentages to the daily averages of net demand deposits and time deposits, respectively, to define its regulatory reserve position. The currency and coin held as vault cash during that week are subtracted from the required reserve to determine the reserve deposit that the bank must maintain with its Reserve Bank. Therefore, a member bank's reserve currently required for operations lags two weeks behind the week designated for its determination.

This method has the advantage of informing the individual member bank before the start of each new week exactly how much reserve balance it must have at a Reserve Bank. However, it can work detrimentally to a member bank in that a decline in its deposits from two weeks earlier is no longer cushioned by a concurrent reduction in reserves required against its deposits.

From a central banking point of view, the method has the disadvantage of giving each member latitude to anticipate its loan and deposit position and its reserve position. If the majority of the member banks (especially large city banks) anticipate that total bank reserves will expand or contract over the two-week period, and this expectation is not fulfilled, short-run fluctuations of member bank credit and deposits may be accentuated, making more difficult central bank guidance of longer-term monetary trends.

These technical specifications of the reserve requirements have been generally accepted by member banks as incidental to fractional reserve commercial banking. However, changes in banking organization and in banking and regulatory practices in recent years have raised them above merely incidental importance.

Once these technical specifications are determined, the Board of Governors is empowered under the law to establish required reserve percentages within the following limits:

Deposit Category by Class of Member Bank	Range of Percentage Requirements	
	Minimum	Maximum
Against net demand deposits		
Reserve city banks	10	22
Country banks	7	14
Against time deposits		
All member banks	3	10

The percentages against demand deposits may be changed separately by deposit category alone or by deposit category and class of bank, but they must be uniformly applied to all banks within a bank class. Individual member banks in centers designated as reserve cities, however, may be permitted to apply the ratios required of country member banks when this is "reasonable and appropriate" in view of "the character of business" transacted by them or in view of their size.

Rationale of the demand deposit differential

The appreciable differential shown above in the level and range of demand deposit reserve ratios for reserve city banks as compared with country banks in part merely carries forward into the contemporary period regulatory precepts for banking reserves that antedate the establishment of the Federal Reserve System. More fundamentally, however, the differential reflects the conspicuous difference between the two classes of member banks in character of business and typical composition and size of deposits.

The reserve city banks are few in number and very large in average size (as pointed out in Chapter 2). They hold most of the commercial banking system's interbank balances, which constitute the bulk of the cash reserves nonmember banks are obliged to hold under state banking law, and on every business day they must be prepared to redeem these balances on demand. Also, they are the major depositories of U.S. Government funds, the current and accruing funds of state and local governments, the operating funds of most regional or national nonbank financial institutions, and the cash balances of large commercial and industrial corporations for which they also provide other domestic and international banking services. Finally, they are major intermediaries and borrowers of Federal funds, and primary or secondary dealers in U.S. Government securities. Any of these activities can result in abrupt and unpredictable fluctuations from day to day and week to week in their total assets and deposits. In addition, these city banks typically experience on average a much higher rate of deposit turnover (velocity) than do the country banks, and the short-run variation in their deposit turnover is much wider.

In contrast, the country member banks are generally of much smaller size and are widely scattered in rural and suburban communities. They provide a limited range of services to local households, small businesses, and farm enterprises; have more stable deposit totals (except perhaps seasonally) and a more stable deposit turnover; hold a larger percentage of savings deposits of individuals; and usually have relatively higher average operating costs per deposit dollar than city banks. The differential in reserve requirements between the two bank classes finds its rationale, therefore, in the general character of business conducted by the banks belonging to each and in the typical bank size.

Graduated pattern of requirements

In recent years, the Board of Governors has become concerned about the use of the variable reserve instrument because it changes simultaneously and arbitrarily the reserve position of all member banks affected, irrespective of their individual situation and operating standards at the time, and because there is no way for its application to make allowances for differences among banks in their activities or the composition of their deposits. Its application may therefore appear unfair and inequitable to member banks. To adjust for this problem in bank relations, the Board concluded some years ago that a graduated pattern of reserve requirements, if progressively extended, could eventually lead to a separate schedule of requirements applicable to each category of deposit (demand or time) held by any member bank. Under this plan, a low ratio would apply to the first few million dollars of demand or time deposits and progressively higher ratios would apply to successively designated brackets of either type of deposit above this minimum.

A fully graduated plan, it was believed, could have the effect of reducing: (1) inequities among member banks incident to any use of the variable reserve instrument; and (2) variations in the total required reserves of member banks resulting from shifts between time and demand deposits and between banks of different size in the same bank class (reserve city or country). Moreover, the first of these advantages might induce Congress to accept a graduated pattern as a formula for extending the reserve requirement authority to all banks, nonmember as well as member, thus strengthening the Federal Reserve's regulative power over total bank credit and the money stock. The second advantage, to the extent realized, might reduce somewhat the volume of Federal Reserve open market operations required to cushion or facilitate deposit shifts within and among banks without affecting the supply of bank credit.

The Federal Reserve's preliminary and modest move toward a graduated pattern of reserve requirements, taken in mid-1966, applied to both the net demand deposits and time deposits of member banks. This limited initial graduation was retained for six years, but after November 9, 1972 a more elaborate graduated pattern of requirements was adopted against net demand deposits, while the existing graduation against time deposits was continued (Table 11).[2]

This elaborated graduation of reserve ratios against demand deposits relieved the Board of Governors of two onerous administrative tasks stemming from the statute. The Board made size of net demand deposits ($400 million and over) in a member bank the single criterion of status as a reserve city bank, regardless of the population and financial activity of the center in which it is located. This restructuring automatically classifies as country banks all members, wherever located, having less than $400 million in net demand deposits. Thus, the Board of Governors had relieved itself of (1) a politically sensitive duty of designating urban centers as reserve cities on the basis of their population and commercial and financial characteristics, and (2) any need to exempt a member bank in such a center from the reserve requirements of a reserve city bank on the basis of the character of its business and its size.

---

[2] By amendment of Regulation D of the Board of Governors.

Although each individual member bank, in determining its reserve position, must accommodate itself to the graduated pattern of demand deposit ratios prescribed by the recently amended regulation, its primary interest is the single effective reserve ratio resulting from such computation. The effective ratios computed for selected sizes of member bank by amount of net demand deposits held before and after the November 1972 restructuring are compared in Table 12 and Chart 8.

The table shows that all member banks, regardless of size, gain some reduction in effective reserve ratios from the new graduated pattern of required reserves; the reductions, however, are largest for banks under $400 million in net demand deposits and become smaller as banks increase in deposit size above that level, with the very large city banks realizing the smallest reduction. In practice, this new graduation of reserve ratios arranges the member banks into six size groups, each having a range of net demand deposits within which

Table 11. Basic Reserve Requirements of Federal Reserve Member Banks Before and After the Restructuring Effective November 9, 1972

Reserve Requirements of Member Banks by Type and Size of Deposit	Required Reserve Percentages	
	Country Banks	Reserve City Banks
Amount of net demand deposits		
Before restructuring		
$5 million or less	12.5	13
Over $5 million	13	17.5
After restructuring		
$2 million or less	8	8
Over $2 million to $10 million	10	10 [2]
Over $10 million to $100 million	12	12 [2]
Over $100 million to $400 million	13	13 [2]
Over $400 million	—	17.5 [2]
Amount of time deposits [1]		
Time deposits		
$5 million or less	3	3
Over $5 million	5	5
Savings deposits	3	3

Source: Board of Governors, Federal Reserve System, *Federal Reserve Bulletin*, July 1972, pp. 626-33 and November 1972, p. 994.

[1] These reserve requirements were unchanged by the restructuring of November 9, 1972.

[2] These reserve requirements were raised by 0.5 percentage point, effective July 2, 1973.

Chart 8. Effective Ratios of Reserve Requirements Before and After Restructuring, November 9, 1972

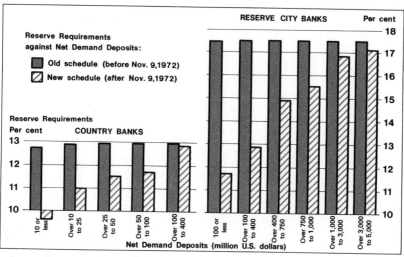

Source: Based on Table 12 below.

Table 12. Effective Ratios of Reserve Requirements Against Demand Deposits of Selected Federal Reserve Member Banks Before and After the Restructuring Effective November 9, 1972

Net Demand Deposits in Member Banks Selected by Size and Class (U.S. dollars)	Approximate Effective Ratios on Demand Deposits	
	Former Reserve Requirements	New Reserve Requirements
	(per cent)	
Deposits in country banks		
$10 million or less	12.75	9.60
Over $10 million to $25 million	12.90	11.00
Over $25 million to $50 million	12.95	11.52
Over $50 million to $100 milion	12.98	11.76
Over $100 million to $400 milion	12.99	12.89
Deposits in reserve city banks		
$100 million or less [1]	17.47 [1]	11.76 [1]
Over $100 million to $400 million [1]	17.49 [1]	12.89 [1]
Over $400 million to $750 million	17.50	14.93
Over $750 million to $1,000 million	17.50	15.58
Over $1,000 million to $3,000 million	17.50	16.86
Over $3,000 million to $5,000 million	17.50	17.12

[1] After the restructuring of reserve requirements, banks with $400 million or less of net demand deposits were classified as country banks.

effective reserve ratios are fairly narrowly equalized. The six categories are under $25 million, over $25 million to $150 million, over $150 million to $400 million, over $400 million to $750 million, over $750 million to $3 billion, and over $3 billion.

The introduction of this graduated plan for demand deposit reserve ratios, as the Board of Governors expressly stated, was intended to be neutral in regard to Federal Reserve monetary policy. Since the action had no immediate policy objective, it appears to have been based on one or more of the following aims: (1) to make the pattern of reserve requirements more equitable among member banks; (2) to combat structural tendencies in banking organization that were adverse to a federally regulated monetary mechanism;[3] and (3) to make variation in member bank reserve ratios against demand deposits a more flexible and usable instrument of monetary policy. As the graduated increase of reserve requirements tends to complicate decision making involving an increase in the member reserve ratio against demand deposits (the third aim), it may be assumed that the first and second aims were of paramount importance in determining the Board action. Moreover, as the reserve restructuring turned out to be broader and larger than might be necessary to attain more reasonable equity alone, the second aim appears to have been the more important one. Only an inclusive reserve requirement reform could make member banking status more attractive to smaller banks than nonmember status.

Joint reform of check clearance

A graduated pattern of member bank reserve requirements that would temper and possibly halt or even reverse past structural trends in banking organization (while at the same time it would relieve the feeling of many bankers that they were receiving inequitable treatment) also opened up the prospect of a very large one-time release of reserve funds to the commercial banking system. But such a release of funds could hardly be justified in circumstances when inflationary dangers were a continuing threat, as they were in 1972.

Fortunately, at that time the Federal Reserve was introducing automated processing of regional and interregional money transfers through

---

[3] Such as progressive erosion of membership in the Federal Reserve System and the steadily declining share of the money stock accounted for by the demand deposits of member banks (see Chapter 2).

the facilities of Reserve Banks. It had already made a sizable investment in this new technology and was prepared to invest more to foster a more efficient national payments mechanism.[4] Although progress in such automation had not yet alleviated significantly the overload of regional and interregional payments resulting from a dramatic growth in check-clearing volume over the past decade, money transfers held promise of being more rapidly expedited by applying the present and developing technologies in the fields of transport, computerization, and communication.

Only one regulatory step was needed: Federal Reserve initiative in modernizing its Regulation J governing Reserve Bank practice in check clearance and collection. If this one-time step were taken simultaneously with a restructuring of reserve requirements, the bulk of the reserves made available by the restructuring could be automatically absorbed by an appreciable cutback in Reserve Bank credit extended in check collection (Federal Reserve float). The entire adjustment might then be kept essentially neutral in terms of the Federal Reserve's current monetary policy. Meanwhile, the regulatory modernization of Federal Reserve check collection would make the process of regional and interregional money payments more efficient for the public, more equitable among banks and bank depositors, and more economical for the entire banking system as automated check collection became more common.

The basic check clearance action taken by the Federal Reserve on November 9, 1972 was purely technical, applying to the payment of checks cleared through Reserve Bank facilities.[5] It simply required

---

[4] In fact, the Board of Governors in September 1972 authorized the Reserve Banks to establish a series of regional check-clearing centers, equipped with electronic and mechanical installations that would permit most of the 62 million checks written daily by bank depositors to be cleared and paid by the opening of business the day after the check was deposited. Each regional center is to have telecommunication facilities to make overnight check settlement between centers and with banks in reserve cities. The centers will cooperate with all banks and established local clearing centers which seek their help in expediting check clearance.

[5] Both the reserve requirement restructuring and the check clearance modernization were originally scheduled to become effective on September 21, 1972, but implementation was delayed because of court action brought by nonmember banking groups to enjoin the check clearance reform. Upon court denial of this injunction a few weeks later, the Board of Governors set November 9th for the application of both changes. To facilitate their introduction, the Board of Governors authorized the Reserve Banks to waive penalties on member bank reserve

every bank—city and country, member and nonmember—benefiting from use of their Reserve Bank's check-clearing service to make payment the same day in immediately available funds for all out-of-town checks drawn on it and presented that day for collection by its Reserve Bank. Since automated collection would increasingly be utilized in clearing intertown checks, the Reserve Banks' standard collection time for many, and eventually most, such checks could be cut back from two days to one day; thus, banks utilizing Reserve Bank check-clearing facilities would receive (be credited with) collected funds earlier than was feasible before the action of November 1972.

Previous Federal Reserve practice in clearing out-of-town checks permitted outlying country banks [6]—nonmembers as well as members— to remit collection settlement one day after a Reserve Bank presented the checks drawn earlier for outside payment by depositors of such banks. In view of this privilege, these banks could charge such checks to customer accounts on the day they were presented for collection settlement, while they actually settled for them in "good funds" one day later. In this way, they earned an extra day's interest on funds in fact owed to the collecting banks.

The modernized practice of Reserve Banks in check collection was expected to affect directly only about 15 per cent of the present dollar volume of check transactions. Although this percentage appears almost too modest to call for a change in bank check clearance practice that was costly to country banks, it was then estimated to account for two thirds of the $3 billion daily average of Federal Reserve check collection float—which in effect advances funds to banks that have not yet made payments to the Reserve Banks for checks already presented to them.

Thus, while the November 1972 restructuring of member bank reserve requirements released an estimated $3.4 billion of reserve funds to the banking system, the check collection reform at the

---

deficiencies (greater than 2 per cent) attributable to the regulatory amendments and also to make their "discount window" available to nonmember banks when a nonmember's liquidity and ability to serve its community would be impaired by the new check collection rules.

[6] Banks outside urban centers not having access to city clearing facilities. The heavy cost burden that this check clearance action would impose on these rural country banks (including larger ones) is one reason for the greater reduction in reserve ratios that the proposed restructuring of reserves would give to them than it would give to large city banks.

same time was counted on to absorb an estimated $2 billion, leaving about $1.4 billion to be absorbed partly by open market operations and partly by allowing some of the released reserves to support current bank credit and monetary expansion.[7] If and when achieved, a large one-time cutback in Federal Reserve float will have other advantages to the Federal Reserve System, such as alleviating problems in administering its more flexible instruments of monetary policy. The most important direct effect should be on open market operations —by contracting the needed volume of Federal Reserve market transactions for an orderly market rather than for policy purposes. Such a technical change could strengthen considerably the Federal Reserve's control of its own credit and of money creation.

From the beginning of the Federal Reserve System, it has been difficult to develop a coherent regulation of bank credit and money under the federal authority because of the U.S. multiple banking system—regulated in part by the Federal Government and in part by the 50 states, with some general consistency but with a few critical inconsistencies in regulatory standards between the two divisions of jurisdiction. Over the years, jurisdictional rivalries between the federal and state authorities have given rise to successive phases of relaxation and tightening in their respective regulation of banking. The Federal Reserve's concurrent reserve requirement and check clearance reforms succeeded in joining elements of both relaxation and tightening of regulations applicable to member banks, while at the same time penalizing modestly the thousands of nonmember banks. Whether the reform will accomplish all that Federal Reserve officials hope, in terms of a stronger and more equitable administration of

---

[7] However, sharp reduction in Federal Reserve float was not quickly achieved (as anticipated) through the changing of Reserve Bank practice in clearing checks. Large city banks responded to the change by discontinuing out-of-town check collection service to their correspondent banks, while smaller banks adapted by shifting to Reserve Bank collection facilities, swelling sharply the volume of checks to be cleared through the System's facilities as a result. An unforeseen buildup of uncleared checks immediately occurred at the Reserve Banks, delaying for an unknown number of weeks the full contraction in their float as earlier estimated and handicapping the Federal Reserve System's pursuit of its bank reserve targets during these weeks. Although the Federal Reserve's officials could take some satisfaction that the short-run response of the banks would hasten the stage when out-of-town clearings for all commercial banks could be handled through the computerized clearing facilities that the System was sponsoring, they were also made aware that initial estimates of the volume of checks to be cleared through Reserve Bank facilities after the check clearance reform were much too low.

the monetary system, will depend on two factors: (1) how individual member and nonmember banks assess their short-run interests in adapting to them; and (2) how state authorities respond over time by endeavoring to restore the competitiveness of their nonmember bank regulatory standards in relation to those now applying to the member banks.

SPECIAL PROBLEMS OF THE VARIABLE RESERVE

The variable reserve authority has advantages and disadvantages that set it apart from the other two instruments of central banking in the United States that directly affect bank reserve positions, making it more of a supplementary and infrequently used instrument than a companion tool for current implementation of monetary policy. Undoubtedly, some problems relating to it arise from the membership composition of the Federal Reserve System—encompassing as it does several thousand independently owned and managed banks, many of which have the option of withdrawing if membership advantages become less beneficial to them.

Distinctive features

Since the cash reserve required for commercial banks is a nonearning asset, the earnings forgone because of it represent a cost of engaging in the banking business. In a sense, the cash reserve requirement is an exchange for a quasi-monopolistic business privilege granted by charter. It has three interrelated reasons for its existence: (1) assurance to the public that their deposits and checks can be readily redeemed in other forms of money or readily transferred to other banks; (2) limitation of the expansion of bank credit and money on the basis of any given volume of reserves held by the commercial banking system; and (3) use as base for central banking regulation of additions to a country's total bank credit and money stock. The first provides a practical liquidity and solvency support for a payments mechanism relying heavily on money transfer by checks drawn on private banks; the second, a safeguard for the public at large against unbridled inflation of private bank credit; and the third, a central banking fulcrum for discretionary variation of monetary policy as national need may indicate.[8]

---

[8] To identify these functions is not to contend that the existence of a cash reserve requirement is sufficient for these broad purposes,

A change in the required reserve ratio of the member banks actually produces no change in the volume of the cash balances held by the member banks at that time, but four important changes do take place. First, an immediate change occurs in the availability to member banks of cash for their banking operations, because a reduction in the ratio releases cash otherwise tied up in required reserves while an increase in the ratio absorbs bank cash (excess reserves, if any).

Second, a change takes place simultaneously in the liquid asset or secondary reserve position of the member banks. For example, when the reserve ratio is decreased, banks with no sizable reserve deficiency find that they have excess reserves for investment in earning assets or for retiring nondeposit borrowing (including that from the Reserve Banks). Since individual banks normally seek to maximize their earnings by avoiding nondeposit debt, their usual initial response to a windfall of excess reserves is to retire pressing short-term indebtedness, including discount debt, and then to acquire liquid assets readily available from the national money market. On the other hand, when the reserve ratio is increased, banks with no excess reserves must acquire additional reserve funds by selling liquid assets in the money market, by borrowing market funds, by borrowing temporarily from the Reserve Banks, or by reducing their lending. Reserve Bank borrowing might admittedly increase the total volume of bank reserves temporarily, more than offsetting the effects of the increase in the reserve requirement. However, Federal Reserve discount practice should limit this response after a moderately short cushioning period.

Third, there is a change in the potential for multiple expansion or contraction of deposits on the basis of a given quantity of reserves in the banking system as a whole. This changed multiplier has relevance to the Federal Reserve System in estimating the expected effects of a reserve requirement change on the major monetary aggregates— that is, total bank credit and the active money stock (M_1). Also, it will serve as a rough gauge for the financial community of the short-run impact of the reserve change on the demand by banks for money market claims and on rates of interest in the money market.

Fourth, any change in required reserve percentages also has longer-term effects on each bank. For instance, if higher ratios are required, each bank must set aside as nonearning reserves a larger amount from each new deposit. In contrast, if lower ratios are required, a smaller amount can be set aside as nonearning reserves from new deposits over a period of time. Changes in reserve requirements thus affect

bank portfolio planning and banking costs of deposit volume, influencing banking attitudes toward the Federal Reserve's use of the variable
reserve instrument. For the regulatory mechanism as a whole, these
continuing effects give Federal Reserve open market and discount
instruments greater or lesser leverage. A lower percentage requirement
over an extended period reduces the amount of Federal Reserve
credit needed in order to realize a given rate of change in bank credit
and the money stock, while a higher percentage requirement increases
this amount.

The required reserve percentage then determines the amount of
banking business that a specific quantity of bank reserves can do,
and eventually the amount of such business that increments in
reserves can add. In view of the credit market responses evoked by
a change in the reserve ratio of the commercial banks, discretionary
authority to make such changes appears to be a powerful and flexible
instrument for any central bank.

Administrative difficulties

Because of the thousands of member banks—each seeking to
maximize its profits by keeping its cash reserve position as low as
management considers prudent in relation to its legal reserve requirement—the application of the variable reserve instrument encounters
some administrative difficulties in the central banking system of the
United States. It is easy to make a decision to lower the ratio for
all member banks, because a lower ratio is always beneficial to every
one of them. Nevertheless, an acute equity problem would almost
certainly arise if the reduction applied to only one bank class or
differed in amount between reserve city banks and country banks.
Furthermore, if the lower ratio needed substantial cushioning or offset
at the time by Federal Reserve open market operations to absorb the
reserves it released, it could arouse objection from Congress as a
"give-away" to private banks of Reserve Bank interest earnings that
might otherwise flow to the U.S. Treasury.

On the other hand, it is not easy to make a decision to raise the
reserve ratio, because few member banks are likely to be in a
"comfortable" excess reserve position to meet a higher ratio. Although
some banks may hold a modest margin of excess reserves, there are
always others in reserve deficiency, and most of the larger banks ordinarily try to maintain a close reserve position—being neither in excess
nor in deficiency by any large amount. The many banks forced into

reserve deficiency or into larger deficiency by the raising of the ratio will voice vigorous criticism, even though they have Reserve Bank advances or purchases of Federal funds available to meet their deficiencies in the short run. However, such funds are available only at a price—although usually a relatively low one, and adjustment of bank assets or liabilities must follow without delay. Besides, the price set results from an action by the authorities that the member banks view as arbitrary. In short, any increase in the ratio seems almost certain to raise the issue of equitable treatment among member banks, deriving from statutory precept that calls for it.

Moreover, the very nature of the variable reserve instrument makes it mandatory that changes in required reserve ratios become applicable on some designated date or dates, at which time a discrete sum of reserve funds is absorbed from or released to banking use. If the ratio is increased, a multiple problem arises. Are the member banks as a group (typically fully invested) to obtain the additional reserve funds needed from (1) market sale by banks of liquid assets; (2) maturity of some loans and investments without replacement; (3) Federal Reserve open market purchases of U.S. Government securities to offset bank sales of liquid assets; (4) member discounting with their respective Reserve Banks; (5) member sales of CDs; or (6) a combination of sources? If the reserve ratio is reduced, the problem will be the reverse—how to dispose of excess reserves. Unless the adjustment problems resulting from a ratio change can be readily solved by the member banks, the impact of the variable reserve instrument can be harsh or abrupt. Therefore, no change in the ratios can be made without gauging its effects in terms of possible marginal and multiplier effects of the bank reserves released to or absorbed from the money and credit markets in the very short run. If the market considers these effects likely to be large, the result can be severely disruptive to an orderly market.

The size of a change in reserve requirements and its coordination with other major instruments of monetary policy may cause another difficulty. Since each of the leading monetary policy instruments is under Federal Reserve regulative control, in principle there should be little difficulty in coordinating their joint use. However, when central banking is under the control of three separately identified statutory bodies, although within the Federal Reserve System, a problem of coordination may arise—and actually has arisen. Coordination has perhaps been of little importance when a change in the reserve ratio would release or absorb a relatively small amount of reserves, but experience over the 1950s, when five out of six successive reserve ratio actions intentionally resulted in large marginal reserve and multiplier effects, demonstrated the need for closer coordination in using Federal Reserve policy instruments than was the practice during that decade.

Two further technical factors influence any Federal Reserve decision to use the variable reserve ratio instrument. One pertains to increases in the reserve ratios: in particular, how any increase may affect the attractiveness to banks of membership in the Federal Reserve System. (Nonmember bank cash reserve ratios applied by the states, as explained in Chapter 2, are generally lower than those applying to member banks.) The other grows out of the recently established and more elaborate graduated pattern of reserve requirements against member bank demand deposits. If the reserve ratio against these deposits is to be varied, will one ratio be changed or will all need to be changed in order to retain an equity arrangement earlier found acceptable by the banks? Whatever the answer, this graduated pattern has made the variation of reserve requirements against demand deposits somewhat more complicated.[9]

Use of reserve requirement change

In practice, four deterrents have limited Federal Reserve use of the variable reserve instrument up to the present time: (1) a close dovetailing of open market and discount operations can produce the same banking effects in a less precipitate way; (2) there are numerous difficulties in administering this instrument; (3) member banks have a strong antipathy to increases in the reserve ratios; and (4) small banks are discouraged from maintaining membership in the Federal Reserve. From its long experience with reserve requirement changes, the Federal Reserve has come to regard this instrument as clumsy and blunt. The infrequent occasions for its use, as one may judge from the record and from reasonable expectations for future uses, would include situations where:

---

[9] For example, if reductions applied to all graduated reserve brackets of demand deposits, they could only amount to 1 percentage point, as the statutory minimum for the lowest bracket (7 per cent) would be reached after that change. Further reductions applicable only to the next higher bracket and above would raise a perplexing equity problem, which the original graduated pattern was intended to solve.

(1) A large and abrupt change is called for (amounting, say, to 5 to 10 per cent of currently required member bank reserves) to counter inflation or recession;

(2) A smaller action (providing or absorbing around 3 per cent of the required reserves of members) will communicate to a large number of banks, widely spread geographically, the Federal Reserve's determination to make its existing policy fully effective, that is, either to accelerate or sustain current bank credit and monetary expansion or to curb expansion of these aggregates;

(3) An action of comparably moderate size will encourage banks to give more or less emphasis to such areas of lending as business finance, housing finance, or foreign lending;

(4) A similarly moderate-sized action may help either to: (a) avoid the direct money market effects of open market operations; (b) cushion unusual international capital flows; or (c) cope with exceptional flows of currency into or out of circulation.

Individual situations leading to a change in member bank reserve ratios are usually complex, and more than one operational purpose may actuate any given change.

Over the past 22 years of flexibility in policy action after World War II (beginning in 1951), the Federal Reserve Board of Governors applied the variable reserve instrument 14 times, six times in the 1950s and eight in the next 12 years. All of the six changes in the 1950s were counter-recessionary in intent (see first situation above), and five of them (averaging 6 per cent of then-required reserves) could be regarded as of large size. Two of these five reductions and the sixth, which was small, were also to implement legislation (1959) that allowed member banks to count vault cash in meeting their reserve requirements and that combined two city bank classes into one reserve city class. In making only successive reductions in the first decade of discretionary action, the Board of Governors apparently felt that it was in part adjusting ratios from wartime to peacetime levels and in part adhering to a then-held view that increases in reserve ratios were undesirable as measures to counter economic boom.

In contrast to the six uses of the instrument in the first decade, the eight applications in the following years (mainly during the 1960s) were all of more moderate size, averaging about 3 per cent of currently required reserves. Also, use in the second decade was evenly divided, with four decreases and four increases. Five of the changes applied to reserve requirements for time deposits and only three to those for demand deposits, whereas in the earlier period, all six changes applied to reserve requirements for demand deposits. Finally, use of the instrument in the second decade was chiefly motivated in one or more instances by the first two of the four situations listed above. Together, these differences reflected a fundamental reassessment of the usefulness of the variable reserve instrument in monetary policy.

Another aspect of the Board's use of the variable reserve instrument from 1951 to 1973 may be noted. The actions taken over the first decade involved a cumulative release of reserve funds totaling nearly $6.5 billion; in the absence of these actions, the member banks at the close of that decade would have required $25.8 billion in reserves instead of the $19.3 billion they actually reported. That is to say, when the Federal Reserve System first regained full discretion in its monetary actions following World War II, each dollar of reserves held by the member banks could support $5.20 of demand deposits, while at the end of the decade it could support as much as $6.70 of such deposits. During the second decade of flexible monetary action, in contrast, the amounts of reserves released and the amounts absorbed by reserve action about counterbalanced each other, so that the deposit multiple of member bank reserves stood at about the same figure at its close as it had at the beginning.

ADAPTATIONS IN THE REQUIREMENT BASE

During most of the 1960s, major sectors of the economy made strong demands for bank and other credit in face of a rising trend in market interest rates. These developments gave an extra profit incentive to large city member banks to reduce or avoid the cost burden of their high reserve requirements against demand deposits. Therefore, these banks sought to finance their loan and investment expansion either through time deposit liabilities subject to much lower reserve ratios than demand deposits or through nondeposit liabilities entirely free of any reserve requirement under the long-standing reserve regulations of the Federal Reserve System.

Techniques of large city banks

These large banks used various techniques for such financing. An early innovation was the sale to deposit holders of negotiable certificates of deposit (CDs) in large denominations—subject to the lower time deposit reserve ratio—and the encouragement of a secondary trading market in these negotiable bank CDs to make them liquid ahead of their maturity. One objective of these CDs was to attract excess demand balances of nonbank holders in interior city banks or outlying local banks into money market paper issued by nationally known banks; another was to obtain a competitively attractive and marketable time liability for temporary placement of excess demand balances of large corporate customers at a time when these customers were increasingly preferring Treasury bills to demand deposits.

A second technique, which became more important in the 1960s, was for the larger city banks to encourage correspondent banks in outlying centers or communities to keep any holdings of excess reserves, as well as some part of their secondary reserves, regularly invested in day-to-day or very short-term loans to city banks through the facilities of the market for Federal funds. The large city banks later encouraged nonbank customers with temporary excess demand balances to use this technique, and they served as agents for the transactions. The Board of Governors subsequently judged this latter practice tantamount to paying interest on demand deposits and therefore prohibited it.

In 1966 and again in 1969, the city banks became actively interested in nondeposit funds when the Board of Governors decided, with legislative sanction by Congress, that interest ceilings on bank time deposits should be kept relatively unattractive to all depositors who wanted temporary placement of funds in the low-risk assets being supplied by banks, even though short-term market rates had risen above the bank ceilings (see Chapter 7). A special motive behind the decision, however, was to avert bidding by the commercial banks of savings, other time deposits, and insurance equity values away from nonbank thrift institutions (mutual savings banks, savings and loan associations, and life insurance companies). As a consequence, the commercial banks issuing negotiable certificates of deposit in large denominations were priced out of the market, since money market interest rates exceeded what they could pay under the interest ceilings then in effect.

Under these conditions, city banks relying on the issue of such money market claims to finance an appreciable margin of their loans and investments faced both sharply increased redemptions of maturing CDs and correspondingly sharp liquidation of their earning assets. Thus, the city banks urgently needed to replace such funds from nondeposit sources or by borrowing from Reserve Banks. Considering the inequity (in their view) of the established ceiling rates on time deposits and the constraints on borrowing from Reserve Banks, they chose to exploit all accessible "outside sources of funds."

Practices adopted by large city banks

Accordingly, the larger city banks adopted a succession of innovative practices to attract nondeposit funds and especially to avoid the cost burden of reserve requirements against their demand deposit liabilities. The new practices included:

(1) Offering to investors short-term and medium-term promissory notes or debenture obligations, unsubordinated to claims of depositors.

(2) Borrowing of funds from the Euro-dollar market through branches and correspondent foreign banks—incidentally gaining extra reserve economy because checks drawn for transfer and repayment of short-term borrowing could then be deducted from the deposit base.

(3) Sale of loan assets to nonbank investors, including affiliate companies, either outright or under repurchase agreement.

(4) Offering to money market investors for their purchase bankers' acceptances ineligible for Federal Reserve rediscount.

(5) Sale of commercial paper (unsecured promissory notes) in the market by a bank's affiliates, subsidiaries, or the parent holding company for the purpose of channeling the funds back to the bank to finance the continued expansion of its credit.

These new practices developed by the large city banks to avoid or lessen the burdens and banking costs of reserve requirement regulation illustrate the practical problems in using the variable reserve instrument when banks are under strong competitive and regulative pressure as well as cost incentive to avert its incidence. By escaping partly from the restraints of reserve requirements, however, the large city banks also made inequitable the reserve requirement burdens borne by other member banks. Such avoidance tactics called for counteraction by the Federal Reserve to prevent their cumulative effect from weakening the reserve instrument itself and undermining its accepted equity among member banks, thus eroding seriously its usefulness as the fulcrum for the lever of Federal Reserve monetary policy. The problem became particularly acute after discount and open market instruments had already been applied to the point of creating stringent credit market conditions. Further increases in reserve requirements, moreover, could not resolve so basic a problem, since it resulted directly from the official specification of those bank liabilities that should be counted by each Federal Reserve member as falling within the "deposit category."

Regulatory reaction by the Federal Reserve

Federal Reserve reaction was bound to be slow, in view of the technical problems to be dealt with in amplifying the basic reserve specifications for member banks. The technicalities, moreover, required a number of actions, and for two of them, Congress would have to and eventually did provide needed statutory authority. The several regulatory amendments made by the Board of Governors within the four years 1966-70 encompassed the following:

(1) Inclusion in gross deposits subject to reserve requirements of all bank liabilities arising from the sale to investors of promissory notes and related forms of bank debt (unsubordinated as to depositor claims), initially having maturities of under two years but later extended to seven-year maturities.

(2) Inclusion in deposits subject to required reserves of all bank liabilities on repurchase account with nonbank customers but excluding repurchase sales of U.S. Government securities or those of its agencies.

(3) Exclusion of all checks drawn by banks to transfer or repay borrowed Euro-dollar funds from items deductible by banks from gross demand deposits in determining net deposits subject to reserves.

(4) Application of a marginal reserve requirement against increases in member bank Euro-dollar borrowings over borrowings outstanding on a selected base date, initially set at 10 per cent and later raised to 20 per cent with a forward shift in the base date.

(5) Application of a 5 per cent reserve requirement against outstanding commercial paper of bank affiliate companies when issued to channel funds to a member bank to finance its activities.

Each of the above actions was designed to close a regulative loophole already discovered by city bank technicians and managements in the Federal Reserve's reserve requirement regulation. The actions thus constituted structural modernizations of the Board of Governors' equity and regulative specifications for required reserves. Although the amendments were adopted in a phase of restraint on bank credit and monetary expansion, their intent was not to add to that restraint. Since the actions resulted in increasing total required reserves of the member banks, the Federal Reserve felt obligated to facilitate banking adjustment by supplying through open market operations on their effective dates an amount of reserves equal to that which the city banks as a group would then be required to set aside to meet the required increase in their reserves. This did not allow the city banks affected to escape reserve adjustment necessitated by a regulative change; rather, it simply assured that the supply of available reserve funds in the market would be sufficient to enable them to trade earning assets for reserve funds through the market without undue penalty.

Recurrence of stringent monetary restraint to cope with inflationary boom conditions in 1973 brought on new problems arising from the Federal Reserve's basic specifications for bank liabilities subject to reserve requirements. In the strong upswing in activity, large banks had been actively increasing their dependence on CD liabilities and had begun to issue corporate customer notes bearing bank endorsement (finance bills) for market sale; they had also shown signs of looking with renewed favor on Euro-dollar borrowings. To deal with these developments, the Federal Reserve Board of Governors in mid-May took the following additional regulatory actions affecting member banks:

(1) Imposition of a marginal reserve requirement of 3 per cent against any increase in large CD liabilities (over $100,000 in denomination) from the then existing levels, thus making the reserve requirement 8 per cent against liabilities incurred after imposition, compared with a requirement of 5 per cent on the outstanding CD liabilities acquired prior to that time (see Chapter 7).

(2) Application of a similar marginal requirement to increases in commercial paper issued by bank affiliates to finance the lending of a member bank (subject, however, to later final action).

(3) Application of a 5 per cent reserve requirement against bank-issued finance bills or working capital acceptances (ineligible for Federal Reserve Bank discount) plus a marginal reserve requirement of 3 per cent on increases in such liabilities from mid-1973; and

(4) Conversion of the existing marginal reserve requirement of 20 per cent against increases over a base date in Euro-dollar borrowings by U.S. banks to a straight 8 per cent reserve requirement against currently held Euro-dollar liabilities—the existing reserve free (base

date) Euro-borrowings to be eliminated within the following nine months.[10] Concurrently, foreign-owned banking institutions operating in the United States which were not members of the Federal Reserve System were requested to conform voluntarily to a marginal reserve requirement of 8 per cent against increases in funds borrowed abroad over the average of such borrowings during May 1973.

The 1973 actions differed in purpose from those taken in 1966-70 in that they were expressly restrictive in intent. Their joint aim was to help moderate the current expansion in bank credit—which by then had gathered strong momentum—while relying on resulting interest rate pressures to help keep U.S. interest levels aligned with those in the Euro-dollar market. Thus, the Federal Reserve did not provide reserve funds through concurrent purchase transactions in the open market for the purpose of facilitating individual city bank adjustment to the new requirements.

PROPOSED LEGISLATIVE REFORM

Two-way flexibility of the variable reserve instrument in U.S. central banking, as emphasized before, has long been seriously handicapped by the division of the commercial banking system into 51 jurisdictions, only one of which is federal. Moreover, the effective cash reserve ratios of the federal jurisdiction are higher than those applying to nonmember banks in the many state jurisdictions. In the mid-1960s, the Board of Governors proposed legislation to remove this handicap by authorizing the application of uniform reserve requirements to all commercial banks, at least to all federally insured banks. In 1971, the Board recommended that required reserve percentages for member banks against their demand deposits be applied to all institutions that accept such deposits, and further that the Reserve Banks be authorized to open their discount facilities to nonmember institutions subject to the new requirements on the same terms as to member banks. This broader recommendation reflected an incipient trend for mutual savings banks and savings and loan associations to seek state legislative authority to provide their customers with checking accounts as well as

---

[10] While this reduction in requirements against Euro-dollar borrowing results in parallel treatment with large CDs, bank-related commercial paper, and bank-issued finance bills, it was officially stated at the time of the action that departure from such parallel treatment might be desirable at some future date.

savings accounts.[11]

These proposals for reform of the variable reserve instrument now rest on the legislative table of Congress. Meanwhile, the Federal Reserve authorities have taken action to make the reserve requirement structure more equitable to its smaller banks in comparison with the state-chartered banks. At the same time the Board acted to give smaller banks some special advantages in check clearance services, while imposing a new cost penalty on the use of these services by both members and nonmembers. In addition, the Federal Reserve System has been investing actively in furthering the automation of check clearing and in expanding the use of wire transfer facilities, with benefits both to the efficiency of the national payments mechanism and to the System's control over its own credit and money creation.

Thus, it is entirely possible that pressures stemming from basic operating and administrative costs in banking will soon be sufficiently relieved to arrest, if not reverse, structural trends in banking organization that discourage voluntary membership in the Federal Reserve System and weaken the required reserve base for implementing national monetary policy. The proposals for broader statutory authority over the reserve requirement, which are legislatively controversial, may therefore continue to rest as they are until further developments bearing on the basic issues are brought into sharp enough focus to engage the attention of Congress.

---

[11] This proposal was endorsed in the *Report of the President's Commission on Financial Structure and Regulation* (1971), p. 65. However, the Commission would go further and make Federal Reserve membership mandatory for all commercial banks and for any mutual savings banks or savings and loan associations providing a checking deposit service to customers. For the latter institutions, the Commission proposed a lower preferential reserve requirement against demand deposits than that for commercial banks initially, with uniformity being accomplished gradually over a five-year period. The Commission also urged that both the statutory brackets within which the Board of Governors may fix demand deposit reserve ratios and the actual ratio levels should be gradually reduced over a period of time. Against savings and time deposits, it recommended complete elimination of required reserve ratios.

7

Instruments for Selective Regulation

THE FEDERAL RESERVE SYSTEM presently has three means of supplementing its primary instruments of credit policy in order to regulate selectively specific types of credit. However, when directed by the President of the United States to prevent or control inflation, the Federal Reserve may apply selective regulation to "any or all credit extensions" (Chapter 1).

Two of these supplementary instruments are under continuing statutory authority, and the other is under a temporary statute. One of the continuing statutes directs the Board of Governors to regulate stock market credit, and the second (found in recent years adaptable to selective regulation) directs it to establish ceiling rates that member banks are permitted to pay on savings and time deposits. The temporary regulation, instituted in 1965 at the request of the President of the United States, is designed to elicit the cooperation of banks and other financial institutions in voluntarily limiting or even reducing their international lending and investing; it is, however, scheduled to be discontinued by the end of 1974.

REGULATION OF STOCK MARKET CREDIT

The Securities Exchange Act of 1934, one of the far-reaching financial reforms of the early 1930s, authorizes the Federal Reserve System to regulate stock market credit. It was enacted because of the destabilizing impact on the stock market and on the economy of the United States of highly leveraged credit extended for purchasing or carrying corporate stocks. Its purposes were twofold: (1) to forestall recurrence both of speculative stock market boom financed by credit (as happened during the 1920s) and of subsequent stock price collapse accentuated by forced security sales from financing on too slim margins of equity (as happened in 1929-32);[1] and (2) to moderate in the future abrupt instabilities in stock market trading and prices by regulating the amount of credit made available to stock investors.

Accordingly, the Board of Governors was directed to prescribe rules and regulations governing the amount of credit extended to any borrower by any lender making loans in the ordinary course of business to finance the purchase or holding of designated types of equity securities, including convertible bonds as well as stock shares.[2] Under this authority, the Board of Governors determines the maximum loan value that may be extended to a borrower for the purpose of purchasing or carrying such securities. In so doing, it establishes the amount of cash or equity that a borrower must deposit with a lender when purchasing or carrying such securities on credit—an amount called the borrower's margin. This margin is the difference between the market value and the loan value of the security or securities used as collateral in a credit transaction.

The Securities Exchange Act broadly empowers the Board of Governors to use its discretion in lowering or raising from time to time the maximum loan value that a lender may assign to stock securities when used as collateral for purchasing or carrying securities. However, the Act specifies that different purposes should motivate these two actions. When it lowers the loan value (and thus raises the required stock margin), the Board's purpose must be that of "preventing the excessive use of credit for the purchasing or carrying of securities," and the

---

[1] Speculation in securities trading is used here in the dictionary sense of buying, carrying, and selling in expectation of profit from market fluctuations. Credit financing in such speculation increases the leverage of the investor in profiting from price changes if they should prove to be in the expected direction.

[2] For an authoritative and comprehensive review, see Frederic Solomon and Janet Hart, "Recent Developments in the Regulation of Securities Credit," *Journal of Public Law*, No. 1, 1971, pp. 167-212. Both authors have had long experience in advising and assisting the Board of Governors in the regulation of stock market credit.

higher required margin also serves as a warning to lenders and to borrowers that they should exercise greater caution in extending or using securities credit. When it raises the loan value (and thus lowers the required stock margin), the Board's purpose must be to act "for the accommodation of commerce and industry," having "due regard for the credit situation of the country," perhaps in admonition to the Board that due deliberation should be observed in taking a liberalizing action.

Initially, the margin requirement was applicable only when credit financing was extended against stock securities registered and listed for trading on recognized national securities exchanges and when credit was extended by member brokers of these exchanges, by other brokers or dealers transacting business through them, or by banks. In recent years, special problems in securities credit have indicated that there was a need for an important broadening and extension of the regulation, and the statutes have been amended to support some extensions to meet this need.

One extension under the original Act applied a margin requirement for purchasing or carrying registered convertible bonds, because the equity feature of these securities appeared to influence significantly their market activity and prices. A second extension applied the stock margin to shares issued by mutual funds which were investing in registered equity securities (later extended further to the share issues of all mutual funds). A third extension, also under the original Act, required adherence to the margin requirement by lenders other than brokers, dealers, and banks.[3] A fourth extension, under an amendment to the Act, applied the required margin to selected securities unlisted on any national exchange but "actively traded" outside such exchanges on the unorganized and decentralized securities market, known as the over-the-counter (OTC) market.[4]

---

[3] This regulation applies to factoring companies, collateral lenders, insurance companies, tax-exempt organizations, credit unions, finance companies, savings and loan associations when authorized, and agents in loan transactions against securities.

[4] The securities which the Board of Governors has selected for its list of OTC margin stocks are those in which investor interest is of national scope as determined on the basis of regulatory criteria. Such criteria include incorporation in the United States, registration of the stock under the Securities Exchange Act of 1934, company size of at least $5 million in capital and surplus, at least 1,500 public stockholders who are not "insiders," five or more dealers who regularly "make a market" in the stock, a six-month record of public trading, daily availability to

A recent extension (also under amended authority) requires all persons borrowing against regulated securities in the United States and all U.S. persons borrowing against such securities abroad to comply with the margin requirement.[5]

How the regulation works

Under present law, therefore, all securities brokers and dealers whether they are members or nonmembers of a national stock exchange, all banks whether they have a federal or state charter, and all others engaged in the business of lending against corporate equities as collateral must comply with the required stock margin in extending credit for the purpose of purchasing or carrying any securities covered by the regulations. Furthermore, all borrowers against regulated securities from a U.S. lender as well as all U.S. persons borrowing against such securities abroad must comply with this margin.

Stock market credit is regulated by directly restricting the amount of credit that any lender can extend and that any individual stock purchaser or holder can seek against marginable securities. Thus, if the Board determines that any securities pledged as collateral have no loan value that can be covered by credit extension, then the required margin against them is 100 per cent; if the Board sets the maximum amount of credit that a securities borrower can obtain at 45 per cent, the margin is 55 per cent; and if the loan value is fixed at 50 per cent, the borrowing margin and the loan value of securities put up as collateral would be the same, that is, 50 per cent. By explicitly limiting both the amount that any lender can loan to any buyer or holder of securities and the amount that the buyer or holder can lawfully demand on loan, the regulation attempts indirectly to affect the total amount of credit that all lenders and borrowers in the stock market can use to finance transactions in equity securities.

---

investors of the stock's price quotations, and 500,000 or more shares of stock publicly held having a market price of at least $10 a share and a total market value of at least $10 million. There are also criteria which any covered OTC stock must continue to meet in order to remain on the Board's list of OTC margin stocks. Of the approximately 20,000 equity securities estimated to be unlisted on any national securities exchange, just over 600 currently meet the criteria for OTC listing as identified by the Board.

[5] U.S. persons residing permanently abroad are exempted for borrowings up to a maximum of $5,000 in one year, as are foreign borrowers who are controlled by or acting on behalf of such persons.

An individual who wishes to purchase securities on credit through a broker or dealer must open a margin account with that particular firm. The account is subject to the margin regulations of the Board from both the broker's and the borrower's side. If the collateral put up by the borrower to obtain credit from the margin account rises in market value after he has incurred his debt, he can redeem that value in cash if he does not impair his regulatory margin position against the market value of his collateral or he can add to the securities collateral in his account by fresh purchases equal to his increased loan value. Furthermore, up to mid-September 1972, he could sell and purchase securities on the same day, thereby substituting collateral against his credit. This privilege is no longer available whenever his debtor position exceeds a specified fraction (60 per cent) of the market value of his collateral. If a debtor whose borrowing position is less than the required margin (that is, under-margined) liquidates at net value some part of his collateral, he is obliged to apply a percentage (called the retention requirement) of the sale proceeds to reduce his indebtedness.

The debtor's required equity in the margin account determines the maximum amount of credit he may obtain in advance at the point of a credit transaction. If the market value of his collateral at that point subsequently declines, he will not be required to restore the initial margin by promptly making a cash payment to reduce his indebtedness or by putting up more securities collateral—in other words, the regulatory margin is not a maintenance margin. The broker, dealer, banker, or other lender extending the credit to the borrower may require, for his own protection, that the margin determined by regulation—or some other maintenance margin, such as one fixed by a stock exchange of which the broker is a member— be observed. Again, if the Board of Governors raises the required margin after a purchase has been consummated, the borrower is not obliged to meet the higher requirement by reducing his loan or pledging more securities as collateral. On the other hand, the debtor's position becomes restricted when it is less than the required margin, whether because of price decline or of Board action to raise the margin. The debtor is obliged thereafter to apply the retention requirement to the proceeds of any sale of pledged securities (other than for one-day substitution, if his margin account is eligible for it) in order to reduce his indebtedness to the level of the permitted credit extension or loan value.

Administration of margin requirements

The Board of Governors has found it expedient to issue four separate margin requirements for regulating the stock market credit: (1) *Regulation T,* applying to brokers or to brokers and dealers in securities listed on national securities exchanges or included on the Board's list of OTC stocks; (2) *Regulation U,* applying to all banks (nonmember as well as member) that extend credit on any equity securities, and imposing margin requirements in cases where the loan is for purchasing or carrying margin stocks; [6] (3) *Regulation G,* applying to lenders other than brokers and dealers and banks engaging in credit transactions with individuals for purchasing or carrying margin securities, if the credit has such securities as collateral; (4) *Regulation X,* applying to all domestic borrowers of credit and to U.S. persons borrowing abroad to finance transactions in domestic securities.[7] Though cumbersome, these four regulations cover all types of lenders and borrowers against equity securities that the Board has determined that its legislative mandate should reach.

It was desirable to have separate Regulations T and U—one covering stock exchange brokers and brokers and dealers and the other covering banks—because banks make loans against stock collateral for a variety of purposes, while virtually all such credits by members of national stock exchanges or of the National Association of Securities Dealers (OTC dealers) are presumed to be for the purpose of purchasing or carrying listed securities. Regulation G, first adopted in 1968, was found necessary because of the growing number of specialized lenders against securities who believed that their lending against listed stock collateral was exempt from margin requirements because they were not classified as brokers, brokers and dealers, or banks. When authority for margin regulation was extended in 1969 to cover borrowing to purchase or carry officially listed over-the-counter securities, all three regulations required some modification to cover the financing of OTC securities that were actively traded and

---

6 Under Regulation U, a bank must always have a prescribed statement of purpose by a borrower against any stock used as collateral. However, bank loans extended without collateral or on collateral other than stock for purchasing or carrying securities are not covered by this regulation.

7 These regulations are technical and complex in form, and they have become more complicated since their initial formulation because of a need to close loopholes in them or to extend their coverage.

had a national investor interest. Because infringement or circum-
vention of margin requirements at borrowcr rather than lender
initiative threatened the effectiveness of the three foregoing regulations, a new Regulation X under amended statute in 1971 was designed
to cope with this situation.

Every lender covered by Regulation T, U, or G is required to
submit reports on his lending against securities as required by the
Board. In addition, all lenders subject to Regulation G are required
to register with the Board. Under Regulation X, every borrower
against regulated securities who obtains credit from an unregulated
foreign lender must retain a full record of his borrowing for at least
six years after its extinguishment.

At the end of 1972, the initial margins that all lenders and borrowers
had to observe were 65 per cent against stock purchases, portfolio
holdings pledged as collateral, or short sales, and 50 per cent against
listed bonds convertible at some point during their life (the lower
margin reflecting the debt instrument aspect of the financing transaction). On the other hand, the retention requirement against
nonsubstituted sales of collateral was 70 per cent.

Criteria for margin changes

The aim of these interrelated margin regulations is not to make
it unduly difficult to obtain credit or to deny access to it either for
financing transactions in securities or for financing holdings as pledged
collateral in borrower loans or margin accounts. Rather, these
regulations are designed to limit the initial credit extended against
securities used as collateral to amounts and types that (when
prudently related to the value of the collateral) would not have a
potentially destabilizing effect on the market if market prices should
fall sharply in response to an adverse development to which investors
in stocks are acutely sensitive. Market experience has repeatedly
demonstrated that such price declines often reach a point where
lenders call for additional collateral to fortify their extensions of
securities credit; if such collateral is not forthcoming from borrowers,
the lenders exercise their right to sell pledged collateral in self-
protection. If such actions are taken by enough lenders at the same
time, they can further accentuate and extend a fall in market prices.

Therefore, the preventive emphasis of stock margin requirements
tends to relate margin changes, with some lag, to a prolonged rise
or decline in stock market prices, accompanied by a marked increase

or cutback in credit-financed transactions or holdings of equity shares, as reflected by the growth or decline of the volume of securities credit and of market trading activity. A prolonged bull market, for example, increasingly attracts speculative investors who seek to maximize their leverage gains by credit financing; hence, at the point when such borrowing becomes excessive in the advancing market, the Board of Governors imposes successively higher initial margins on current stock purchases, and these tend to be retained until the margin credit is no longer considered excessive. Raising the average equity in stock market transactions thus serves to protect the stock market against excesses in the use of total securities credit with its potentially severe destabilizing effects if the stock price level abruptly changes course.

Thus, the movement of total securities credit in relation to that of market trading activity and the course of average stock prices are significant criteria as to whether reliance on credit financing is becoming excessive and, accordingly, a destabilizing threat to the stock market. Moreover, any long-sustained movement in the level of stock prices upward or downward will have a bearing on the "credit situation of the country," because of its effects on the net worth positions (that is, the asset-liability relationships) of both individual and institutional investors. Lenders look to the net worth of an applicant for credit as a key factor in their assessment of his credit standing. In addition, the net worth positions of all holders of corporate stocks are altered by an extended "bull market" rise or an extended "bear market" decline in the level of stock prices, and the resulting changes in portfolio (net worth) values will influence the willingness to spend of these holders. The credit situation, therefore, is always an important consideration in any Board decision to either raise or lower the required margin in securities credit.

In regulating stock market credit over the period 1951 through 1972, the Board of Governors varied the margin requirement 14 times, with 50 and 90 per cent as the outside limits of the required margin. Seven of the changes involved an increase and seven a decrease in the margin. None of the increases halted further expansion in stock market credit over the months immediately following their effectiveness, but they usually slowed the pace of expansion.

After a margin increase, stock prices generally continued to advance for a time, and then downward price adjustment occurred, accompanied by contraction in stock market credit. Decreases in the required margin tended to be followed after a varying lag (depending in part on the size of the change) by both an appreciable increase in credit to finance stock purchases and a strong advance in stock prices. Thus, the Board of Governors has adhered closely to the above empirical criteria in changing the margin requirement. However, it is interesting to note that increases in the margin have generally taken place just before or during periods of restrictive monetary policy, while decreases have usually occurred at times when policy was either accommodative or stimulative.

INTEREST RATE CEILINGS ON TIME DEPOSITS

The Federal Reserve Act as amended in 1935 directs the Board of Governors to establish a ceiling on interest that member banks may pay on savings and other time deposits. This amendment was one of the products of the financial reformation of the early 1930s. Since the Board's authority is applicable only to member banks, the same legislation vested in the Federal Deposit Insurance Corporation a parallel authority to fix a ceiling on the interest rates that insured nonmember commercial banks may pay on time deposits.

The rationale of two parallel authorities for this control was to keep member and insured nonmember commercial banks from competing against each other in attracting savings and time deposit funds and to avoid money flows between them for reasons of interest differentials. Accordingly, the two federal agencies promptly adopted the practice of informing one another of any contemplated change in their respective interest ceilings on time deposits, and, when feasible, they have taken concurrent action to change them. Because of the dominant role of member commercial banks as time deposit debtors to the public, any change made in the ceilings has been commonly attributed to the initiative of the Federal Reserve rather than to that of the Federal Deposit Insurance Corporation. Therefore, ceiling changes are now usually identified with the applicable regulation of the Board of Governors (Regulation Q).

Administration of ceilings

For many years after the authority was vested in the two regulatory agencies, officials of both agencies regarded its basic purpose in the administration of interest rate ceilings on time deposits as the prevention of destructive interest rate competition between banks, because many in Congress and throughout the country in that period believed that such competition was an important cause of the many bank failures during the 1920s and the early 1930s. In competitively attracting savings and other time deposit funds at relatively high interest rates, the banks in these early years were allegedly under pressure to lend or invest the funds in high-risk, high-yield assets; as a result, they jeopardized the soundness of their asset positions and risked ultimate insolvency. But this conception of the purpose of the law was neither consistent with the establishment of only two authorities (one for regulating member banks and one for regulating insured nonmember commercial banks) nor altogether applicable to later banking and monetary developments.

Since interest rates in financial markets were historically low in the years when the two agencies first promulgated their interest rate ceilings, they set the ceilings comparatively low to be compatible with the market rates.[8] These low market rates persisted, and when the United States entered World War II in December 1941, they were accepted as the base upon which government wartime deficits were to be financed. This meant that the existing interest rate ceilings on commercial bank time deposits were frozen for what proved to be an extended period. After postwar stabilization of market interest rates on U.S. Government securities was abandoned in early 1951, a gradual rise in interest yields in the money, securities, and mortgage markets permitted a modest lifting of ceilings in 1957, and further rises followed over the early 1960s.[9]

It was in this period that city banks introduced large-denomination negotiable certificates of deposit (CDs), which made the city banks more aggressive competitors for interest-sensitive funds. Consequently, continued rises in financial market yields during the 1960s encouraged the banking community to press for further increases in ceilings, and the Board of Governors willingly took action to allow them—to as much, in fact, as 4 per cent on savings deposits and 5½ per cent on other time deposits by the mid-1960s.

But interest rate ceilings had by then become so closely related to market rates that both member banks and nonmember insured

---

[8] In 1936, for example, the interest rates were set at 1 per cent on time deposit maturities from 30 to 89 days, 2 per cent on those from 90 days to 6 months, and 2½ per cent on those over 6 months and on savings deposits.

[9] Since 1962, the time deposits of foreign governments and of certain monetary and financial authorities have been exempted from these ceilings.

commercial banks could compete more actively with other institutional sources in providing to the public an attractive interest-bearing asset redeemable at par or, if marketable, at only a modest penalty. This more active bank competition soon motivated flows of funds to commercial banks, especially from the numerous insured savings and loan associations and the insured mutual savings banks. However, these institutions found themselves in no position to respond to fresh competition in savings deposit rates to customers, as their asset yields were heavily weighted by earlier participation in home mortgage financing at lower market rates than the current ones. Accordingly, they sought relief through federal legislation.

Congress took only a few months to respond to their requests. In September 1966, it enacted temporary legislation to authorize ceilings on dividend or interest rates that federally insured savings and loan associations and mutual savings banks, respectively, could pay on their savings accounts. Administration of ceilings for insured savings and loan associations was assigned to the Federal Home Loan Bank Board and that of ceilings for insured mutual savings banks to the Federal Deposit Insurance Corporation. These ceilings were to be set in appropriate relation to the ceilings for commercial banks. The legislation therefore instructed the Federal Reserve Board of Governors and the Directors of the Federal Deposit Insurance Corporation to consult with the Federal Home Loan Bank Board in setting mutually compatible ceilings that would also be consistent with credit market and economic conditions.[10]

For banks, this consultation in September 1966 resulted in maintenance of a 4 per cent interest rate ceiling on savings deposits of individuals redeemable on short notice or on time deposits having a maturity of under 90 days, a reduction from 5½ per cent to 5 per cent

---

[10] The *Report of the President's Commission on Financial Structure and Regulation* (1971), pp. 23-27, proposed that all authority for interest rate ceilings be abolished, but that the Federal Reserve Board be given an interim stand-by authority to reimpose ceilings on a temporary basis on consumer-type liabilities of banks and other thrift institutions should their ability to function as effective intermediaries again threaten to become a serious problem as it had in 1966 and 1969. Under this stand-by authority, the Board could impose an interest rate ceiling for banks and thrift institutions offering a checking account facility that differed from the ceiling applying to those thrift intermediaries not offering such facility, but later the Board could apply only one temporary interest rate ceiling to all depository institutions. After ten years of effective experience under the stand-by authority, however, the Commission proposed that it too be abolished.

in the ceilings on all time deposits of multiple or fixed maturity of larger size up to $100,000, and retention of a 5½ per cent ceiling on single maturity deposits of large size ($100,000 and more, typically in negotiable certificate form). For insured savings and loan associations and mutual savings banks, the consultation permitted ceiling rates to be set a little higher than the commercial bank ceilings on all time liabilities designed to attract individual consumer-savers.

Regulation Q ceilings and city banks

While these actions alleviated the problem of unusually large flows of funds from savings and loan associations and mutual savings banks to commercial banks, the Federal Reserve's decision to hold firm to its higher ceiling on large, single maturity, negotiable CDs brought on another problem. Under pressure of the Federal Reserve System's tightly restrictive monetary policy in 1966, money market interest rates by the fourth quarter of that year so far exceeded the 5½ per cent interest rate ceilings (and continued to escalate) on these deposit funds of large amounts that the negotiable CDs, sold to investors by city banks predominantly, were no longer competitive with other money market paper. City banks, therefore, experienced what they regarded as a sharp runoff in their marketable CD liabilities over the few months following the initial interest rate ceiling agreement among federal regulatory agencies.

Whatever problems resulted for the city banks, the Federal Reserve authorities realized from this experience that, in a period when Federal Reserve policy was sternly restrictive of bank credit expansion, the Board ceiling on the CD rates of city banks tended to operate as an instrument of selective regulation of a specific type of credit which these banks issued to draw liquid funds from the money market.

In light of this experience, the Federal Reserve Board reviewed its ceiling rate schedule in the spring of 1968, with the result that it retained the ceilings established in the early fall of 1966 on time deposit accounts below the negotiable CD minimum size ($100,000), but accepted new rates for the CD category ranging from 5½ per cent on maturities of 30 to 59 days to 6¼ per cent on maturities of one year or more. Early in the tight money stringency of 1969, the federal agencies responsible for interest rate ceilings at competing thrift institutions agreed that maintenance of the ceilings on consumer-type savings and time accounts was needed to keep interest rate competition from leading to undue flows of funds from one class of institution to another. For its part, the Federal Reserve Board decided, as it had in 1966, to hold firm to the existing (1968) ceilings applying to city bank CDs (up to ¾ percentage point higher than in 1966) as a support to the restrictive and anti-inflationary monetary policy then taking form.

At that time, the expansion of bank credit was being propelled by bank lending to business customers primarily. As these demands gathered strength for reasons of inflationary boom, market interest rates were soon driven far above time deposit rates applicable to negotiable CDs. In this situation, city banks in ensuing months experienced a drastic liquidation of their CD liabilities to some $14 billion from a peak of $24 billion—a liquidation seven times greater than that which occurred in 1966.

This 1969 use of interest rate ceilings to support restrictive monetary policy had been so severe in its effect on city banks that after nine months the Federal Reserve authorities early in 1970 gave some relief by raising the ceilings applicable to large negotiable CDs, depending on maturity, and a few months later gave optimum relief by lifting them entirely on large CDs of 30 to 90 days in maturity. The action also introduced new categories and rates by maturity for multiple maturity CDs of less than $100,000 in denomination. In a further phase of restrictive monetary policy more than three years later (mid-May 1973), the authorities took the further step of suspending all remaining interest ceilings on large CDs regardless of maturity range,[11] coupling it, however, with the imposition of an 8 per cent reserve requirement against increases in such liabilities, compared with a 5 per cent requirement on amounts outstanding at the point of suspension (Chapter 6). Thus, any future use of this regulation as a selective measure to restrict city bank lending is questionable, but the regulative authority still permits such potential use.

RESTRAINT ON FOREIGN LENDING AND INVESTING

Restraint on foreign lending and investing started in 1965 as one phase of a broad national attack on the persisting shortfall of the

---

[11] The Federal Home Loan Bank Board at the same time announced that it was removing its interest rate ceilings on savings certificates in denominations of $100,000 or more issued by insured savings and loan associations; these ceilings had formerly ranged from 6½ to 7½ per cent, depending on maturity.

United States in its international payments. To limit the role of U.S. credit and capital outflows in the payments disequilibrium, the U.S. Government introduced two companion programs of restraint. One program applied to banks and nonbank financial institutions and was designed and administered by the Federal Reserve Board of Governors; the other, applying to direct foreign investment by business corporations, was planned and administered by the Department of Commerce. Although both programs initially called for voluntary compliance, only the Federal Reserve program has continued on this basis; compliance under the business corporation program was made mandatory in 1968 by Executive Order of the President. Under the order, regulation of any transfers of funds covered by the Federal Reserve program, could also be made mandatory, if desired.[12]

Both programs have necessarily affected the expansion of domestic credit. The business corporation program has limited the demand of U.S. companies for domestic credit to finance their direct investment abroad, and the bank and financial institutions program has limited the availability of dollar credits in foreign lending and investing, whoever the borrower may be. The latter program, administered by the Federal Reserve, has probably diverted some credit from foreign to domestic borrowing and use.

Since the net domestic effect of both programs is impossible to trace and the main purpose of their adoption was to restrain dollar flows abroad, the discussion below is focused on this aspect alone. Also, it is limited to the program administered by the Board of Governors because (1) the Board's program has provided essential support for the business corporation program; and (2) in years just preceding the introduction of the Federal Reserve program, bank lending abroad had become increasingly important in the persisting U.S. foreign deficit.

The Federal Reserve program

The Federal Reserve program to restrain the foreign lending of U.S. bank and nonbank financial institutions mainly relies on performance guidelines for foreign lending and investing with which the Board of Governors asks these institutions to comply voluntarily.

---

[12] *Federal Reserve Bulletin,* January 1968, pp. 80-82.

However, from its inception the program has been partly supported by the application of the interest equalization tax to acquisitions by such institutions of foreign obligations and loans having a maturity beyond one year. The Board requests that each cooperating institution report periodically its respective current holdings of foreign debt obligations and equity investments in relation to a target ceiling that applies against holdings on a selected base date, or to the institution's size in the case of some banks. Each participant is also requested to conform to its target and, if the target is exceeded, to report any corrective action to its Reserve Bank. Though technically applying to all banks and all nonbank financial institutions, the program has in practice had its principal effect on the very large banks and on the relatively few nonbank financial institutions that had already attained sizable holdings of foreign assets at the time of its first application.

The guidelines for the program are tailored to the characteristics of banks and nonbank financial institutions, with distinctive guidelines applying to each type of institution. However, both the bank and nonbank types comply with ceilings on holdings of foreign assets. By law, both now exempt export credits from ceilings. Also, both types give priority to lending and investing in developing countries, and participants are instructed to observe special restraints on new credits or investments in developed countries (with the exception of Canada)—particularly on long-term credits to, or investments in, countries of continental Western Europe.[13] They are likewise asked not to hold liquid assets abroad in excess of working balances. In addition, both types exempt investment in obligations of international institutions of which the United States is a member, and both pay attention to the possibilities of loopholes and to equity between banks and nonbanks. Finally, both banks and nonbanks require participating institutions to report their current foreign credit and investment positions quarterly (when the holding or change in holding is large enough to justify a report).

There are many technical differences between the bank and nonbank financial institutions in the program. For banks, it has been found desirable to ask participants to avoid sell-offs of assets to U.S. residents

---

[13] Banks are currently to make no new long-term loans to countries in continental Western Europe, and nonbank institutions are not to increase investments in that area to an amount exceeding their holdings on December 31, 1968.

without recourse and, if sold with recourse, to continue to count them as covered assets; to specify when foreign assets of bank subsidiaries, affiliates, and holding companies should be consolidated under the reporting bank's ceiling and when they might be kept separate; to make certain that the claims due to the head office from its foreign branches and subsidiaries are covered under its ceiling; to discourage bank customers from placing liquid funds outside the United States; and to avoid lending that would infringe on the business corporation (direct foreign investment) companion program of the Department of Commerce. Whereas before 1972 the domestic branches or agencies of foreign banks in the United States were merely asked to act in accord with the program's intent, beginning in that year they were requested to conform to it under explicit ceilings.

For the nonbank financial institutions, participants are requested to refrain from substituting their loans for those that the commercial banks refrain from making and to avoid loans either to foreign subsidiaries of U.S. corporations that the foreign direct investment program would not have permitted the parent company to make, or to U.S. borrowers who in turn would make loans to foreign companies that could substitute for funds otherwise obtained abroad. They are also requested to count under ceilings: (1) net investment in foreign branches, subsidiaries, or affiliates; (2) long-term credits to developing countries to finance the construction or operation of foreign-built vessels, primarily oil tankers; (3) all long-term credits to foreign obligors in developed countries other than Canada; and (4) the equity securities of foreign companies in these countries, except those acquired from U.S. investors.

Record of the Federal Reserve program

Under the Federal Reserve program covering both banks and nonbank institutions in force at the end of 1972, the aggregate regulative ceiling of foreign credits extended by the lenders covered by the program stood at nearly $14 billion, about $2 billion more than the ceiling at the beginning of the program eight years earlier. Of this total, domestic banks were allowed a little over $10 billion, agencies and branches of foreign banks $1.8 billion, and nonbank financial institutions another $1.8 billion. However, outstanding foreign credits of participating domestic banks were short of their aggregate ceilings by $1.5 billion, those of agencies and branches of foreign banks were in excess of their recently established ceilings by $500 million, while those of nonbank financial institutions apparently approximated their ceilings.

The contribution of the program to the correction of the foreign payments deficit of the United States is difficult to assess. During the five years preceding its adoption, there had been a surge of foreign lending and investing by U.S. banks and other financial institutions. It was to be expected, therefore, that it would be followed by an initial curtailment of their foreign lending to industrial countries abroad, especially in Europe. The program then permitted a resumption of moderate growth in the total foreign asset holdings of participants within the ceilings to be used as guidelines, but it was intended to hold (and apparently did hold) such growth to a negligible amount.

Against this performance record, there must be recognized any offsetting secondary effects that may have accentuated continuing payments deficits. One of these was probably the tendency to transfer the foreign lending of some institutions covered by the program to branches abroad engaging in Euro-dollar activities, and such transfer may have tended not only to enlarge this market's role but also to help swell the U.S. payments deficit by its effects on interest levels there. Not all such effects can be easily identified and probably some will never be recognized. In formally extending the program of voluntary restraint on the foreign lending and investing by U.S. financial institutions at the time of foreign exchange realignment on December 18, 1971, one motive may possibly have been to assure the major industrial countries concerned that the agreed realignment of their currency values with the dollar would not expose them to the risk of resumed large dollar inflows to their economies on capital account from the domestic lending operations of U.S. financial institutions.

However helpful such assurance may have been in late 1971, when the U.S. Government announced on February 12, 1973 a further devaluation of the dollar by 10 per cent, it also announced that it planned to phase out—by the end of December 1974 at the latest—the interest equalization tax, the direct foreign investment program of the Department of Commerce, and the voluntary foreign credit restraint program of the Federal Reserve System. The view then taken by the U.S. Government was that these measures would no longer be needed in view of (1) the beneficial effect that the cumulative impact of dollar exchange rate changes would likely have within the intervening period; (2) the continued success the Federal Government expected to have in curbing inflationary tendencies; and (3) the prospect that the U.S. economy would prove increasingly attractive to investors from abroad.

8
Coordinated Use of Policy Instruments

EFFECTIVE COORDINATION in the use of the several Federal Reserve policy instruments—open market operations, the discount rate, the variable reserve requirement, and the instruments for selective regulation—depends on both statutory and financial considerations. The legislative design of the Federal Reserve System, with statutory specification for the use of each instrument, imposes important constraints on how these instruments are coordinated in practice. Also, although the multiple unit banking and financial structure in the United States exhibits marked tendencies toward concentration of deposits in large banks and groups of smaller banks under single management, it is still a vigorously competitive system and this profoundly influences the coordination process.

Furthermore, coordination is affected by the linking of diverse types of financial activity into a close-knit web of local, regional, and national credit markets, with New York City serving as the national and international financial center of the United States. Related to this influence on coordination is the important role of the few very large city member banks (46 in number) in providing vital payments and liquidity services to nonmember banks and to the central money and credit market, which has numerous financial and nonfinancial participants. Finally, the Federal Reserve's coordination of its policy

instruments is affected by the large-scale fiscal and debt operations
of the U.S. Government.

FINANCIAL AIMS IN INSTRUMENT COORDINATION

While all of the institutional elements mentioned above influence
Federal Reserve application of its instruments in a subtle manner,
financial concerns related to the performance of the economy are of
more direct relevance. With varying emphasis, these financial concerns
receive attention at virtually every meeting of the Federal Reserve's
most important policy forum, the Federal Open Market Committee,
although indications of such attention may be limited in the formal
policy record of each forum meeting to the statement of those aims
considered paramount at a given time. Briefly, the interrelated
financial aims of the Federal Reserve System are:

(1) A pace of monetary expansion consistent with the optimum
and balanced real growth of the U.S. economy over the longer run,
but adapted, as appropriate, to moderate any cyclical fluctuation in
economic activity and to cushion any potential financial emergency.

(2) A supply of bank credit funds sufficient to supplement those
otherwise supplied by the private sector in financing a volume of
producer and consumer investment that will sustain and support the
economy's optimum growth.

(3) A pattern of interest rates and a range of their fluctuation
consonant with current financial forces and flows of funds, both
domestic and international, and also compatible with the overall
stabilization policy of the Federal Government.

(4) Avoidance of pronounced inflationary or deflationary trends—
both cyclical and secular—in producer and consumer price levels.

(5) A reasonable balance in the economy's foreign payments.

In addition to these five aims, there are two others relating
primarily to operational aspects of the financial process. If these
are not realized, the functioning of the real economy may be seriously
disrupted. These aims—the first of which is short term and the
second, long term—are:

(6) A continuing, orderly functioning of the money market to
permit needed liquidity adjustments by private financial institutions
and business corporations, while facilitating short-term borrowing by
the U.S. Treasury as well as reliance by the Federal Reserve on open
market operations as its major instrument of monetary regulation.

(7) A prudently balanced relationship between the asset structures and the liability commitments of financial institutions and businesses and a soundly administered banking system to act as a safeguard against national financial emergency.

These basic aims have complex implications. Moreover, since they are interrelated in varying degree and some inconsistencies may develop among them (at least in the short run), concurrent realization of all the aims is difficult. Official participants in policy making may stress one or more of the aims in the context of a given proposal to change Federal Reserve policy. Thus, the resulting consensus statement of policy may reflect quite differing weights or trade-offs in the decision making. Nevertheless, the Federal Reserve keeps these aims in mind when determining and coordinating the use of its major instruments.

However, no Federal Reserve officials would ever claim that these financial aims could be accomplished through discretionary monetary action alone, but would contend only that monetary policy, as implemented by the System's statutory instruments and directed to these aims, is indispensable to any broad government effort to achieve economic stabilization. Whether this broader effort—of which Federal Reserve policy is a part—attains such a goal to the satisfaction of the public must depend both on the balance and effectiveness of the overall economic program pursued by the Federal Government and on the forces generated in response to it, which may frustrate the program's full realization.

STRATEGY IN INSTRUMENT COORDINATION

By its very nature, the task of dovetailing monetary policy into the Federal Government's broader stabilization program calls for judgment on the part of Federal Reserve policymakers, particularly in deciding upon meaningful targets for application of their policy instruments. In recent years, this problem has become one of judging what emphasis is to be placed on aggregate monetary quantities and on money market conditions and interest rates. To determine the desired emphasis, Federal Reserve authorities have had to weigh and consider three vital elements: (1) the need of an advanced economy to have adequate liquidity available at all times; (2) the heavy dependence of an active monetary policy on a well-functioning market for liquid claims; and (3) the need for a properly guided growth of the key monetary aggregates in relation to the official stabilization policy. In the end, the authorities settled their guidance problem—at least for an interim period—by adopting a mixed strategy taking into account both the monetary aggregates and the interest rates. Thus, ultimate monetary aggregates (M_1 and M_2) are taken as main targets for a longer-term objective, whereas for short-term guidance the twofold targets are the desired course of the member bank reserve position against privately held deposits (including interbank deposits) and the judgmental constraints set by the Federal Reserve authorities themselves on the fluctuation of money market conditions and interest rates. If proven faulty, the short-term targets may be adjusted by the Federal Open Market Committee or, when he is given latitude to do so, by its Account Manager in relation to the longer-term targets.

In view of the Federal Reserve's long experience in monetary regulation, the adoption of a mixed guidance strategy is hardly surprising. Such a strategy represents a choice suited to the System's eclectic tradition. For one thing, it recognizes that quantitative factors and interest rates constitute joint channels for the transmission of monetary impulses set in motion by central banking action. For another, it leaves the Federal Reserve authorities free to emphasize whichever approach to policy strategy they deem most relevant in dealing with their constant problem of avoiding disruptive imbalance between monetary and interrelated financial developments on the one hand and real economic activity on the other. Thus far, the Federal Reserve's practice in applying a combination strategy—considering the uncertainties of existing knowledge and future events—has been experimental and subject to modification through experience. Any priority assigned to a guidance perspective has thus been explicitly confined to a given context, taking into account defects shown in earlier patterns of performance.

COORDINATION OF BANK RESERVE INSTRUMENTS

Since authority over the use of the bank reserve instruments is shared by three different statutory bodies within the Federal Reserve System, its organizational structure appears less than ideally suited for the simple and direct coordination of the bank reserve instruments. The instruments themselves, however, are closely interdependent in function, and the statutory entities having final authority over their application either have interlocking membership with (or representation on) other bodies or share authority with another body. As pointed out earlier, the Federal Reserve has found that it is necessary for the achievement of desirable instrument coordination not only to develop a distinctive role for each instrument but also to make such reasonable organizational adaptation as would be judged permissible under governing law.

Recast of the instruments after World War II

The Federal Reserve System's first opportunity after World War II to reintroduce a flexible monetary regulation came in the early 1950s. Over that decade, the Federal Reserve's major instruments received critical re-examination with a view to modernizing the central banking role of the Federal Reserve and establishing a new pattern of instrument coordination for it.

Since the open market operation had served chiefly as a support for prices and yields in the U.S. Government securities market during World War II and the immediate postwar years, it received initial attention. Against the experience of the preceding decade, a Federal Reserve consensus crystalized from this re-examination—that the open market instrument should serve as the Federal Reserve's main tool in flexible monetary regulation. This consensus apparently rested on five major considerations:

(1) The Federal Reserve System's primary assignment for the longer term was to foster the orderly and noninflationary growth of the economy in an active manner.

(2) The open market instrument affected the lending and investing position of the banking system indirectly through the market process and involved no direct Federal Reserve member bank transactions or communication with individual banks or groups of banks.

(3) It was the most flexible of the bank reserve tools on a short-term (even day-to-day) basis and lent itself readily for application in situations when the functioning of the banking and monetary mechanism called for decisive initiative by the Federal Reserve in supplying reserve funds to the banking system or withdrawing them from it.

(4) The viability of the private commercial banking system with thousands of independent unit banks might be sustained with minimal risk of contagious bank insolvency,[1] if the bank reserves needed to

---

[1] Such as had marred the U.S. banking record in the nineteenth century, in the 1920s, and in the early 1930s.

finance the expanding money transactions of a growing economy could be largely provided by the central bank at its own initiative through open market purchases. This would leave the member banks substantially free from priority liability for repayment as debtors for Reserve Bank credit.

(5) The huge federal debt outstanding (a legacy of war finance that was held partly by the banks) warranted the Federal Reserve in acquiring over the years a growing amount of this debt through its open market transactions. The amount of debt to be acquired by the Federal Reserve would be determined by the noninflationary growth of the banking system, rather than by the size of any government deficits.

The Federal Reserve authorities proceeded to operate experimentally under this consensus, but they soon found that new ground rules were needed for the discount instrument. They concluded that member bank access to the Federal Reserve discount facility had to be kept optimally uniform between the twelve Reserve Banks and at the same time subordinate to initiatives taken by the System in supplying reserve funds through the open market channel. To this end, the Board of Governors in the mid-1950s modernized its discount regulation (Regulation A) to limit member bank borrowing from Reserve Banks primarily to occasions of short-term or transitional banking adjustment (see Chapter 5).[2] Faced with constraint on the use of Reserve discount debt to finance expansion, individual member banks would have to rely more heavily on their own competitive efforts to acquire reserves for growth by either attracting customer deposits or raising additional capital. When their reserve positions needed temporary supplement, individual member banks could ordinarily and readily adjust through money market transactions that would draw on the funds available in the money market, partly as a result of Federal Reserve open market operations. If such adjustment was not feasible or was deemed too costly, the member could seek short-term discount accommodation from its Reserve Bank.

Regarding the variable reserve instrument, which had been available to the Federal Reserve System only since the mid-1930s and had had only limited use until the 1950s, Federal Reserve authorities found experimentation and analytical assessment the only paths to guidance

---

[2] Amended as of mid-April 1973 to permit seasonal borrowing by member banks up to eight weeks (see Chapter 5).

in raising or lowering reserve percentages. Gradually, consensus was reached (see Chapter 6) on the following points:

(1) Use of the instrument in a banking system such as existed in the United States was handicapped both by technical considerations and by difficulties in relationships between the Federal Reserve System and its member banks. Because of these problems, it was impractical to make flexible two-way changes in member bank reserve ratios for short-run purposes.

(2) As the short-run effects of reserve ratio changes on bank reserve positions could be accomplished through open market and discount operations, the variable reserve tool could indeed be used only occasionally.

(3) The variable reserve instrument's primary usefulness in coping with monetary tendencies was mainly limited to unusual situations, when a large and abrupt change in reserve availability to member banks was called for by actual or threatened adverse banking and economic developments. But as such situations might be infrequent, the Federal Reserve would need to experiment with interim use of the variable reserve instrument by making more moderate changes.

After such determinations had been made for each instrument, it was clear that optimum coordination of their use would depend on a flexible adaptation of the coordination pattern as special problems developed and on more direct, frequent, and formal communication between the entities responsible for applying the instruments. It was further agreed that the Federal Open Market Committee could be a helpful medium for better communication. Accordingly, it began to function as the Federal Reserve policy summit (see Chapter 1), that is, the body giving formal expression to the goals of Federal Reserve policy, which, until modified by the Committee, would guide decision making as to the use of other instruments as well.

Coordination in the short run

With these instrument and policy-making adaptations, the Federal Reserve felt that it would be able to evolve a fairly consistent pattern of instrument coordination in the short run. Open market operations would be used continuously as the main instrument of monetary regulation to cushion seasonal and irregular organic monetary factors affecting bank reserve positions and the orderliness of the money market. Open market operations would not only narrow the range of day-to-day fluctuation in money market conditions and money rates but also make it easier for credit market participants to gauge the trend of these rates as influenced by basic liquidity forces and Federal Reserve monetary actions. The Reserve Banks would then align discount rates with money market rates, and the credit market itself could be counted on to align the position of its other rates (that is, bond rates, customer loan rates, mortgage rates, etc.) with its more sensitive short rates.

Furthermore, open market operations would be the principal means of actively injecting or absorbing bank reserves for short-run policy objectives—that is, to facilitate the adaptation of the banking system to variations in domestic money flows, in general business activity, or in rates of economic growth. The discount mechanism, though subject to standard rules at each Reserve Bank in administering the resort of member banks to it, would be available to aid or cushion member bank reserve adjustment to these market operations. Because of its limitations, the variable reserve instrument would have appropriate application primarily when short-run and longer-run policy objectives merged. Moreover, its application would invariably present coordination problems with the other two bank reserve instruments.

Problems in coordinating reserve ratio changes

The application of the variable reserve instrument (see Chapter 6) contrasted sharply between the 1950s and 1960s. In the 1950s, the changes were downward and mostly large, while during the 1960s they were two-directional (four increases and three decreases), of more moderate size, and more deliberately coordinated with other policy action. This difference in application reflected experimentation in the use of the instrument to supplement open market operations in particular.

Of the seven reserve ratio changes during the 1960s, five were based on member bank time deposits and two based on demand deposits. The base chosen by the Federal Reserve authorities for a change depends mainly on the policy aim of the action. From the standpoint of the response by a member bank, a change in either the time or demand deposit base removes or makes available reserve funds—a matter of prime importance for its operations. These changes, with their effective dates and expressed purposes, are listed in Table 13.

Table 13. Changes in Member Bank Reserve Ratios, 1962-70

Year	Announced	Effective	Time Deposit	Demand Deposit
	Dates		Type of Change	
1962	October 18	October 25 and November 1	Decrease	

Purpose: To encourage monetary growth and to temper incentives to capital outflow by relieving pressures on the short-term interest level that could result if the reserves to be supplied were wholly provided by open market operations.

| 1966(1) | June 24 | July 14 and July 21 | Increase | |

Purpose: To reinforce monetary restraint and generally tighten credit conditions.

| 1966(2) | August 17 | September 9 and September 15 | Increase | |

Purpose: To discourage city bank competition in attracting time deposits, to curb expansion of bank lending, and generally to reinforce monetary restraint at the risk of still tighter money market conditions.

| 1967 | February 28 | March 2 and March 16 | Decrease | |

Purpose: To combat recessionary tendencies and to ensure adequate credit availability for resumption of orderly economic growth.

| 1968 | December 27 | January 11 and January 16 | | Increase |

Purpose: To resist a resurgence of inflationary expectations and to mitigate adverse factors affecting the international payments balance.

| 1969 | April 3 | April 17 | | Increase |

Purpose: To support discount rate and open market action in resisting the excessive strength and inflationary tendencies of the economy.

| 1970 | August 17 | October 1 | Decrease | |

Purpose: To offset other reserve action (reserve requirement against commercial paper issues by bank affiliates) and to reactivate monetary growth.

Table 14 shows how Federal Reserve action to release or absorb reserve funds in each of the above cases was related to similar releases or absorptions of funds from open market operations or from net market factors during the period from four weeks before to four weeks after the action. The table also relates these changes to responses in sensitive bank reserve indicators during the overlap weeks and to the rate of change in total bank loans and investments and in the narrowly defined money stock over the three months before and the three months after each reserve action.

Each reserve requirement change exemplifies the complexity of short-run coordination. With regard to specific coordination between reserve ratio change and open market operations, the amount of funds supplied or absorbed by each type of action must be weighed against the amount supplied or absorbed from changes in the complex of net organic factors over the very short period surrounding a reserve requirement action. The latter amount may equal or exceed the amounts injected or absorbed by either a change in reserve ratio or open market operations or by both actions together. A glance at the figures in Table 14 for the three sources of bank reserve funds makes clear the difficulty that coordination may sometimes present to the policymaker and also emphasizes the importance of appropriate timing for any decision to change the member bank reserve ratio.

Coordination with other reserve instruments. In three of the variable reserve actions, reserves were supplied to the member banks. In two of them (1962 and 1967) open market operations, together with other institutional and market factors, reinforced the additions to the reserve supply from reserve ratio action. But in the third (1970) the reserves supplied by open market operations were only a modest reinforcement to reserve action, and other net factors actually absorbed a token amount of reserves. In the first two instances, Federal Reserve monetary policy sought to be overtly stimulative in the application of the two instruments, while in the third it was shifting hesitantly from vigorous general monetary restraint to active stimulation of the monetary situation.

The four instances in which reserve ratio action absorbed reserves were at points when Federal Reserve policy was in the initial or very early stage of monetary restraint, but in three of these (two in 1966 and one in 1968) open market operations and other factors (net) provided enough bank reserves to more than offset the amount

Table 14. Estimated Short-Run Effects of Concurrent Reserve Requirement and Open Market Action on Marginal Reserve Measures and on Associated Expansion of Total Bank Credit and the Active Money Stock, 1962-70

(million U.S. dollars)

Reserve Ratio Change	Reserve Requirement Action	Estimated Reserve Funds Released (+) or Absorbed (−) (4 weeks before to 4 weeks after)		Change in Marginal Reserve Indicators (4 weeks before to 4 weeks after)			Changes in Monetary Aggregates: Compound Annual Rates (3 months before and 3 months after[2])			
		Open Operations[1]	Other Factors (net)	Excess Reserves	Reserve Bank Borrowing	Net Free Reserves	Total Commercial Bank Loans and Investments[2]		Active Money Stock[3]	
							Before	After	Before	After
1962	+770	+938	+405	+104	+32	+72	+10.1	+11.2	+1.6	+4.1
1966(1)	−440	+386	+926	−18	+121	−139	+10.0	+0.6	−9.6	+1.6
1966(2)	−440	+944	+831	−48	+146	−194	+4.1	+0.4	+2.1	+4.9
1967	+885	+961	+700	−63	−208	+145	+13.4	+8.3	−7.8	+11.3
1968	−535	+357	+1,020	+221	+199	+22	+9.2	+7.8	+21.1	+5.1
1969	−660	−399	+745	+7	+207	−214	+5.7	+0.9	+4.1	−2.0
1970[3]	+550	+178	−63	−224	−330	+106	+12.2[4]	+14.3[4]	−2.4	+21.6

Sources: Federal Reserve System, Board of Governors, relevant *Annual Reports*; relevant issues of the *Federal Reserve Bulletin*; and staff articles, "Revision of the Money Stock" and "Revision of the Bank Credit Series," *Federal Reserve Bulletin*, November and December 1971, pp. 880-93 and 971-75, respectively.

[1] Measured by the change in the System Open Market Account.

[2] Based on seasonally unadjusted figures.

[3] This action was announced on August 17, at which time the total release of reserves would have amounted to $770 million, of which about one half ($350 million) was estimated to be absorbed from the application of a time deposit requirement against commercial paper borrowing by bank affiliates for the purpose of supplying funds to the related bank. By the effective date of October 1, the outstanding commercial paper of bank affiliates had been so reduced that the amount of reserves actually becoming available to member banks from the action was re-estimated to be $550 million, a figure less precise than the other figures in this table for 1970.

[4] Including loans sold to affiliates.

absorbed by reserve action. This may have reflected a Federal Reserve emphasis at the time on keeping any change in money market conditions a gradual one, and it probably also reflected the difficulty in estimating even for short periods the amount of reserves provided by the interplay of nonpolicy factors. In the fourth instance (1969) open market operations supported the reserve action modestly. This action, though taken further along than the initial phase of a developing restrictive period (1969-70), was still early, inasmuch as Federal Reserve policy was then becoming exceedingly stern in its monetary restraints.

The relation of discount rate change to reserve requirement and open market action is not conveniently shown in Table 14. However, on the basis of the Federal Reserve's past practice in administering its discount rate, it would be expected that discount rate changes would follow rather than lead any reserve ratio action, since the Reserve Bank discount charge serves no positive role as a deterrent to member bank discounting. Actually, during the 1960s discount rate change was closely timed with reserve requirement action in only the four restrictive instances described above—being almost coincidental in the one in 1969 and lagging by four to six weeks in the two in 1966 and the one in 1968. A further coincidental change was made in late June 1973.

Impact of joint reserve ratio and open market action on bank reserve positions. In assessing the short-run impact of reserve ratio and open market action taken together, the Federal Reserve authorities aparently look particularly at the short-term response of three sensitive indicators of change in the member bank reserve position: excess reserves, Reserve Bank borrowing, and net free or borrowed reserves. In virtually all of the instances covered in Table 14, though the pattern of response was not large for any one indicator, it was consistent with the policy intent of the variable reserve action—that is, a consistent response was never completely obscured either by the concurrent effects of open market operations or by the net interplay of external and random factors, or by these two elements jointly. Even concurrent bank deposit expansion, by tying up new funds in required reserves, could hardly have accounted for much short-run moderation of reserve action impact on these sensitive reserve indicators.

Ratio change and response of the monetary aggregates. The case-by-case short-run response of the major aggregates (total bank credit and the narrowly defined money stock) to reserve ratio change, allowing for adjoining offset or reinforcement both before and after the change from open market operations and from other identifiable reserve sources, reveals fairly marked short-term agreement with the broad domestic monetary goals of the reserve actions. These more general monetary responses, when considered along with the more specific evidence of a moderately positive response of the sensitive reserve indicators to reserve ratio variation, would appear to confirm that moderate reserve requirement changes, as made during the 1960s, can serve Federal Reserve policy at times as a helpful supplement to open market and discount operations in achieving a prompt response in the trend of the monetary aggregates. If properly timed, therefore, a reserve ratio change of medium size can dovetail constructively at specific junctures with other action to regulate the combined reserve position of the banks.

Coordination for longer-run objectives

For longer-run domestic monetary objectives, it seems probable that the Federal Reserve's strategy of coordination—in the light of the searching reassessment that it conducted in the 1950s—would be geared to the general character of the financial development of the economy under certain conditions as described below.

Under balanced economic conditions. Under conditions of balanced economic growth and active utilization of available resources without undue inflation, provision of bank reserves to accommodate concurrent expansion of bank credit and the money stock would proceed through the open market channel with little general reliance on discounting by the member banks. The discount rate would then be kept in "satisfactory" alignment with market rates, and rate changes, if any, would carry no policy implication. On the other hand, the variable reserve instrument would remain available on a stand-by basis.

Under conditions of destabilizing boom with inflationary trends. If a strong destabilizing boom accompanied by inflationary tendencies should threaten or become dominant, an effort would be made to dampen bank credit and monetary expansion by first providing a smaller amount of reserves at the initiative of the Federal Reserve through the open market. If active demand pressures on banks and on other lenders persisted in the credit market, causing market interest rates to rise, member banks in growing numbers (and with a constantly changing composition) would resort to discounting. Reserve Banks would then be required to exercise a more active administrative surveillance over the enlarged volume of borrowing. To control the expansion of such borrowing and to limit the problem of administrative surveillance, the Reserve Bank discount rates would be successively raised as appropriate.[3] At some stage, an increase in the reserve requirement might be imposed to emphasize the policy of monetary restraint and perhaps to swell the numbers of member banks finding it necessary to resort to discounting. Subsequently, the restrictive intent of this higher reserve ratio might be underscored by a further rise in the discount rate.

As member bank borrowing could generally cover only the temporary needs of indebted banks, repayment pressures would soon make themselves felt, bank lending standards would tighten, and the accessibility of bank credit for potential loans (that is, bank credit availability) would narrow. Whenever open market supplies of bank reserve funds are limited and growth in discount credit is slowed down by volume of repayment, the amount of bank credit and the monetary expansion—being essentially dependent in U.S. banking practice on nonborrowed reserve positions—would visibly lessen, perhaps markedly. And if there is less contribution from commercial banks to the total credit supply—that is, less bank credit availability—competition among potential borrowers would intensify throughout the credit market. Interest rates in all sectors of the credit market would undergo sharp advances, with the entire constellation of market rates possibly breaching the last increase in the discount rate. In this tight money environment, some borrowers (perhaps including city banks subject to a statutory interest ceiling on market issues of certificates of deposit) would be priced out of the market, while nonbank sources of funds would be encouraged to supply more credit to it.

Although the broad aim of this restraining effort would be to contain the total expenditures of the economy financed by borrowing, the

---

[3] Too long a delay in raising the Federal Reserve discount rate in relation to rising money market rates, repeated experience shows, will soon result in sufficient "interest cost incentive" for borrowing by member banks to cause both the total volume of borrowing and the number of indebted members to increase markedly. Given such delay, even a more active surveillance of members' borrowing by Reserve Bank officers may not suffice to dampen the response of members to a widening incentive to borrow.

effect between the different borrowing sectors would be uneven. However, such overall containment of borrowed finance would be a necessary objective of Federal Reserve anti-boom and anti-inflation policy. This policy would have to be pressed gradually and persistently to a judgment as to when the disequilibrating and inflationary boom would abate enough to permit all measures of restrictive monetary action to be moderated and then reversed.

Experience has shown that a relatively small amount of member bank borrowing can carry out the Federal Reserve policy objective of slower growth of the monetary aggregates. In fact, an aggregate volume ranging from 3.5 to 5.5 per cent of member bank required reserves in individual weeks (for example, from $1 billion to $1.6 billion during the restrictive period of 1969) and involving discount debt by about one fifth (approximately 1,200) of all individual member banks seems to have exerted considerable restraint on banking and monetary conditions and credit financing in the 1960s.[4] This would compare with a discount volume under stimulative monetary conditions ranging from a few million to $250 million, probably involving borrowing by fewer than one twentieth of the member banks.

To cope with recession and potential deflation. If economic conditions showed a deflationary tendency together with economic recession, the sequence of primary instrument coordination would be broadly the opposite. The turnaround time for Federal Reserve action from restraint to stimulation could well be quite short and decisive, bearing in mind the need to keep adverse tendencies from gathering undue momentum and to foster orderly readjustment to resumed economic growth.

Adaptations in coordination. It would seem that these patterns of coordinated use of policy instruments for domestic objectives could

---

[4] The Federal Reserve's experience with member bank borrowing during the 1960s, however, may not carry over into the 1970s—in part because of the recent revision of Regulation A, applicable to member bank borrowing (implicitly modifying the standard rules of surveillance of member indebtedness adhered to by the twelve Reserve Banks), and in part possibly because of a changing attitude of member banks toward debt owed their Reserve Banks (see Chapter 5). In fact, the upper limit for the borrowing ratio indicated for the 1960s was being exceeded midway in the target money development of 1963.

hardly be expected to remain static over an indefinite future but would be adapted ad hoc to emerging monetary problems. Thus, in a period of recovery from the deflation following an inflationary boom, resource utilization and economic growth might lag behind desired targets for reflation. In the event of such a lag, the provision of reserves through the open market could be enlarged, or a special downward adjustment of the reserve requirement could be authorized, to keep interest rates in the credit market under strong downward pressure—thereby endeavoring to stimulate bank credit and monetary demands—and to accelerate the tempo of economic activity. Any consequent lowering of money market rates could be accompanied by a special reduction in the discount rate or could simply be tolerated without discount rate action. If inadequate investment could be identified as an especially acute domestic problem in such circumstances, Federal Reserve open market operations might be shifted from the money market to the capital market by transferring many short-term open market purchases to the longer-term sectors of the U.S. Government securities market— thus trying to exert additional supply pressure on long-term interest rates in order to stimulate longer-term investment.

The effectiveness of these adaptations is seldom clearly evident; either the forces prompting them may be too strong to make the adaptations observably effective or subsequent relaxation may reflect response to other considerations. Whatever the case, such adaptations need careful assessment lest long-run effects cause a more difficult problem than the short-term problem they are intended to help overcome.

One recent change in Federal Reserve practice in open market operations, which will have lasting effect on its pattern of coordinated use of instruments for domestic stabilization, is the decision of the Federal Open Market Committee to place greater emphasis on projected desirable performance of the ultimate monetary aggregates as longer-run targets for its open market operations, while keeping money market conditions and the member bank reserve positions against publicly held nonbank deposits in consistent accord with the targets determined by the Committee. This adaptation will need to permit wider day-to-day variation in money market conditions and interest rates than the Committee tolerated as customary practice throughout most of the 1960s. It will also unavoidably result in the need for market participants, especially banks, to accustom themselves to managing their secondary or liquidity reserve positions in a more variable market without undue adjustment costs. This may increase the frequency with which individual member banks—especially the large city banks—resort to temporary discounting to avoid sales of liquid assets when market prices have moved adversely and may raise somewhat the volume of discounting usually experienced in either easier or tighter credit conditions.

A further adaptation with longer-run implication is the progressive effort of Federal Reserve policymakers to incorporate modern methods of economic forecasting into their decision-making process. The desire to achieve two immediate goals has motivated this effort: (1) to reduce the lag between the recognition of the need for action to change policy and the application of such action; and (2) through earlier and perhaps stronger action following policy change to achieve the minimum practicable lag (at best, of uncertain duration) between the timing of a change in policy followed by action and the visibility of the response to such a change in the real economy.

Judgmental and econometric models are utilized to project the economy's forward performance. The models take into account both possible adverse economic developments and feasible alternative adaptations in fiscal and monetary policy in order to assess their effects on performance of the economy. While these models can never really give the answer as to what will actually happen to economic development in the period ahead—because there is never available full knowledge of the past, let alone of the future—they can aid in identifying potentialities and risks more sharply. While forecasting technique has already reached an advanced stage, it still has many limitations (for example, the varying lag effects over time of similar patterns of monetary action). Therefore, Federal Reserve technicians must constantly engage in new experimental work to make forecasting a more useful tool in the making of monetary policy.

Coordination with Treasury debt management

The Federal Reserve not only faces the problem of coordinating the use of its three primary or bank reserve instruments in accordance with prevailing credit and monetary conditions, but also that of coordinating their use satisfactorily with Treasury management of the U.S. Government's large public debt. Every year the Treasury must refinance billions of dollars of maturing debt and may also need to issue billions of dollars of additional debt obligations. As the successful placement of these securities in investor portfolios is a matter of national interest as well as of considerable technical interest in monetary regulation, the Federal Reserve authorities have felt that they must temper, if not avoid, overt policy change during periods between offering and settlement of a Treasury issue that would possibly upset the fixed interest securities market.

The financial markets have colloquially referred to this self-restraint on the part of the Federal Reserve during Treasury financing periods as an "even keel policy," for the Manager of the Open Market Account typically has refrained during this time from any strategy that might suggest an imminent change in monetary policy. At this time also, the Reserve Banks have refrained from proposing a discount rate change, and the Board of Governors has withheld approval of any earlier proposed rate change. And no change in member bank required reserve percentages by the Board of Governors has been scheduled to become effective in the "even keel" period. In more positive terms, "even keel policy" means that during the time spans of Treasury financings Federal Reserve open market operations are mainly limited to transactions designed to keep the money and securities markets orderly, though not actually stabilized. Since market distribution of any new Treasury issue may involve temporarily larger inventory holdings on the part of securities dealers or perhaps some very temporary swelling of bank portfolios of Treasury securities, a modest bulge in Federal Reserve credit through market transactions—to be extinguished after completion of the financing—may have been tolerated at the time by the Federal Open Market Committee.

Federal Reserve "even keel policy" presents a twofold problem for overall monetary policy. On the one hand, market time becomes unavailable for implementing instrument action that would otherwise be appropriate. On the other hand, experience shows that a temporary bulge in Federal Reserve credit to assist Treasury financings may not be easily extinguished by reverse monetary action in the subsequent period if official concern about the orderliness of the money market then places priority on avoiding an abrupt rise in its interest rates. The underwriting aid to the Treasury in that case amounts in effect to a leakage of Federal Reserve credit into the reserve holdings of the banking system, thus giving an unplanned stimulus to credit and monetary expansion.

The Treasury is fully cognizant of these risks to monetary policy and action. By careful planning, it endeavors to keep (1) its recourse to the market as infrequent as possible; (2) its offering and settlement dates as close as practicable; and (3) its offering interest rates consistent with yields on comparable debt obligations then outstanding in the market and therefore acceptable to investors. Also, the Treasury makes a practice of seeking the advice of Federal Reserve officials in planning its financing schedule. When market conditions are favorable, it may handle a succession of obligations soon to mature into an advance refunding package, partly to curtail the size and number of Treasury market financings, partly to lengthen the average maturity of the federal debt, and partly to reduce congestion in the short-term floating debt. Furthermore, it looks increasingly to the auction procedure, in which market bidding sets the interest yield, for the issuance of obligations of medium-term and longer-term maturity.

At the same time, the Treasury feels that the Federal Reserve System has a responsibility to facilitate its financings insofar as this can be done without jeopardizing satisfactory attainment of the goals of monetary policy. The Federal Reserve System has long accepted such a duty as a central bank accommodation of government financing. The governing rules should obviously be (1) the competitiveness of the interest rate on Treasury offerings with the levels and tendencies shown by market yields on comparable obligations; and (2) the avoidance of supplying any extra central bank credit to ensure an offering's appreciable absorption into the investment portfolio of the commercial banking system.

COORDINATION OF SELECTIVE AND MAJOR INSTRUMENTS

The use of the three minor and selective instruments with which the Federal Reserve System may implement monetary policy is affected in part by the appropriate legal authority necessary to regulate a special sector's credit volume. It is also conditioned by how well credit volume in a particular sector correlates with or diverges from the generation of new credit extension in the economy as a whole. In the case of stock market credit, the legal format is now well established and the correlation of the sector's credit with the economy's total credit is so close and the regulative technique so readily adaptable that changes in margin requirements for either stock transactions or portfolio investment can be expected to be broadly consistent with Federal Reserve use of its bank reserve instruments. However, Federal Reserve use of interest ceilings on time deposits or of regulation of foreign credits extended by bank and nonbank financial institutions is not so easily coordinated with its primary instruments.

The permanent Federal Reserve authority for regulating ceiling rates paid by banks on time deposits calls for interest ceilings at all times, although legislation applicable since 1966 has dispensed with this formality through 1974 and this period may be extended. In addition, certain technical problems are inherent in the operation of rate ceilings. For instance, if both the rate ceilings and the rates that banks actually pay on time deposits are high enough, holders of demand balances may be induced to transfer some part of them to time deposits, thereby accelerating the rate of total bank credit expansion (M_2) in relation to that of demand deposits and the money stock (M_1). Further, if the rates are too low in relation to those paid by competing thrift intermediaries, money flows may then go from the banks to competitors; or if rates paid by banks and competitors are low in relation to those available in the securities and mortgage markets, money flows may then go from the banks and other thrift institutions to these markets.

As the Federal Reserve has gained experience in administering bank rate ceilings on time deposits, the dominant problem has been to keep a tolerable equilibrium between permissible and actual rates paid by banks and those permitted and paid by competing intermediaries as well as between those rates and rates on longer-term securities and residential mortgages. It is therefore unusual for the Federal Reserve to apply the interest rate ceiling to reinforce a restrictive or stimulative monetary policy by affecting the pace of bank credit and monetary growth. In restrictive use, when ceiling rates are below money market rates, the purpose would be to encourage particularly holders of money balances with banks to convert them into money market claims that entail some risk and transfer cost in reconversion to deposit form. In stimulative use, the purpose would be the opposite. In the former instance, the aim would be to limit the availability of bank credit and to accentuate restraint on monetary growth otherwise being exerted by use of the bank reserve instruments; in the latter, it would be to liberalize bank credit availability and stimulate monetary growth being fostered by the use of these primary instruments. In either instance, use of ceiling rates in reinforcement of the bank reserve instruments would be infrequent.

Voluntary regulation of foreign lending by banks and other financial institutions is cumbersome for the Federal Reserve to administer, as it does not lend itself to short-term adjustment in the way that domestic monetary policy can be adapted to varying national economic and financial conditions. Therefore, it is only useful to apply it when the U.S. economy faces a possibly extended period of adverse effects on the balance of payments, caused by international credit outflows—and perhaps when other industrial countries are apprehensive that credit inflow from the United States may be large and have an adverse effect on their domestic stabilization policies. The fact that use of voluntary regulation has been found at all expedient points up a persistent problem of basic monetary disequilibrium among major trading nations and a need to deal with it through fundamental international monetary reform.

INFLUENCES OF INTERNATIONAL MONETARY DEVELOPMENTS

Federal Reserve actions to implement national monetary policy, as emphasized throughout this study, are directed mainly to the reserve position of the member banks. The overall aim of such policy is to sustain an expansionary trend for the aggregate of member bank reserves that will be consistent with the growth potential of the domestic economy—as indicated by the availability of labor, normal gain in productivity, prospective technological advance, and the objective of optimum stability of domestic price levels. At the same time, international interest rate levels and payments flows must always be taken into account in shaping the strategy of U.S. monetary policy, since the U.S. dollar has long played a key role in the functioning of the international monetary mechanism and since public confidence in the dollar is necessarily affected by its usefulness to, and standing in, the international financial markets.

The international concerns of the Federal Reserve policymakers can be said to center on two aspects of emerging trends in the U.S. economy's money transactions with other countries: (1) the incentives to international capital and credit flow resulting from relative interest rate levels and ease of borrowing in the United States as compared with these factors in major financial markets abroad; and (2) the competitiveness in world markets of U.S. products and services. The forces affecting these two aspects of intercountry financial relations, together with how they are being reflected in domestic trade and financial activity, have much to do with the way that Federal Reserve authorities modify their policy and actions in helping to achieve and to sustain reasonable balance in the country's foreign transactions. To illustrate the first aspect, in periods when imbalance in U.S. international payments appears to be caused primarily by capital and credit outflow, the Federal Reserve may make a number of adaptations in using its major policy instruments.[5] These may include: (1) Offsetting by open market operations the effect on member bank reserves of conversions into gold or other reserve assets of dollar balances acquired by foreign central banks in coping with inflows of U.S. dollars; [6] (2) At times of economic slack, shifting some open market purchases from the short-term to the long-term sector of the securities market to relieve downward pressure on money market rates exerted by the otherwise easy availability of bank reserves; (3) On such occasion, perhaps substituting reserve requirement action for open market operations in providing bank reserves; or on occasion of lessening slack in activity, in raising reserve requirements to enforce higher interest rate levels internally so as to brake the outflow of credit and capital; (4) Accelerating or delaying the timing of discount rate changes and perhaps resorting to a rate change of unusual size; (5) Supporting these actions by applying guidelines to limit the foreign lending and investing abroad by U.S. financial institutions.

The first four types of action would have a low public visibility because, in practice, they would intermingle with policy actions for domestic purposes. Nevertheless, they would be attested to in the policy record of the Federal Open Market Committee. The fifth type, in contrast, would be special and accorded as much publicity as feasible.

Whether this combination of action, if persistently followed over time, could gradually correct U.S. payments imbalances caused by

---

[5] Other steps that might be taken would be intervention in the foreign exchange market to moderate the effect of any unusual spread in exchange rates (spot and forward quotations) on credit outflow, and adjustment of the special reserve requirement on member bank borrowings of Euro-dollars. These steps, however, could have temporary effects only.

[6] It is to be emphasized here that only when foreign central banks convert their dollar holdings into other reserve assets can these conversions be offset by open market operations. When foreign central banks immediately convert their accumulated dollars into U.S. investments in Treasury bills or special Treasury securities, no offsetting open market operations are necessary; that is to say, there is no lasting effect on the member bank reserve position from such dollar investment, but merely a shift in ownership of dollar assets.

capital outflow would depend on a blend of forces, some originating internally and some in foreign developments (particularly in the monetary policies pursued by major central banks abroad). These forces would need to work together within a reasonable period to bring troublesome differentials in interest rate levels and relative ease of borrowing within more compatible limits. Over much of the 1960s, Federal Reserve policymakers had to cope with differentials in international financial incentives that constantly stimulated the outflow of credit and capital. To the extent that their efforts failed to achieve success, that failure could be partly attributed to the development over that period of a highly dexterous Euro-dollar market specializing in mediating interest differentials between major financial markets internationally. As always, it could be attributed in part, too, to the psychological and political forces conditioning financial responses to monetary policy actions in that period.

On the other hand, when balance in international transactions becomes threatened by evident progressive erosion in the competitiveness of U.S. products and services in foreign markets, say from inflationary pressures on domestic costs and prices, the Federal Reserve policymakers are confronted by an especially difficult problem. In this case, the policy effort needs to enforce a limitation on growth of member bank reserves that will be rigorous enough to foster decisive correction of the inflationary source of adverse balance of payments tendencies. This would involve the early and strong coordinated use of the key bank reserve instruments to contain undue economic boom as well as a prompt relaxation of such use to cushion any subsequent reaction and avoid any potentially cumulative deflationary effects. And this strategy for policy may have to be pursued to the point of clear abatement of domestic inflationary trends.

Should the problem prove to be intractable to this strategy of monetary policy or should the strategy itself threaten disruption of the domestic economy, the one alternative remaining under U.S. monetary arrangements is for the Federal Government to take action that will realign the exchange value of the dollar in relation to other major currencies.

OUTLOOK FOR INSTRUMENT COORDINATION

In summary, the use of the Federal Reserve's interrelated policy instruments has undergone many adaptations over the years, as a result both of statutory amendment and of internal decisions. The purpose of such adaptation has been either to make a given instrument more effective or to improve its coordinated use with the other instruments. This process can be expected to continue. That it is continuing is exemplified by the Federal Reserve's recent modernization of the reserve requirements of member banks and at the same time of the Reserve Bank check clearance service to all commercial banks, by a recent liberalizing amendment of the discount mechanism, particularly in seasonal lending, and by advocacy of legislation to extend to all commercial banks the application of the reserve requirement and discount instruments.

These changes will have important consequences for the coordination of the Federal Reserve instruments. For instance, the modernization of member bank reserve requirements, coupled with Reserve Bank check clearance reform, has already reduced somewhat the volume of open market operations needed to maintain orderly money market conditions. Furthermore, the reform of the discount mechanism could gradually alter the relative roles of open market and discount operations—both as processes for facilitating short-term member bank adjustment and as processes through which monetary policy is implemented.

Eventually, such a shift might even relieve the discount rate of its heavy public relations role imposed by custom and practice, allowing it greater flexibility as a price charged to commercial banks that borrow from the central bank. Finally, statutory reforms of the variable reserve instrument, obliging all institutions with demand deposits to adhere to member bank reserve requirements and providing access to the Federal Reserve discount facility for all, would give this instrument more strength and greater potential utility for monetary regulation. However, the greater strength of the variable reserve instrument would, in practice, complicate both its more frequent use and its coordination with the Federal Reserve System's two other— and more flexible—reserve instruments. These possibilities, however, must await future developments.

Also for the future is the broader problem of what adaptations ought to be made in the use and coordination of the instruments of monetary policy for purposes of effective monetary cooperation internationally. The need for paying greater attention to this problem has increasingly become evident over the past two decades, and, indeed, some solid progress has been made in evolving forms and forums for a more active cooperation between the central banks of the major trading countries. To establish a firmer base on which further progress in such cooperation may be made is one of the tasks to which reform of the international monetary system currently in process is directed.

INDEX

References are to pages, and those including the letter *n* are to footnotes.

Bank for International Settlements, 91, 93, 95n, 96
Bankers' acceptances, 40, 46, 58
Board of Governors, 1, 3-10
  Chairman, liaison with Congress, 5-6
  Chairman, liaison with Executive Branch of Government, 5-6
  Chairman, role of, 4-6; *see also* Federal Open Market Committee
  credit regulation, 8-10, 28; *see also* Credit
  foreign credits by U.S. financial institutions, regulation, 9, 147, 159-164
  members, selection and duties, 3-4
  monetary policy formation, 3, 8-10
  monetary policy instruments, administration, 3, 8-10, 100-102, 123-134, 155-159
  operational costs, accountability to Congress, 4
  Regulation Q, interest rate ceilings on member bank time deposits, 9, 147; *see also* Interest rates
  reporting to Congress, 6, 10
  stock market credit, regulation, 8-9, 147-155
  supervisory and regulatory duties, 1, 3, 6-8, 7n
  See also Monetary policy *and* Credit market

Capital market, *see* Credit market
Central banking, U.S., *see* Federal Reserve System
Central banks, foreign, *see* Foreign central banks
Commercial banks
  aggregate bank lending and investing, influence of monetary policy, 8-10
  aggregate cash reserves, 2-3; and open market operations, xii, 29-30, 50-52, 81-82

aggregate demand deposits, 2, 29-31, 38
aggregate time and savings deposits, 29-31, 33-39, 77, 77n
bank float, 35-36
bank holding companies, 8, 33, 38
certificates of deposit (CDs), 156-159
correspondent nonmembers, 3, 33-34, 36
currency holdings, 2, 23-24, 71
federal deposit insurance, xi, 30, 32, 34-35, 37, 155
functions, xi, 28-29, 34-35, 47-49
interbank deposits and balances, 29-30, 33-34
number and size, 28-30, 33, 38
organization and structure, xi, 28-29, 31, 33
Reserve Bank credit, 34n, 37, 48, 51; *see also* Discount operations
supply of funds to credit market, 28-53, 77-79; *see also* Credit *and* Credit market
thrift institutions, competition, xi, 30
Commodity Credit Corporation, 40n
Comptroller of the Currency, 7n
Council of Economic Advisers to the President, Chairman of, *see* Board of Governors, Chairman, liaison with Executive Branch of Government
Credit
  Federal Reserve, 79
  funds, sources of supply and demand, 28, 39-45
  regulation, xii-xiii, 10, 147
Credit market, 39-45
  capital market and, 28-29, 40-42
  debt claims, 39-41, 45-46
  discount facility and, *see* Discount operations
  interest rates, 42-44; *see also* Interest rates

money market and, xi-xii, 28-29, 39, 45-53; *see also* Open market operations
nature and size, xi, 28, 39-42
Reserve Banks and, 28, 41, 43, 50; *see also* Reserve Banks
role, xi, 29, 42
sources of funds, 28, 40-41
Credit unions
commercial banks, competition, xi, 30
federal agency insurance, xi, 32
number, 30
time and savings deposits, xi, 30, 41
Currency, *see* Commercial banks; Federal Reserve System; *and* Treasury

Deposits, *see* Commercial banks *and* Member banks
Discount operations, 97-122
administration, xii, 8, 97-108, 188
credit and monetary conditions and, xii, 97
discount rate changes, xii, 55, 102, 111-114, 176
discount rate, fixing, 100-102; *see also* Reserve Banks
discount rate, other money market rates and, xii, 98-102, 108-114; *see also* Interest rates
emergency advances and, 114-117
major monetary policy instrument, xii, 1, 8, 17, 97, 170, 172
Regulation A, 99, 117-122, 170
reserve position of member banks and, 97-98, 170, 172
U.S. Government and federal agency securities, 97-98

Employment Act of 1946, objectives, 11-12
Euro-dollar market, 48, 142-143, 186n, 187
"Even keel policy," *see* Monetary policy
Executive Office of the President, *see* Board of Governors, Chairman, liaison with Executive Branch of Government
Export-Import Bank, 40n

Federal Advisory Council
function, 18-19
membership, 19
monetary stabilization and, 19
Federal Deposit Insurance Corporation, 30n, 32, 155
ceiling on interest rates of nonmember banks, Regulation Q, 155-158
Federal funds market, 34, 46, 48-49, 51-52, 66, 71
interest rate, range of fluctuation, 59, 60n
Regulation A, 99
Federal Home Loan Bank Board
ceilings on interest rates, administration, 157-58
insurance, 30, 30n, 32n
See also Savings and loan associations
Federal National Mortgage Association, 40n
Federal Open Market Account Manager, 55-83
competitive techniques, 64-66, 65n
market strategy, 55-56, 59-60
matched sale-purchase transactions, 56-57, 61-64, 69
orderly market operations, 60, 69-73, 81-83
outright transactions, 56, 61-64, 69
policy-oriented operations, 60, 68, 72, 75-81, 168
repurchase transactions, 56-58, 61-64, 69
transactions, foreign central banks, 67-68
Treasury transactions, 67-68
Federal Open Market Account, Special Manager, 87-90; *see also* Treasury
Federal Open Market Committee, 10-13, 166-167
agent, 55; *see also* Reserve Bank of New York
Chairman, 5, 11
Chairman, liaison with Federal Government, 5-6
meetings, 12-13, 58, 101-102, 166
meetings, consensus on monetary policy objectives, 12-14
meetings, frequency, 12, 58, 101
meetings, order of agenda, 12-13, 18n, 58-60, 101-102
meetings, policy directives, 58-59

members, 10-11
monetary policy role, xiii, 1, 5, 11-13, 58-59, 72, 74, 166-167, 171-172; *see also* Monetary policy
open market operations and, 10-11; *see also* Open market operations
procedures, 55-56, 84-85
supervision of Account Manager, 1, 10, 12, 60; *see also* Federal Open Market Account Manager
swap network, 90-93, 96; *see also* Foreign currency operations
Federal Reserve Act, 7, 7*n*, 18-19
amendment, emergency reserve ratio changes, 123
amendment, interest rate ceilings on time deposits, 155-160
Puerto Rico, exclusion, 14*n*
Federal Reserve Banks, *see* Reserve Banks
Federal Reserve System, xi-xiv, 1-27
accountability to Congress, 26-27
administration, 1; *see also* Board of Governors
check clearance and collection, 3, 131-134, 188
currency balances, foreign, 70
currency issue, 2
decentralization, xi, 1, 19-22
deficit financing and, 83
discount instrument, *see* Discount operations
Federal Reserve program, 159-164; *see also* Foreign lending and investing
float, 69, 71, 131, 133
foreign currency transactions, 86-96
functions, 20, 22-26, 83
headquarters, 1
independent agency status, 26-27
influence on credit and money, xii, 22-24, 28-29, 51-53, 76
international monetary developments and, 185-189
member bank time deposits, interest rate ceilings, 147, 155-59; *see also* Interest rates
open market instrument, *see* Federal Open Market Committee *and* Open market operations
organization and structure, xi, 1-22
regulation of stock market credit, *see*

Stock market credit
relations with U.S. Government agencies, 5-6
reserve instrument, *see* Reserve requirements
swap network, *see* Federal Open Market Committee
Treasury, collaboration, 25-26, 86-88
See also Member banks; Monetary policy; *and* Reserve Banks
Federal Savings and Loan Insurance Corporation, 32*n*
Foreign central banks, 67-68, 70, 186
cooperation, 86-87, 90-96
gold or other reserve assets, conversion into, 186, 186*n*
investment in U.S. Treasury bills or securities, 186*n*
swap network, *see* Federal Open Market Committee
Foreign currency operations, xii-xiii, 70-71, 93-96, 186; *see also* Foreign central banks *and* Treasury
exchange realignments and, 87, 94-95, 187
Foreign lending and investing
business corporations, mandatory restraints, 160
financial institutions, Federal Reserve program, xiii, 160-164
voluntary restraints, xiii, 147, 159-164, 184-186

Gold, 25, 25*n*, 71, 186

Interbank deposits, 29-31; *see also* Federal funds market
Interbank market, *see* Federal funds market
Interest rates
ceilings on member bank time deposits, Regulation Q, 155-159
changes, 42, 44, 0-71, 74, 78-79
Federal Reserve actions and, xiii, 51-52, 147
member bank time deposits, xiii, 147
monetary policy and, xiii, 167-68
money and bank credit and, 51-52
See also Discount operations
International Monetary Fund, 89, 91, 92*n*, 93*n*, 95*n*
International payments system, reform of, 87

Margin requirements, see Stock market credit

Member banks

borrowing frequency, 118-120; see also Discount operations

cash reserve level, effect on aggregate bank lending and investing, 3, 8, 23

check clearance and collection, 2-3, 130-134

classes, 29-33, 125-126

discounting with Reserve Banks, 3, 29, 97-100; see also Discount operations

demand deposits, 2-3, 29-33, 38, 38n, 123-125, 124n, 127-129

federal deposit insurance, 32

large city, role, 158, 165

number, xi, 29-30, 37-38

obligations and privileges, 3, 29, 31-32, 37-38, 49, 97

reserve city, 30-33

reserve position, 23-24, 29, 31-32, 35, 38, 70-71, 73, 77-79, 172; see also Reserve requirements

reserve position, monetary policy and, xii, 8

stockholders in District Reserve Banks, 3, 3n

supervision, 6-8, 9n, 37

Monetary policy

Board of Governors and, see Board of Governors

capital and credit outflows, 185-187; see also Foreign lending and investing

competitiveness of U.S. products and services in world markets, 185, 187

criticism and review, xiii, 23-24

directives, 11, 13, 58-60, 72

"even keel," 182

formation, xiii, 1, 8, 23, 166-167

Federal Open Market Committee and, 1, 166-167; see also Federal Open Market Committee

implementation, xi-xii, 1, 8-10, 23, 72

instrument coordination, financial aims, 166-167

instrument coordination, outlook, 187-189

instruments for selective regulation, 147-164

interest rates and, xiii, 167-168; see also Discount operations

international interest rates, 185-187

international cooperation and, 189

International Monetary Fund and, 89

major instruments, xii-xiii, 28-29, 54-85, 86-96, 97-122, 123-146

major instruments, coordination, 12, 101-102, 165-181

major instruments, coordination with Treasury debt management, 181-183

member banks, reserve position, 23, 185; see also Reserve requirements

monetary aggregates and, 23-24, 167-168, 177-178

national economic program and, 167, 185

selective and major instruments, coordination, 183-185

U.S. payments imbalance and, 185-187

Money creation, 80-81; see also Money supply

Money market

conditions, 73-75, 77-79, 167-168

definition, xi, 28, 42

Euro-dollar, 48, 187

foreign central banks, transactions, 67-68

interest rate ceilings and large CDs, 158-159

large city banks and, 48, 156-159

monetary policy role, xi-xii, 50-53

U.S. Government and federal agency securities, 49, 61-69

Treasury, transactions, 49-50, 67-68

Money supply, 23-24, 167-168

expansion, 24, 77-81, 175-178, 184

See also Credit; Credit market; Discount operations; Interest rates; Money market; Open market operations; and Reserve requirements

Mutual savings banks

competition with commercial banks, xi, 30, 32, 32n, 157

federal insurance, xi, 30, 32, 32n

interest rate ceilings, 157

number, 30, 32n, 41

savings and time deposits, xi, 30, 32n, 41

source of credit funds, 41

National Association of Securities Dealers (OTC dealers), 152
Nonmember banks, xi; see also Commercial banks

Office of Management and Budget, Director, see Board of Governors, Chairman, liaison with Executive Branch of Government
Open Market Account, see Federal Open Market Account
Open Market Committee, see Federal Open Market Committee
Open market operations, xii, 2, 29, 50-53, 54-85, 169-170, 176, 186, 188
  conditions, 54-55, 73-75
  dominant monetary policy instrument, xii, 8, 54-55, 79-85, 166, 169-172
  policy guidance, xiii, 72, 77-79; see also Monetary policy and Federal Open Market Account Manager
  procedures, 55-61, 70
  U.S. Government securities, 57, 61-66
  See also Federal Open Market Committee
Open market operations in foreign currencies, xii, 86-89
  role of Special Manager, 87-90
  swap drawings, 90-92
  U.S. Treasury and, 88-89

Puerto Rico, see Federal Reserve Act

Regulation A, see Discount operations
Regulation J, see Reserve requirements
Regulation Q, see Board of Governors and Interest rates
Regulations G, T, U, and X, see Stock market credit
Report of the President's Commission on Financial Structure and Regulation, 32n, 145n, 157n
Reserve Bank of New York, 1-2
  agent in foreign currency transactions, 67-68, 87
  agent for System open market operations, 2, 55, 60
  agent for Treasury open market operations, 2, 49-50, 67-68

foreign central banks and international institutions, correspondent accounts, 67-68
  Foreign Department, 87-88
  Securities Department, 61, 67-68
Reserve Banks, 6-7, 13-18
  branch offices, 2, 14
  capital stock, 3
  directorates, 3, 16-18, 100, 102
  directorates, duties, 17-18
  directorates, selection, 16-17
  discount procedures, 17-18, 102-108; see also Discount operations
  discount rate, 17, 100-102
  districts, 2, 13-16
  monetary policy role, 1, 16
  monetary policy, implementation, 1-2, 17
  New York Bank, see Reserve Bank of New York
  number and size, 1-2, 13
  organization and functions, 1-2, 13-16, 14n
  representation at Federal Open Market Committee meetings, see Federal Open Market Committee
Reserve Bank funds, see Federal funds
Reserve ratios, see Reserve requirements
Reserve requirements, xii, 29, 35-36, 123-146, 170-176, 186, 188
  administration, 127-130, 134-138
  basic specifications, 123-124
  changes, xii, 123-130, 138-140, 176
  check clearance reform, Regulation J, 131-134
  coordination with other monetary policy instruments, xii, 137-138, 170-171, 174-176
  cost avoidance, 142-143
  demand deposit differential, 123-126
  effect on credit market, 18, 135-136, 172
  Federal Reserve Act and, 123
  graduation, 126-130
  limitations, xii, 138-139
  proposed legislative reform, 145-146
  rationale, 125-126, 134-140
  regulatory amendments, 143-145
  requirement base, adaptations, 140-143

reserve city banks, 124-126
variable, 123-146

Savings and loan associations
  competition with commercial banks,
    xi, 32, 32n, 157-158
  federal insurance, xi, 30, 32, 32n
  interest rate ceilings and, 157-158
  number, 30, 32n
  savings and time deposits, xi, 30, 41
  source of credit funds, 41
Securities Exchange Act of 1934, 147-
  149
  amendments and extensions, 149-150
  See also Stock market credit
Securities market
  dealers, 56, 61, 63-66, 152
  federal agency (or agency), 56-57,
    61, 63
  U.S. Government, 25, 57, 61-63, 67-
    68, 71-72
Smithsonian Agreement, 93-94
Special drawing rights (SDRs), 69-71,
  94n, 95
Stock market credit, 147-155
  borrower's margin, 148-151
  margin requirements, 152-155
  over-the-counter (OTC) securities,
    149n, 152-153
  regulation, xii-xiii, 147-153
  Regulations G, T, U, and X, 152-153

Treasury
  accounts, 26, 71
  bills, 55, 59, 66

cash balance, 69, 71
currency, 25, 71
dollar convertibility, suspension, 92-
  93
dollar devaluation, 93-95, 94n
dollar stabilization, 25
federal credit agencies and, 25
federal government borrowing, administration, 25
fiscal agent, 67-68
foreign currency transactions, agent,
  88-89
foreign currency transactions, approval, 88
gold, 25, 25n, 71
gold and foreign exchange, authority
  to deal in, 25n
gold and foreign exchange reserves,
  custody, 25
notes and coin, 25
realignment of dollar exchange, 187
Secretary, see Board of Governors,
  Chairman, liaison with Executive
  Branch of Government
Stabilization Fund, 88
U.S. Government trust funds, market
  investment, 25

U.S. Government securities
  open market operations and, see
    Open market operations
U.S. Treasury, see Treasury

About the Author

Mr. Young prepared this study of U.S. monetary policy instruments during the time he served as a consultant in the Fund's Central Banking Service from 1967 to 1973. He came to the Fund from a distinguished career on the staff of the Federal Reserve Board of Governors as Senior Advisor to the Board from 1962 to 1967 and Secretary of the Federal Open Market Committee from 1960 to 1965. After joining the staff of the Federal Reserve in 1946, he held the positions of Assistant Director and then Director of the Board's Division of Research and Statistics until 1960, when he became Director of the Board's Division of International Finance, serving in that capacity until 1966.

2421